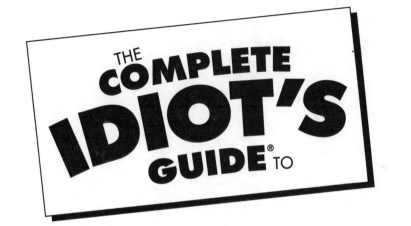

Boating and Sailing

Third Edition

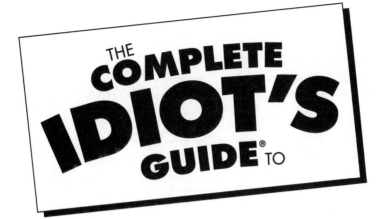

THE COMPLETE IDIOT'S GUIDE® TO

Boating and Sailing

Third Edition

by Frank Sargeant

ALPHA

A member of Penguin Group (USA) Inc.

ALPHA BOOKS

Published by the Penguin Group

Penguin Group (USA) Inc., 375 Hudson Street, New York, New York 10014, U.S.A.

Penguin Group (Canada), 10 Alcorn Avenue, Toronto, Ontario, Canada M4V 3B2 (a division of Pearson Penguin Canada Inc.)

Penguin Books Ltd, 80 Strand, London WC2R 0RL, England

Penguin Ireland, 25 St Stephen's Green, Dublin 2, Ireland (a division of Penguin Books Ltd)

Penguin Group (Australia), 250 Camberwell Road, Camberwell, Victoria 3124, Australia (a division of Pearson Australia Group Pty Ltd)

Penguin Books India Pvt Ltd, 11 Community Centre, Panchsheel Park, New Delhi—110 017, India

Penguin Group (NZ), cnr Airborne and Rosedale Roads, Albany, Auckland 1310, New Zealand (a division of Pearson New Zealand Ltd)

Penguin Books (South Africa) (Pty) Ltd, 24 Sturdee Avenue, Rosebank, Johannesburg 2196, South Africa

Penguin Books Ltd, Registered Offices: 80 Strand, London WC2R 0RL, England

Publisher: *Marie Butler-Knight*
Product Manager: *Phil Kitchel*
Senior Managing Editor: *Jennifer Bowles*
Senior Acquisitions Editor: *Renee Wilmeth*
Development Editor: *Jennifer Moore*
Production Editor: *Megan Douglass*

Copy Editor: *Molly Schaller*
Cartoonist: *Richard King*
Cover/Book Designer: *Trina Wurst*
Indexer: *Aamir Burki*
Layout: *Angela Calvert*
Proofreading: *John Etchison*

Contents at a Glance

Contents

Part 2:   The Basics of Operation   73

5   Getting Underway for the First Time   75

Foreword

I first met Frank Sargeant almost 30 years ago. Both he and I were among a small group of boating writers assembled at a large Florida marina, by one of the country's leading magazines on that subject, to test a dozen or so soon-to-be introduced models from various manufacturers around the country. Sea trials of pre-production boats are hardly the stuff of glory; mostly it's wet, at times hot, gritty work that requires attaching various measuring devices to the engines and other onboard equipment. Sometimes the boats are so new they don't even want to run. By the end of the day you usually smell like a cross between a gasoline or diesel fuel dump and a large dog that badly needs a bath. Your knuckles are scraped from turning wrenches in very tight places; you're sunburned, sweaty, tired, and cranky. Your tape recorder has probably run out of batteries and/or fresh tapes, and you've supplemented this with charts and tables of data and hastily scrawled notes that are so barely legible that your third-grade teacher would probably have failed you for the year.

This can go on for up to a week. Then you're supposed to go home and somehow avoid getting one boat mixed up with another as you write a detailed test report on just what it was that you did with each. And at the same time keep your editor happy by meeting an insanely tight deadline. It takes the right stuff to pull this off, and having shared a cockpit or two with Frank over the years, I can say with certainty he has it.

Frank Sargeant brings many years of experience with boats and the outdoors to the table, and whenever he tackles a project, he's very thorough about getting the job done. As a boating writer myself for 35 years, I can certainly tell you from personal experience that writing a book like this takes a great deal of time and requires enormous attention to detail. Boating writers rarely strike it rich, even from books as good as this one, so it has to be a labor of love.

Don't let the title mislead you. While it is well written in clear, concise terms that any idiot should be able to understand, the information it imparts is detailed enough to cover the subject thoroughly. I consider it good gut-level stuff, with lots of solid information, but also with a light touch of humor strategically injected here and there to make it an easy read.

No one will ever become an instant expert on boating, no matter what the guy down the street with the hot rod boat parked on a trailer in his driveway may think. And you certainly won't either, even if you read this book cover-to-cover. There's just too much information to absorb in one sitting. Thus I see this third edition of *The Complete Idiot's Guide to Boating and Sailing* also as a terrific reference book, one that belongs on your shelf within easy reach. And if it doesn't become dog-eared from constant use within a year or two, the only acceptable excuse is that you sold the boat.

—Bob Stearns

Bob Sterns is the editor at large for *Saltwater Sportsman* magazine. As a writer, he has published almost 1,500 feature articles and columns in magazines such as *Boating, Sea, Yachting, Motor Boating & Sailing, Rudder, Motorboat, Field & Stream, Outdoor Life, Sports Afield, Fishing World, Saltwater Sportsman, Small Boat Journal, Saltwater Fly Fishing* (Boating Columnist), and many others. He is the author of *The Fisherman's Boating Book* and the revision author for the *Saltwater Fisherman's Bible* (with Erwin A. Bauer) He has appeared on television on *The Fisherman* series, the *Outdoor Life* series, and *Sportsman's Adventures.*

Introduction

As Ted Turner once said, "It ain't as easy as it looks." Turner, an accomplished boater and former America's Cup skipper, was not talking about boating, but about his success in business. However, an experienced skipper makes handling a boat look very easy, when in fact it's a combination of knowledge and physical skills that takes a bit of preparation even to get started, and years of study and practice to master.

The Complete Idiot's Guide to Boating and Sailing, Third Edition, offers that preparation, beginning with the basics and then wedding them to some of the more technical topics in the later chapters. (For those who are not novices, skipping chapters is allowed and even encouraged—the convenient chapter outlines in the Contents at a Glance and the many subheads make it very easy to find your way around.) And this third edition includes a look at many modern developments in boating, such as the rapid rise of the four-stroke outboard and the widespread use of electronic charting and computerized navigation. You'll also find lots of new information on personal watercraft, sailboarding, and advances in safety gear.

There will not be a test at the end of the semester, nor even pop quizzes along the way. However, if your state is one that requires you to pass a boating-knowledge test before acquiring a license, this book is designed to give you all you need and lots more.

Boating might not be as easy as it looks, but it's not all that difficult if you have a guide to direct you around the reefs and rough spots.

Most boating books are written as if they are military drill books, which makes sense if you're studying to be captain of a nuclear submarine—there's nothing funny about driving the Sea Wolf into the Bosporus Straits. But recreational boating is supposed to be fun, and I hope this book will be fun, too.

The design of this book means you don't have to read every chapter to make it useful. In fact, if you're a lake or bay boater who never intends to get out of sight of land, you can probably skip right over Part 3 on marine navigation. Ditto for Part 7 on sailing, if you're a confirmed powerboater. And sailors who wouldn't be caught dead in a "stinkpot" might choose to bypass Chapters 2 and 3 on engines and props—though if you run an auxiliary kicker, you might want to make a few crib notes, just in case.

With *The Complete Idiot's Guide to Boating and Sailing, Third Edition,* you can easily locate all the information you need—whether you're just getting started in boating, or you've had some experience on the water and want to know more about the arts of navigation, anchoring, or rough-water handling. And although there's a very specific vocabulary in boating, I've taken care to define every term in everyday language that won't leave you guessing.

This book is a starting point to help you ...

 ◆ Learn which boat is best for you and your family.

 ◆ Save you money when buying a boat.

 ◆ Understand the legal requirements for safety equipment aboard.

 ◆ Get through that unnerving first launch.

 ◆ Avoid problems afloat.

 ◆ Build your confidence for taking on longer voyages and bigger waters.

 ◆ Navigate like an old salt.

 ◆ Keep your boat shipshape.

 ◆ Understand basic engine troubleshooting.

 ◆ Master the basics of sailing.

How to Use This Book

The Complete Idiot's Guide to Boating and Sailing, Third Edition, details all the important things you need to know to get started. Read the book and learn the basics, and then take it with you on your first voyage and put them to work. The important details are covered in seven parts:

Part 1, "Getting Started in Boating," walks you through selecting a boat that will be right for your family, whether their idea of fun is a day on the beach, chasing the big ones, diving on a colorful reef, or simply enjoying a quiet day of sailing. And it takes a look at the advantages and disadvantages of four-stroke and two-stroke outboards, of diesel versus gas, and of sail versus power.

Part 2, "The Basics of Operation," helps you with the details of getting underway for the first time, handling a boat around the docks, anchoring your boat, tying proper boating knots, and moving a boat with both paddles and engine power.

Part 3, "Getting from Point A to Point B: Marine Navigation," covers the use of charts, the marine rules of the road, the tools of navigation, and making your first long cruise. It also covers the use of the latest marine electronics, which make pinpoint navigation far easier than ever before.

Part 4, "Nature's Triple Play: Wind, Weather, and Tides," teaches you to understand the signals that bad weather is coming and how to protect yourself. It also covers the ins and outs of tidal flows in coastal areas, and how they can work for or against you.

Part 5, "Staying Safe Afloat," reviews safety gear required by federal law for recreational boats, reminds you of some basic measures to avoid getting into trouble in your boat, and offers some tips on how to deal with emergencies that could someday occur aboard.

Part 6, "Boating Maintenance," gives a review of the tools you need to keep your boat running right, plus advice on keeping your boat clean, neat, and at maximum resale value. It also covers engine maintenance and fixing some common but simple problems.

Part 7, "Sailing, Sailing ...," clarifies the sometimes confusing vocabulary of sailboaters; reviews the types of sailboats, rigging, and sails; and instructs in the basics of getting started in sailing in anything from an 8-foot sailboard to a 50-foot ketch.

Extras

Like your information in a nutshell—forget the verbiage and give you the facts? *The Complete Idiot's Guide to Boating and Sailing, Third Edition,* does the job with lots of compact, easy-to-find, and quick-to-read tips. Look for these elements throughout the book:

Boat Bytes

These are tips that make boating easier, more fun, or safer—a bit of advice from those who have been there and done that and can show you a better way.

Look Out!

You need to keep a sharp lookout when you go boating, and these sidebars will tell you exactly what to watch for when a situation can be difficult, expensive, or risky.

Salt Talk

If you want to understand boating, you need to speak the language. Seasoned sailors are often referred to as "Old Salts"—and you can get your sea legs by learning how to talk like they do. Read these sidebars and your boating and sailing vocabulary will bloom.

Nautical Notes

The devil might be in the details, but so is a lot of the interest. These segments give you added depth on topics that will help you navigate your way from being a boating novice to a seasoned skipper.

Acknowledgments

There have been so many people who have helped me along the way, both in learning boating and in becoming a writer, that it's hard to fit them all in a few paragraphs—but I'll try not to miss anyone.

Thanks to Marty Luray, who got me started in writing about boating when he bought my first story for *Rudder* more than 30 years ago. Thanks to Chris Caswell, who was my boss at *Sea* magazine for several great years; and to Harry Monahan, managing editor at *Sea*, who taught me lots of boating terminology, some of it printable in a family publication. (Harry, I finally learned to spell "accommodation"—two c's and two m's, right?)

Thanks to Tom McEwen, who hired me at the *Tampa Tribune*, and who has been a guide and mentor to me and so many other sportswriters for so many years.

Thanks to John Owens, Richard Stepler, and Randy Steele, my editors at *Boating* magazine over the last decade; and to features editors Jeanne Craig and David Seidman, who buried me with assignments; and to associate editor Lenny Rudow, who keeps me busy these days.

Thanks to Karl Wickstrom at *Florida Sportsman*, for founding one of the nation's finest fishing and boating magazines, and for letting me be a part of it so often. Thanks to Jeff Weakley, editor of *Florida Sportsman*, for all his guidance the past five years.

Thanks to Colin Moore, who so ably edits my boating columns for *Outdoor Life* magazine—but who inevitably outfishes me. Thanks to Larry Larsen of Larsen Outdoors Publishing, who convinced me to get into the book business for the first time almost a decade ago, and has now published 10 of my books.

Thanks to Steve Hargis, producer at *Outdoor World*, who took a chance with an untested scriptwriter, and wound up creating a team that won a basketful of awards in the TNN years.

Thanks to Dan Atwood at Pro-Line Boats, who put me up for the NMMA Award and be damned if we didn't win it.

Thanks to Earl Bentz, former president of OMC Boat Group and now CEO of Triton, who backed two of my early boating books and has offered lots of encouragement. Thanks to Alex Leva of OMC/Hydra-Sports for countless assistances and advice. Thanks to the staff at Brunswick's Mercaibo Test Center for years of education. Thanks to Walker Agency and Yamaha, Bear Agency, and particularly tech wizard Dave Greenwood of Suzuki, and all the other boat and motor companies who have been so helpful on so many stories. BOAT U.S. was helpful in providing price data and other useful material from their excellent catalog, and Steve Colgate of the Offshore Sailing School got me interested in sailing for the first time more than 30 years ago.

Thanks to all the skippers and guides who have taken me under their wings all these years, glossed over my errors, and corrected my perceptions with their experience and good humor.

Special Thanks to the Technical Reviewer

The Complete Idiot's Guide to Boating and Sailing, Third Edition, was reviewed by an expert who double-checked the accuracy of what you'll learn here, to help us ensure that this book gives you everything you need to know about boating and sailing. Special thanks are extended to Brian Battuello. Brian met his partner, Frances Ross, at the Cal Sailing Club in Berkeley, California. They've raced double-handed from San Francisco to Hawaii and cruised to Maine, Bermuda, and the Caribbean. They have too many boats.

Trademarks

All terms mentioned in this book that are known to be or are suspected of being trademarks or service marks have been appropriately capitalized. Alpha Books and Penguin Group (USA) Inc. cannot attest to the accuracy of this information. Use of a term in this book should not be regarded as affecting the validity of any trademark or service mark.

Part 1

Getting Started in Boating

Help! Where do you start?

Right here. Part 1 helps you and your family decide which boat will best let you do the things you'd like to do on the water.

Prefer to cruise, ski, dive, fish, or simply relax on a secluded beach? There's a boat that's just right for each of these activities. Ditto if you're into sports that use your muscles as power, or your technical skills to harness the winds.

Do you need one motor or two? Gas or diesel? Two-stroke or four? And what sort of propeller will give your boat the best performance—you'll find all the answers here.

And if you'd prefer to "dock" your boat in your garage, I'll tell you how to do that, too, as well as give you details on which trailer is right for your boat and how to handle it—and maintain it.

Chapter 1

Welcome to the Wet–And Wonderful–World of Boating!

In This Chapter

- ◆ Finding the right kind of boat for you
- ◆ Learning the vocabulary of boating
- ◆ If you have to ask how much it costs … you're smart!
- ◆ Buying your first boat: New or used?

You've looked at the boating magazines and mooned around the boat shows long enough. Now it's time for *you* to be the guy or gal next to that smiling, deeply tanned model with the mirrored sunglasses and the wind-rippled hair, cruising across that emerald sea toward adventure, romance, and a monthly payment book.

Or maybe your vision is a bit more domestic: the spouse, the kids, the Boston terrier, a jug of Gatorade, and a picnic basket full of pastrami on rye, off for a visit to a sandy beach. Sailing, water-skiing, snorkeling, a visit to the next port down the river, or maybe a cruise to that island over the horizon—*you* are the skipper ... you decide.

You're in command in a world where there are no yellow lines and no traffic jams, where fish and birds and wonderful marine mammals such as porpoises and manatees are frequently part of the scenery, and where you can find true solitude when you want it. No wonder people love boats and boating.

There's an aura of mystery to handling a boat, cultivated in part by the arcane language of the old salts of the sea. But getting started is a lot easier than you might imagine, and learning the basics for competent, safe operation takes a minimal investment of time and energy.

But first, you need a boat.

What type of boat is really best for you and your family? Read on.

Start at the Bottom Line

Whatever your boating dream, realizing it starts with facing the realities of affordability, space, affordability, seaworthiness, affordability, comfort, affordability, and affordability.

It's the money, friends. Everybody knows that.

With boating, as with everything else in life, you will soon find that you always want just a bit more than you can actually afford. That said, it *is* possible to go boating at some level on just about any budget that features discretionary income. I currently own a 15-foot Lowe aluminum skiff with a 25-horsepower outboard, which I can afford, and a $25,000 Sea Pro fiberglass center console with a 150-horsepower outboard, which I can't. (If a man's reach does not exceed his grasp, what are 12-year payments for?)

> **Boat Bytes**
>
> If you can manage just $100 per month, you can go boating in style. In fact, if you enjoy "people-powered" boats such as canoes and kayaks, you can be a boat owner for under $50 per month!

Because boats last a long time and don't go out of style rapidly, you can get long-term financing, up to 15 years, on most models. This makes the payments relatively easy for anyone with steady employment. You can get a rough estimate of 5-year payments at 8 to 10 percent by multiplying the number of thousands by $20—that is, a $5,000 boat will have payments around $100, a $10,000 boat will run around $200, and a $20,000 boat will cost around $400 per month. Check out the following table for examples.

(And note, at present, if your credit is good, you can probably get a lower interest rate—and lower payments. Many large dealers will set up the financing for you right at the dealership—but it may pay to shop around to get the best interest rate.)

What Kind of Boat Will Your Money Buy?

Payments on a $1,000 Canoe at 10 Percent Interest

Term	Monthly Payment	Interest Over Full Term
60 months	$21.25	$275.00
120 months	$13.22	$586.40
180 months	$10.75	$935.00

Payments on a $5,000 Bass Boat at 10 Percent Interest

Term	Monthly Payment	Interest Over Full Term
60 months	$106.24	$1,374.40
120 months	$66.08	$2,929.60
180 months	$53.73	$4,671.40

As you can see, longer payments mean lower payments. But they also add up to lots more interest—an amount almost equal to the principal in the case of the 15-year term.

Cash is usually the best buy on any depreciable asset—that is, any asset that loses value over time—but if you can't manage, the long-term payments make it possible to enjoy the boat of your choice within your budget.

Nautical Notes

I own two boats because, for me, one is never enough, and sometimes two are not enough. I have owned as many as seven boats at one time, until the zoning people came knocking.

The problem, as you soon discover when you get into boating up to your chin, is that the boat that's just right for a solitary paddle into a yard-wide tidal creek where the scarlet ibises nest is not the right boat for crossing a 25-mile-wide bay with four or five aboard. That's why many long-time boaters wind up with a backyard that looks like a boat basin.

However, there are lots of boats that will meet the basic needs of most beginning boaters. The question is, out of all the thousands of designs and sizes, which one will be the best fit for you and your crew?

Maintenance Costs

If you opt for a 15-foot fiberglass canoe, maintenance costs won't ever be a concern. But the larger and more complex the boat you buy, the more you have to consider repair and maintenance expenses when deciding how much boat you can afford. If you'll be storing it in a slip or at a high-and-dry marina (where the boats are lifted out and stored on racks, usually inside a large building), don't forget about those monthly fees. If you're a powerboater or a sailboater with auxiliary power, you'll need to budget for regular oil changes (with four-stroke and diesel engines) and tune-ups. Fuel costs will be part of the picture—particularly if you choose a boat with big twin outboards. And don't forget the cost of insurance—your finance company will require it, if common sense does not.

Boats that are stored in the water need anti-fouling paint every year or two, and sailboat rigging and sails have to be maintained or replaced as they wear. For a 20-foot-long powerboat that's stored on a trailer at your home, these costs can be as little as $15 per foot, per year—i.e., around $300. If your community association bans boat storage in your yard, budget at least $25 a month to store the boat on a trailer at a commercial storage facility. For larger boats stored at a marina, costs can run to $200 per foot per year and more.

If the Sloop Fits, Buy It

Boat Bytes

Englishman Izaak Walton wrote *The Compleat Angler*, the first widely read book on recreational fishing, in 1653. It's a celebration of angling, conservation, and the pastoral lifestyle, and has made Walton the patron saint of anglers everywhere.

The trick to buying a boat that's right for you is to get one that has enough space for everybody you'd normally bring aboard, and that fits the "mission" you and your crew envision.

If you want silence and communion with nature, you're probably going to be a sailor, or perhaps a paddler of your own canoe or kayak. If you want the thrill of mile-a-minute speeds, big-engined muscle boats might be for you. If you have budding Izaak Waltons in the family, a fishing boat will do the trick. If you like boats so well you want to live aboard, a trawler or houseboat might be in your future.

What to Call the Pointy End (and the Rest of a Boat)

Before delving any further into what type of boat you want, you need to learn a bit of "boater-ese"—the language of boaters. (Cursing doesn't count.) Some of the basic definitions are found in the following figure. More definitions are scattered throughout the coming chapters as "Salt Talk" margin notes. After you learn the lingo, you'll sound like an old salt when you talk about boats!

The following two figures show you the various parts of the boat. (Sailboats have their own terminology, which we'll discuss in Part 7, "Sailing, Sailing ...." And you'll find many added terms in Appendix A.)

The vocabulary of boaters can be as confusing as Russian at first, but it becomes more familiar after some time aboard.

Here are the basic terms to describe the various parts of most boats—use them as often as you can when aboard, and soon they'll be second nature:

- **aft** Toward the back part of the boat.

- **amidships** The middle part of the boat, between aft and forward.

- **beam** The width of a boat, usually measured at its widest point.

- **bow** Rhymes with "ow"; this is the pointy front end of a boat. (Most canoes have two pointy ends. The one in front is the bow.)

- **chines** Where the bottom of a boat meets the sides.

- **draft** The distance from the waterline to the lowest point of the hull—the shallowest depth in which a boat will float without any part touching bottom.

- **forward** Toward the front part of the boat.

- **freeboard** The distance from the waterline to the gunnels.

- **gunnel** The top of the hull, where the inner liner joins the outer hull. (It's also spelled "gunwale," but still pronounced "gunnel.")

- **inwale** The inner side of the gunnel.

- **keel** The junction where the two halves of the bottom meet. Structurally, the main center frame member of the hull. In sailing, the fin projecting from the bottom to reduce leeway is also called the keel.

- **length overall (LOA)** The distance from the tip of the bow to the end of the stern.

- **stern** or **transom** The squared-off back end of the boat.

- **waterline** Where the surface of the water meets the hull.

Even the floors and doors have special names aboard a boat.

Here's the rundown on each of the terms in the preceding figures:

- **hatch** A horizontal door, usually on a storage compartment.

- **sole** The part of the boat you stand on, the floor.

- **outboard motor** A self-contained engine and propulsion system that mounts on the stern. Historically these were two-cycle engines, which burned oil along with gasoline to make power, but four-cycle outboards are now rapidly becoming dominant due to quieter operation and lower emissions.

- **sterndrive** Also known as an "inboard/outboard" or "I/O," this system combines a four-cycle automotive-type engine or a small diesel engine inside the boat with a drive unit on the transom.

- **inboard** A four-cycle gas or diesel engine mounted inside the boat, which drives the boat through a shaft in the bottom.

What Kind of Boat Are You Looking For?

Boats can be broadly classified into "power" and "sail," according to their forms of propulsion. In addition, there are many divisions within the classes (and people-powered boats are a whole class by themselves—see *The Complete Idiot's Guide to Canoeing and Kayaking* for lots more information).

Powerboats generally have large engines and depend entirely on a motor for propulsion. Sailboats might or might not have auxiliary engines, but they always carry a mast and sails that enable them to harness the wind. Sailboats are not quite "turn-key" rigs like powerboats; it takes considerable instruction to learn the basics, but those who take the time to learn are rewarded with a lifetime of wonderful recreation—and no noisy exhausts.

Power to the People: Boats with Motors

For most families, that first boat is a small powerboat powered by an outboard motor of 50 to 90 horsepower. Powerboating takes less study and requires less physical work than sailing, so it's a quick, easy way to get started.

Powerboats range from slow as a turtle to fast as a flying fish. They can be broken into many subclasses, including the following:

- Runabouts, ski boats, and performance boats

- Fishing boats

- Live-aboard cruisers, trawlers, and houseboats

- Pontoon and deck boats

- Personal watercraft (PWCs)

- Inflatable boats

Powerboat prices range from under $2,000 to millions of dollars, and sizes range from diminutive 8-footers powered by 1-horse electric motors to stately 150-footers driven by multiple diesel engines with thousands of horsepower.

Many powerboats in the popular 14- to 17-foot class are available at prices from $5,000 to $14,000, including a trailer that allows you to "dock" them in your garage and tow them to the ramp each weekend. These are great starter boats.

One Model Fits All: The Runabout

The runabout is what most of us think of when we think of a one-model-fits-all family boat. It has a closed bow, a windshield, back-to-back seats that fold down into a sun lounge, and space to store water skis and life jackets under the sole or main deck.

Salt Talk

A walk-through windshield has a hinged section in the middle that swings open to give passengers easy access to the bow.

A variation on the runabout is the bow-rider, which has the same hull and aft layout, but with seats replacing the closed bow and a *walk-through windshield* to enable passage forward. An advantage of the bow-rider is that there's more seating space—you can carry six or eight passengers, depending on the depth and beam of the boat and your tolerance for close company.

Bow-rider boats feature "walk-through windshields" that enable easy access to seating up front. These are good for relaxing or fishing, but it's best to ride behind the windshield when the boat is traveling at speed.

(Lund Boats)

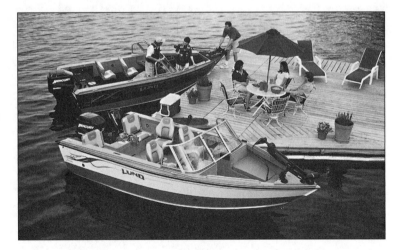

The front section of a bow-rider creates a great "kiddie-pen" where you can keep little sailors under your watchful eye with just a bit of separation provided by the windshield. It's no place for kids once the boat is underway, however—the ride is rough, and they'll be safer back in the cockpit.

Dedicated ski boats are a specialized form of runabout. They're usually inboard-powered, 18 to 22 feet long, and have fairly flat bottoms so that they *plane* easily when pulling several skiers.

Some feature special fins on the bottom that enable them to turn very sharply, a ski pylon or post near the center to attach the tow rope, and a rear-facing seat so that one passenger can keep an eye on the skier without turning around. Ski boats tend to be fairly expensive for their size, ranging from $25,000 to $50,000.

Boat Bytes

The National Marine Manufacturers rating, listed on a sticker placed on the dash of all powerboats, gives the safe load capacity in terms of persons estimated at 150 pounds each, plus gear. It also lists the safe power rating of any powerboat.

Salt Talk

When a boat **planes**, it lifts near the surface, increasing speed and decreasing drag.

The Need for Speed: Performance Boats

Performance boats also share the general configuration of runabouts, but there's a difference in the engine room. They're also called "muscle boats" for their powerful engines relative to their weight, and they're dedicated to white-knuckle speeds. A runabout might be powered by as little as 70 horses; muscle boats sport engines of 225 to 1,000 horsepower.

Performance boats usually have a deep vee bottom to provide a soft ride at speed, but the aft several feet of the keel might be flattened into a planing pad. This pad functions like a slalom ski as speed increases, elevating the boat very high in the water and allowing it to reach speeds of 60 mph and higher.

It's not uncommon for performance boats only 20 feet long to wear outboard engines of 250 horses. Those in the 30- to 35-foot range might have twin 500-horsepower sterndrives and run close to 100 mph in the hands of a highly skilled driver! Because of the cost of

Look Out!

Sixty miles an hour is fairly sedate cruising down the interstate in your Chevrolet, but on the water, mile-a-minute speeds are exciting, challenging, and possibly dangerous. The rapidly changing contour of the surface, unmarked shoals, and the unique handling forces that develop as a boat accelerates demand added caution, experience, and skill from the driver.

high-powered engines, these boats are also expensive, ranging from $30,000 to well over $450,000.

Something Fishy: Boats for Anglers

Fishing can be as intriguing as golf and slightly more addictive than chocolate. Consequently, fishing boats of all sorts are top sellers.

Of course, many fishing boats are also used regularly as ski boats, dive boats, and casual day-cruising rigs. One variety known as the "Fish 'n Ski" includes a ski pylon, walk-through windshield, and bow-rider seats as well as fishing seats, rod boxes, trolling sockets, and live wells. It serves double-duty.

Fishing boats can be divided into those suited for freshwater, which include rigs specifically designed to chase largemouth bass, walleyes, crappies, and other species, and those designed for coastal use.

Up the Creek: Freshwater Fishing Boats

Bass boats, so called because they're popular in fishing for largemouth and smallmouth bass, are often high-performance hulls designed to travel across big reservoirs at speeds better than a mile a minute. (Fast fish, those bass!) Bass boats tend to be javelin-shaped and powered by big V6 outboards producing 150 to 275 horses. Most run on a narrow "pad" near the transom, which causes them to plane up on top of the water much like a slalom ski, increasing speed and reducing fuel use (but not by much!). They're usually equipped with a silent electric trolling motor at the bow to provide low-speed maneuvering as the angler probes cover for his quarry. Prices range from $7,000 to $50,000.

Smaller boats, some with squared-off bows known as "jon boats," are popular for pursuit of all sorts of finny critters from catfish to sturgeon. Most of these boats are lightweight aluminum, which means they can be pushed with motors from 5 to 40 horses. Overall prices are affordable, starting as low as $2,500 including a trailer but without a motor. (The motors are portable and can be added or removed as needed.)

Monsters of the Sea: Saltwater Fishing Boats

Coastal fishing boats fall into three general divisions determined by size, seaworthiness, and price.

Most seaworthy are the biggies designed for fishing well offshore. They range in length from 20 to 65 feet and are priced anywhere from $20,000 to several million dollars. These boats have lots of freeboard, lots of beam, and often twin or even triple engines.

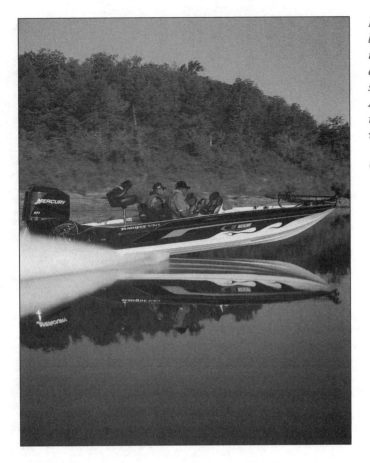

Lots of speed allows bass boaters to reach distant fishing areas in a hurry. Raised casting decks at the bow and stern make for easy casting. An electric trolling motor at the bow provides silent power while fishing.

(Ranger Boats)

Layouts vary. Many from 20 to 35 feet are center consoles, with the wheel in the middle of the boat and fishing space both fore and aft—the preferred arrangement for those who cast to their fish.

Cuddy-cabin boats have a low cabin under the bow—usually space for bunks and a dinette, but not enough head-room to stand up. Full-cabin boats, also known as "sportfisherman" rigs, have standup head-room, usually a full bath or "head," and a kitchenette or "galley." If you dream of catching marlin bigger than a pickup truck, this is your boat.

The "walk-around," shown in the following photo, is a popular variation of the cabin boat. It has space around the sides of the cabin to allow anglers to walk to the bow to fish, thus giving it some of the advantages of the center console, yet preserving the amenities of the full "house."

Walk-around cabin boats have full cabins but also provide walkways to the bow for easy fishing and anchor handling. This model, from Robalo, includes a built-in motor bracket at the stern.

(Yamaha Outboards)

Cabin rigs make it possible to spend the night afloat. Camping out on the water has a special charm (if the mosquitoes aren't too thick) and cabin rigs make it possible to extend the range of your cruises beyond the distance you can travel in a day.

Bay boats have moderate vee bottoms, moderate freeboard, and usually a single engine. Lengths of 17 to 24 feet are common, and prices range from $15,000 to $50,000. They're usually center consoles. These are boats designed to take on sizable waters, and they're often used along the ocean and gulf beaches in moderate weather.

For the Shallow-Minded: Flats Boats

Flats boats are designed to pursue trophy saltwater species in depths of one to four feet. Some of these boats float in only eight inches of water and can run in as little as a foot. Elusive, metallic creatures known as bonefish spend a good part of their time in water barely deep enough to float a tadpole. They are as neurotic as turkeys the day before Thanksgiving, ready to speed for deep water at the bump of a pushpole against a gunnel, very difficult to fool, and inedible when caught. In the perverse way of anglers, they are considered wonderful game fish. Similarly obnoxious species include the permit and the six-foot-long tarpon, also avidly chased by flats anglers.

Salt Talk

Draft refers to the depth from the waterline to the deepest portion of the keel. It measures the minimum depth in which a boat can operate without going aground.

Flats boats are stealth fighters devised to sneak up on these species. Most have a nearly flat bottom (the boats, not the fish) to give them a shallow *draft*.

Flats rigs have low freeboard so that they don't catch the wind and drift excessively. Lengths range from 15 to 21 feet. Center or side consoles are common, although some are simply operated from near the transom via a tiller. Prices range from $7,000 to as much as $45,000 for special lightweight models with particularly shallow draft.

Boat Bytes

The National Marine Manufacturers' Association (NMMA) is both a boating industry booster and watch-dog. Members includes thousands of companies that build boats, motors, and accessories, and it also helps to set boating standards for construction and safety. Check them out online at www.nmma.org.

Leisure Afloat: Cruisers, Trawlers, and Houseboats

For those who can afford them, these floating houses turn boating into a much more leisurely, even luxurious, affair that those not into salt in the hair and sardines in the swimsuit can appreciate.

Cruisers and trawlers differ from houseboats in that they have deeper-draft hulls and are more suited to taking on offshore waters and big inlets. They also usually have more power and more seaworthy fittings. Consequently, they're expensive, with prices starting at about $1,500 per foot and going into the stratosphere.

Cruisers have *planing hulls*, which means they offer speeds not possible with *displacement hulls*. They're often equipped with twin engines and can cruise at better than 20 mph, reaching maximum speeds of near 40 mph with adequate power. The level of interior finish can be superb in these boats, and the prices reflect the quality fittings. Lengths from 30 to 55 feet are common, with prices from $80,000 to several million dollars.

Salt Talk

Planing hulls have flattened sections on the aft bottom that allow these boats to rise near the surface of the water, reducing drag and increasing speed. **Displacement hulls** have rounded bottoms and chines that prevent these boats from reaching plane. This makes them slower than planing hulls, but they're more economical to operate, can carry heavier loads, and often have far greater range than planing hulls.

Trawlers nearly always have displacement hulls, rounded bottoms where speed is limited by the waterline length, as opposed to flatter aft portions that allow for planing. No matter how much power you put on a round-bottomed trawler, it still chugs along at a speed somewhere south of 10 knots. (A knot is 1.15 statute miles per hour, thus 10 knots is 11.5 mph.) This means you need plenty of time to go anywhere in a trawler. However, the round hulls are extremely seaworthy (though some are "rolly" in beam seas, or waves coming from the sides). Displacement or nonplaning hulls tend to be very fuel-efficient—they travel a long distance on each gallon of gasoline or diesel. This is the reason that many long-distance travelers choose trawlers. Equipped with a small diesel inboard, some can travel over 1,000 miles between refueling. Lengths range from about 28 to 50 feet, with prices from $100,000 to $500,000.

> **Nautical Notes**
>
> The largest boat-owners' association in the world is BOAT U.S., which frequently lobbies for boating causes at both the state and federal levels. The association offers special insurance packages and maintains its own mail-order catalog. They can be reached online at www.boatus.com or by phone at 703-461-2864.

Houseboats are the camper-trailers of the watery world—slow, unlovely, and unexciting, but with all the comforts of home for those who do most of their boating in protected waters. And they're amazingly affordable.

Many houseboats ride atop a pair of aluminum cylinders known as pontoons, although some models have vee-shaped fiberglass, aluminum, or steel hulls. Lengths range from 25 to more than 100 feet. Power is usually an outboard of 30 to 100 horses, although the larger rigs have inboard power. Prices range from $25,000 to $400,000. You get actual conventional rooms aboard—kitchens, dining rooms, living rooms, bedrooms, and bathrooms, all on one level. Houseboats feel like a home ashore, but you can take a swim off the back porch.

Houseboats Without the House: Pontoon and Deck-Type Boats

Pontoon boats and deck-type boats feature couches, dinettes, sinks, refrigerators, and usually portable marine toilets, but no sleeping areas and no permanent roof. Weather protection is usually from a convertible top known as a Bimini. It's tall enough to stand under, but with no side panels to prevent air circulation. A pontoon with a front deck for fishing is shown in the following photo.

Pontoon boats ride on the same sort of aluminum cylinders as many houseboats. They can be powered by motors as small as 10 horsepower but rarely more than 60 horsepower, and they're cheap to buy and operate. Because of the great amount of floor space and comfortable seating, pontoon boats are a favorite with families. Prices are surprisingly reasonable, starting at around $12,000 for an 18-footer and ranging up to $25,000 for a 30-footer.

Pontoon boats ride on aluminum or fiberglass "logs" or cylinders that are usually filled with flotation foam. These boats are inexpensive, roomy, and comfortable. Although not quite so graceful in appearance as other boats, they're a great value.

(Triton Boats)

Deck-type boats look much the same as pontoon boats from the deck upward, with couches, lounge chairs, tables, and maybe even a portable TV and barbecue grill. But below the deck is a semi-vee hull that allows full planing operation with adequate power. They can handle motors of 50 to 150 horses and speed along at 30 to 50 mph, making them good ski boats. Deck-type boats range in length from 18 to 24 feet. They cost considerably more than pontoons, with prices of $15,000 to $35,000 common.

Motorcycles on the Water: Personal Watercraft

Personal watercraft, also known as PWCs, are the newcomers in the boating world, but have rocketed to near the top of the fleet in sales since their introduction in the mid-1980s. They're also the motorcycles of the boating world, designed for thrills and speed

CAUTION

Look Out!

PWCs account for a disproportionate share of boating accidents nationwide. Although PWCs are safe if driven carefully, inexperienced drivers pushing them to the limit frequently run into trouble. Use the same care as you would when skippering any watercraft, particularly in crowded waterways, and you can enjoy these sporty little boats safely.

rather than comfort. They offer special appeal to the young and the young at heart who want excitement in their boating.

Most PWCs are under 10 feet long. The seats are saddles, just as in a Harley-Davidson, and you steer via handlebars. The power for these boats is via a water-jet instead of the open-bladed propeller found on conventional boats—a safety measure that also makes the craft capable of spectacular end-for-end turns.

The power ranges from 40 to 165 horsepower. Given the light weight of these boats, this results in speeds to 70 mph or more with some models. Prices begin at around $5,000 and go to a bit over $10,000. Turn to Chapter 10 for a detailed look at PWCs.

Boating on Air: Inflatable Boats

Inflatable boats are basically waterborne balloons, but they're a lot tougher. Multiple air chambers and very stout skins on modern inflatables make them extremely durable. In fact, some of the heaviest-duty boats used by the Coast Guard are inflatables, and they take these boats through outrageous weather where lesser boats with conventional hulls wouldn't stand a chance.

Inflatables have incredible buoyancy for their weight and can carry many times the load of conventional boats of equal size. Let the air out of them and you can carry them in the trunk of the family car and stow them in the hall closet.

Inflatables like this Zodiac are favorites as yacht tenders because their light weight makes it easy to get them aboard, and they can be stored deflated to save space. The soft sides also don't mar a yacht's finish as a hard-sided dinghy might.

(Zodiac of North America)

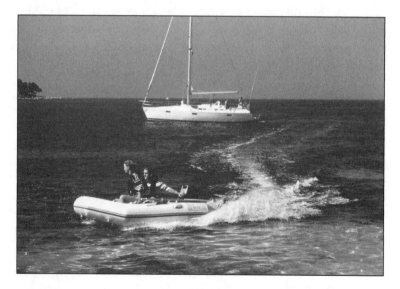

Add a fiberglass bottom, as many larger inflatables have, and you have a boat within a boat—a vee bottom to soften the ride and the giant sponsons to provide that remarkable flotation and capability to bump into things without scratching or bending. Some large inflatables have twin outboards so they can really fly.

The downside is it's expensive to make a really good inflatable—the best ones cost about as much as a fiberglass boat of equal size. Lengths range from 7 to 22 feet, with prices from $300 to $20,000.

Powered by the Wind: Sailboats

Boats powered by the wind are a totally different genre than those powered by machinery and seem to appeal to an entirely different group. In sailing, the voyage is often as important as the destination. Of course, there are a lot of boaters who enjoy both types of boats.

The basic configurations of sailboats range from the tiny, flyweight sailboards to majestic double-masted ketches capable of crossing all the world's oceans. Sailboats vary in price from as little as $1,000 to millions of dollars, and their designs vary as much as the price.

We'll delve into the basics of selecting a wind-powered craft that fits both your budget and your interests—and take a closer look at the categories of these boats, based on their mast and sail arrangement—in Part 7.

Single-masted sailboats like this one are known as "sloops." They're the most common sailboat, more economical to buy and easier to sail than two-masted ketches and yawls.

(Beneteau Yachts)

Buy New or Used?

Boats, like cars, have negotiable prices. It's rare to have to pay the sticker price. You can often get 10 percent off the list price, and maybe more if the dealer needs to make a sale to pay the rent. If you buy used, you can save lots more. Here's a look at the advantages and disadvantages of buying new versus buying used.

Look Out!

Some dealers price rigs without trailers to get you in the door. But unless you're going to store the boat at a marina or the dock in back of your house, you're going to need a trailer. This adds $1,200 to $3,500 to the base price—ask about the trailer, right away.

Buy new and …

◆ You can order exactly what you want, including a special engine, electronics, and interior trim.

◆ You get a full warranty—the dealer, not you, has to worry about the repairs.

◆ Some companies offer special package deals with lots of extra equipment at bargain prices.

◆ You pay new-boat prices and take the initial depreciation hit of 10 to 25 percent.

Buy used and …

◆ You save big money—25 to 50 percent!

◆ You get lots of extra gear added by the first owner, at no extra cost.

◆ Sailboats virtually never wear out, though you might have to repair some rigging on used boats. On powerboats and sailboats with auxiliary power, the engines can be more problematic, however. In general, fiberglass hulls last far longer than most owners want to keep them.

◆ There may be hidden faults that will have to be fixed—and you have to pay to fix them.

Boat Bytes

It's a good idea to have a marine mechanic take a look at any used boat you're considering. They can tell you in an hour what you couldn't figure out for yourself in weeks—or until the engine stranded you. The fee might be $100 to $200, but it's well worth the price.

There's more "wiggle room" in the price of a used boat than in the price of a new one. The difference between the wholesale price (what the dealer gives you for your used rig) and the retail price (the price he wants to charge the next buyer) is usually 20 to 30 percent.

You can talk him out of some of that difference, particularly if you're interested in a boat that's not a hot property. It's not uncommon, after some negotiation, haggling, arguing, and sometimes begging—to buy a two-year-old boat in excellent shape from stem to stern for 60 percent of the original price.

One of the best ways to shop for a used boat is via the Internet; numerous sites list literally thousands of boats, and you can search their databanks by make, length, price, year, and so on. You can also ask to see just boats that are in your home state or even in your area code. Two of the largest sites are www.boattraderonline.com and www.boats.com.

The Least You Need to Know

- No one boat is perfect for all families or all applications. Choose a boat that suits most of your needs, but be aware that it has limitations.

- Boaters have a vocabulary specific to watercraft. Learning what to call the parts of a boat makes operation simpler for all aboard.

- Boats, like cars, have negotiable prices. If you don't haggle, you don't get the best deal.

- New boats might give the dealer headaches, but you don't have to worry about them.

- Used boats save you money, but any headaches that come with them belong to you.

Chapter 2

Power to the People: Marine Engines

In This Chapter

- ◆ Understanding outboard motors
- ◆ The basic parts and how to work them
- ◆ Inside-out and outside-in: sterndrives and inboard engines
- ◆ Determining whether you need twin engines for your boat
- ◆ The advantages of diesel engines

Most boats on the water today are powerboats. Even most sailboats (except racers, who like to keep weight to a minimum) carry inboard or outboard motors to get them easily in and out of harbors, and for those days when the wind just doesn't blow.

Good thing, too, or a lot of people wouldn't be boating—oars don't do the job when it comes to heading 20 miles offshore, and even experienced sailors need a little power backup sometimes. Sailing is an art not learned quickly or casually, and the engine on a sailboat can be very important for the neophyte.

Several forms of unpowered boating such as kayaking, windsurfing, and outrigger canoeing have experienced periods of very rapid growth in recent years Nonetheless, the dominant forms of recreational boating involve power.

The power in a powerboat comes from many sources. In this chapter, we'll look at the types of motors used in boats and consider how much it costs to purchase and operate them.

Portable Power—Outboard Motors

Most first-time boaters buy boats with outboard motors.

Outboards feature an integral drive system, which includes a drive shaft and propeller in a single unit that can be moved from boat to boat. (In practice, outboards above 15 horses are rarely removed from the transom, however.) All of them still look more or less like the motor designed by Wisconsin inventor Ole Evinrude and patented in the United States on September 16, 1910. Evinrude went on to found Outboard Marine Corporation (OMC), which was the world's largest manufacturer of outboards for many years before being purchased by Bombardier.

An outboard motor includes a gasoline *engine* mounted at the top of a long shaft and gears, *prop shaft*, and *prop* mounted at the bottom. The *motor* clamps on the stern of a boat, and the whole thing—motor, shaft, gears, and prop—pivots to steer the boat.

 Salt Talk

The propeller on a boat is commonly referred to as the **prop**. The horizontal shaft that connects it to the vertical drive shaft from the powerhead is called the **prop shaft.**

In nautical parlance, an **engine** is the power unit itself without the drivetrain and propeller. A **motor** is a complete power unit including a drive shaft and prop. Thus, inboard and sterndrive power plants are usually referred to as engines, while outboard power plants are usually called motors. (And just to make things more confusing, a motor is also an energy-conversion device such as an electric or hydraulic motor that draws power from an engine located elsewhere on the boat.)

Outboards today offer the advantages of high performance, low weight, and *power trim* and *tilt* of the lower unit. Trim can control the running attitude of a boat—the angle of the boat bottom to the surface of the water—and makes it easier to operate in shallow water. Outboards are also easy to steer due to the "vectorable" thrust— that is, the propeller itself can be angled to push the stern to one side or the other.

Salt Talk _____

Power trim is an electrical and hydraulic system for moving the lower unit of an outboard or sterndrive in or out relative to the transom. Trim is used for minor adjustments while underway to help improve the running attitude of the boat. **Power tilt** is part of the trim system. It enables the motor to be tilted to almost 90 degrees while at the dock or on a trailer.

The following figure shows the lower unit of an outboard.

The lower unit of an outboard and a sterndrive are nearly identical. The power put out by the engine turns the prop, which causes the boat to move through the water.

Let's run through the parts of the lower unit of an outboard:

- **Tab.** The tab offsets the tendency of a prop to "walk" sideways slightly at some trim positions and balances the steering force (not to be confused with "trim tabs" that control running trim, usually found on larger boats with inboard power).

- **Bullet or nosecone.** The bullet or nosecone houses the forward and reverse gears and prop shaft.

- **Propeller.** The propeller, or prop, grips the water and propels the boat by pushing water backward. Three-bladed props are most common.

- **Skeg.** The lowest extension of the lower unit, the skeg protects the prop from striking obstructions and also helps the boat track straight.

- **Lubricant fill hole.** The lower unit requires oil to provide lubrication. The lubricant fill hole allows for oil to be drained and refilled.

- **Anti-ventilation plate.** This flat plate helps prevent the prop from drawing in surface air and losing its grip on the water. It is often called the "cavitation plate," a usage that is technically incorrect but common enough to be widely understood.

◆ **Cooling water pick-up.** This small intake allows the water pump to pull water through the lower unit and up into the cooling passages of the *powerhead*. It must be kept free of debris at all times.

Salt Talk

The **powerhead** includes the combustion chamber, ports, and cylinders where power is made by burning fuel.

Tabs on outboards and sterndrives are usually made of zinc, which acts as a "sacrificial anode" in salt water. The "sacrifice" it makes is to literally be eaten up by galvanic corrosion in order to protect the more important aluminum and steel parts of the motor. When a tab becomes severely depleted, it can be replaced by loosening one bolt. Inboards usually have a similar zinc anode bolted in place on their shaft, and it, too, must be replaced periodically.

Four Strokes: The Wave of the Future?

Until recently, there was no choice in outboards—nearly all were two-stroke, also called two-cycle, and they all burned a small amount of oil as lubricant along with their fuel. They also released a significant amount of unburned fuel and oil mixture into the water. The resulting air and water pollution eventually led to federal regulations calling for a considerable decrease in emissions by 2006.

Motor manufacturers took two different routes to achieve the improvement. Some, including Bombardier, Mercury, and Yamaha, built what are known as "high-pressure direct-injection" two-cycle engines, which squirt atomized fuel directly into the cylinders at very high pressure via a very precise timing system. The result is that very little unburned fuel blows out the exhaust ports, and the motors greatly decrease use of both fuel and lubricating oil. These motors typically beat conventional two-strokes by 40 percent in fuel efficiency at low- and mid-range rpms and decrease pollutants accordingly.

A second approach, which now dominates the industry for motors above 50 horsepower and is rapidly becoming favored in smaller motors, was to build four-stroke outboards. These are very similar to automotive engines, with valves, cams, and oil-bath lubrication; they do not require oil to be injected into the cylinders, so they produce very little pollution. They are quiet, smoke-free, very dependable, and achieve 40 to 50 percent better fuel efficiency than conventional two-strokes. However, most are slightly heavier and cost considerably more than their two-stroke counterparts, and they also present the problem of what to do with the used oil when it is changed, typically after every 100 hours of operation.

For performance-minded boaters, most four-strokes don't rev up as fast as two-strokes, so they don't provide head-snapping acceleration. However, Mercury's new Verado series, the world's first supercharged outboards, get around this weakness with take-off that's a match for anything on the market. The motors are expensive and relatively untested as of this writing, but if the technology holds up, this could become a very popular way of improving four-stroke performance.

This V6 outboard from Mercury is the world's first supercharged outboard. The Verado four-stroke is available in outputs from 200 to 275 horses. The motor is environmentally friendly, fuel-efficient, and exceptionally powerful, particularly on take-off.

(Mercury Marine)

These days, you can buy any of the mainstream engines with confidence. These include the Bombardier (formerly OMC) brands Johnson and Evinrude, Mercury, Honda, Suzuki, and Yamaha. They range in price from as little as $800 for the smallest to more than $20,000 for the largest. Nissan and Tohatsu offer fewer models of outboards and there are fewer dealers, but they are significantly less expensive than the more widely known brands. Some builders offer both two- and four-stroke models; review what you want in performance before choosing.

Carbureted two-stroke engines, which will all be phased out by 2006, are selling for as much as 40 percent less than four-strokes and direct-injection two-strokes. Remember, though, that if you keep the motor a long time, you'll spend lots more for gas and oil with the carbureted motors. And you won't be doing your part in helping to decrease pollution created by exhaust gases.

Carry-Out Outboards: Mini-Motors

Mini-outboards offer portable power in weights as light as 23 pounds, which makes them light enough for most kids to carry. Most minis have the same quality as the larger motors except that they don't offer oil injection, power tilt and trim, or electric start. (If there's no electric start, how do you start it? Muscle-power. There's a pull-cord, just as on your lawnmower. For most pull-start motors, you close the choke, pull the cord until the motor pops briefly, and then open the choke partway and give one more pull to kick it off.)

We're talking motors from two to about eight horses here, with the two-horsepower motors weighing just over 20 pounds, and the eight-horsepower motors weighing about 60 pounds in most makes. Prices range from just under $1,000 to about $2,000.

Boat Bytes _____

A big plus of the two- and four-horsepower motors is their light weight—their power is modest, but you can lift them off a dock with one hand. Sailboaters like them because they can remove them from the stern and stow the weight more efficiently while sailing—and to a sailor's eyeball, there's nothing as ugly as an outboard motor on the back of a boat under sail. Of course, that motor can be beautiful to behold if the wind dies.

Many small motors have the fuel tank built right into the cowling. These little tanks don't hold a lot of gasoline, but they're adequate for short trips and fishing outings, and you don't have to tote a separate fuel tank. You can fish two or three days on a three-gallon tank of fuel, another big plus of the mini-motors. For two-strokes, the lubricating oil is added to the gasoline prior to putting the fuel into the tank.

Compact Motors

Compact motors are like compact cars, big enough to get you from point A to point B, but not big enough to provide much in the way of comfort or performance. A 100-pound motor is more than most people want to carry down the dock, and this weight kicks in at about 10 to 15 horsepower for most brands.

CAUTION Look Out! _____

Portable outboards come with portable gas tanks, either three or six gallon. The tanks have a hose that connects to the engine. Most are clip-on, and they only go on one way. Try putting them on upside down, and fuel will come shooting out the ball valve in the connector.

Anything over 15 horses is definitely not portable and will require you to either have a motor cart, or to put the boat on a trailer and leave the motor in place. (I know, those husky Canadian fishing guides sometimes manhandle 125-pound, 30-horse motors onto the back of their big square-ender freighter canoes, but the rest of us will probably find that a bit much.)

Prices range from $2,200 for a 10-horsepower compact motor to about $7,500 for a 50.

Some inexpensive portables, like those from Briggs and Stratton, are air-cooled rather than water-cooled. An air-cooled engine is cooled by air passing over aluminum fins on the cylinders. A water-cooled engine is cooled by water passing through molded water passages around the internal parts of the powerhead. The powerhead on an air-cooled engine looks and sounds like a lawnmower motor. These tend to be hard on the ears, but they are also very light and very cheap. If you must pinch every penny, they're okay, but you'll probably be happier in the long term buying a small water-cooled motor.

Jet Power

Jet drives are available from several of the major outboard builders and are also used on all personal watercraft or jet-type sterndrives. They are not nearly as impressive as they sound. In the first place, they are not true jet engines—only the drive system operates on the jet principle, creating propulsion by shooting a narrow stream of water out a nozzle. The powerhead is a conventional gasoline piston engine, either two- or four-stroke.

The lower unit of a jet outboard has an "impeller" inside the housing, rather than a propeller on the back of a prop shaft. Water is drawn through the square intake on the bottom and jetted out the back at great speed, driving the boat forward.

(Frank Sargeant)

Jet drives waste horsepower and fuel—the horsepower rating is automatically reduced by about 25 percent on all these motors by the maker to account for their lack of performance. That is, when you buy a 100-horse jet, you get the performance of a 75-horse prop engine—but you burn fuel like a 100! Jets are also much noisier than prop engines and extremely hard to steer at low speeds—docking one is like playing bumper cars.

So why does anyone buy a jet? For operation in extremely shallow, rocky water, these motors are unbeatable. They can bounce off rocks and shoals and skip over water that's only inches deep—they're a favorite for river-running in the Pacific Northwest. And for personal watercraft, the fact that there's no dangerous propeller spinning under the rider is a huge safety factor. Jets are also capable of making 180-degree turns in a heartbeat, a big plus for those who enjoy the thrills of personal watercraft riding.

In most other venues, though, jets are not the ticket. (I tried one in the shallows of Florida for a time. The motor skimmed over the flats beautifully, but every time we stopped, it sucked weeds into the impeller and couldn't get back on plane without a major cleanout.)

Two-Cycle Outboard Oils

With two-cycle motors, the oil is mixed with the fuel and burned in the firing chamber. It's critical that the oil maintains its lubricating capabilities right up to the moment it's fired off, and then that it burns along with the gasoline, leaving behind a minimal amount of carbon, which can foul the plugs or gum the rings.

These days, most two-stroke motors from 40 horses up have automatic oiling systems, which means you put the oil in a separate tank and the motor meters just the right amount for various speeds, ranging from as little as 200:1 (200 parts gasoline to 1 part oil) at idle up to as much as 50:1 at full throttle.

This results in less oil consumption and less fouling than with the old way of doing things, which was to pour the oil directly into the gas tank at a ratio of 50:1 and hope it mixed adequately with the fuel to keep the motor from frying.

> **Look Out!**
>
> Automatic oiling systems work great—as long as you remember to keep the oil reservoir filled. Keep an eye on the warning light on the dash, and as a safety measure, refill the oil tank each time you fill the fuel tank. (A warning horn will tell you if you're dangerously low on oil, but by the time it goes off, damage might have already occurred.)

Nautical Notes

The outboard companies would love you to buy their particular brand of oil at $15 a gallon. It's top-flight stuff, to be sure, but any oil that is rated TCW-3 by the Society of Automotive Engineers meets the requirements of the warranty, and you can get no-name oil for about half that price. Particularly with larger motors, the savings can be huge over a year of running.

Or, if you'd prefer the quality spread but at a reduced price, take your own clean gallon container to the nearest dealership and have him pump it full from his 50-gallon stock drum. The price will be about two thirds to three quarters of the price of buying it off the shelf.

Innies and Outies: Inboard/Outboards

Inboard/outboards (I/Os), also called sterndrives, have become the second most popular form of propulsion for recreational boats. Basically, they combine an inboard engine with the lower unit—the gear case and prop—of an outboard, coupled through a waterproof housing in the transom. They offer the following advantages:

♦ Automotive-type engines are available in larger sizes than outboards, up to more than 500 horsepower.

♦ Four-cycle inboard/outboard engines are more economical on fuel than conventional two-cycle outboard engines and don't require oil to be mixed with the fuel.

♦ Because the lower unit can be steered, trimmed, and tilted like an outboard, maneuverability and performance are better than with most conventional inboards.

♦ Inboard/outboards are usually quieter than two-stroke outboards.

The inboard/outboard combines an inboard engine with the lower unit of an outboard. Advantages include better maneuverability and control of trim than found in inboards, more potential power, and quieter operation than found in outboards.

(Mercury Marine)

The Volvo Penta DuoProp system is a special kind of sterndrive that features two propellers that counter-rotate on a single shaft. This system gives outstanding perform-ance and cuts steering wheel torque.

(Volvo Penta Corporation)

Inboard Engines

Inboards are primarily automobile and truck engines, slightly modified to fit the marine application. They supply power to the prop via a shaft through the bottom of the boat. The inboard power system enables the use of engines much larger than those available in outboard power, so they're the universal choice for big sportfishing boats and yachts.

The disadvantage of inboards is that the prop and drive shaft are fixed in place, straight ahead. They can't be adjusted or trimmed to improve the running attitude of the boat, and they require more draft, or water depth, to operate without touching bottom. Also, steering is less positive at lower speeds because a rudder is used for directional control, rather than moving the prop thrust to one side or the other as in outboards and I/Os.

Inboards like this Crusader are modified versions of auto and truck engines. They provide lots of power for larger boats.

(Crusader Corporation)

Power Without Spark Plugs: Diesel Engines

In 1892, a German engineer named Rudolph Diesel invented an engine that required no spark plugs to set off the fuel charge. Instead, heat created by compression caused the fuel to ignite. Thus the diesel engine was born.

Most diesels are four-cycles, like the gasoline engines used in automobiles. However, on the intake stroke, the diesel sucks in only air. And the compression stroke will squeeze that air charge down to at least $1/14$ of its initial size, making it very hot. A fuel injector at the top of the cylinder then shoots in a small amount of fuel, generally kerosene-like light oils, and the heat ignites it immediately. The power and exhaust strokes are like those of gasoline four-cycles.

Diesels burn less-expensive fuel than gasoline engines, and they burn it more efficiently. They must be built heavier than gas engines due to the forces of compression, but they last longer—in fact, a well-maintained diesel might outlive three or four gasoline engines before requiring a major rebuild. However, they are considerably more expensive to buy, they are far noisier than most gas engines, and they produce a smelly exhaust, though this has been reduced considerably in the latest versions.

Boat Bytes

Diesels are available in power to more than 1,200 horses, which makes them the only reasonable choice for large yachts. Very small diesels of 50 horses or less are sometimes fitted to oceangoing trawlers because of their extreme stinginess with fuel—there are no fuel docks in the middle of the Pacific Ocean!

Diesels like this Caterpillar are available in sizes large enough to power even 200-foot yachts. They're heavy but very durable, normally far outliving gasoline engines.

(Caterpillar Corporation)

Fuel Economy

Gasoline two-cycle outboards put out about 10 horses per gallon of fuel burned at full throttle. For example, a 200-horse motor will consume somewhere near 20 gallons an hour at full throttle, while a 150-horse motor will eat somewhere around 15 gallons an hour. It's not uncommon for motors to be a couple of gallons over on this, with a 150 taking, say, 18 gallons an hour at 5,800 rpms. Four-cycle outboards can cut this fuel use up to 60 percent in the mid-ranges, though they use nearly as much as two-cycles at full speed.

Top-End Performance

Although all gasoline motors of a given horsepower are similar in power output at maximum rpms, they're not the same. Some do better on fuel and still manage excellent performance. The test results run in magazines such as *Boating* give you exact numbers for comparison.

The idea that you get there faster at full throttle and, therefore, don't run the motor as long and don't burn as much fuel, doesn't work out in reality. It's common to see fuel usage double from mid-range to full throttle. Of course, speed goes up, too, but the miles-per-gallon figure usually shows 30 to 50 percent better efficiency at the lower rpms.

Better at Cruising Speed

True to the operating manual, most outboard motors get their best fuel economy—that is, the most miles per gallon—somewhere between 3,500 and 4,500 rpms, with most gas inboards achieving maximum efficiency at between 2,500 and 3,500. For diesels, the economy range is likely to be around 1,800 to 2,400 rpms. (Big diesels are never run as fast as gasoline motors—most redline at 2,200–2,700 rpms. However, some of the smaller models may be run close to 4,000 rpms without damage.) The most fuel-efficient speed for a given boat is called its "cruising speed."

One Engine or Two?

Redundancy is bad in writing, but good in boat motors. People like dual engines on boats because they can't pull over to a service station if one quits. That's a big reason for having two motors, particularly on offshore boats. However, the redundancy factor has to be weighed against a lot of other factors when you decide whether to buy one engine or two.

The most obvious factor is cost. Outboard motors are outrageously expensive, averaging from $10,000 to $20,000 for a V6 of 150 to 300 horsepower. Buying two motors instead of one can add 30 percent to the price of a boat. Inboards and sterndrives are similarly costly. Two engines also burn a lot more fuel—basically twice as much, although you might also go faster.

If you go with two motors, choose them so that *each* motor can plane your boat. You might have to buy somewhat larger motors to have this capability, but it's money well spent when you really need that extra power 50 miles offshore and want to come home at 25 mph instead of 5. Twin engines have the added advantage of making for easy steering around the docks (see Chapter 6 for details).

Is one big engine better than two small ones? Could be, if you're interested mostly in speed. A pair of 90s won't usually match a single 200 and maybe not even a 175, because the single has less drag due to there being only one lower unit. It's also much less expensive to buy one big single rather than two smaller motors that put out an equivalent power combined.

One popular approach is to use a single main engine, and also carry a "kicker" or small, low-horsepower outboard for emergency low-speed propulsion.

Twin engines provide security when you head offshore. If one breaks down, the other will bring you home. However, if you're pinching to buy a boat in the first place, that second engine might put you way over the top.

(Honda Marine)

The power you choose for your boat depends on the "mission" you hope to pursue. Balance the initial costs, fuel economy, and dependability factors when you make a selection. Fortunately, nearly all modern engines are far more dependable and more fuel-efficient today than they were just a few years back.

The Least You Need to Know

- Two-cycle outboards are the usual motor for most beginning recreational boaters.
- Outboards, sterndrives, and inboards are suited to different boats and boating needs.
- Most motors deliver their best economy at about three-quarter throttle.
- Single engines are more economical than twin engines, but twins provide more security.

Picking a Proper Prop

In This Chapter

- What a propeller does
- The importance of diameter and pitch
- Prop designs and materials
- Propping problems

The propeller, known by almost everybody in boating as a "prop," is the tires of your boat, the part that hooks up to the medium through which you travel—water—to convert motor power to propulsion. If the prop isn't right, it can make a dog out of the finest hull and motor combination. (And we're not talking a greyhound—a basset, more likely.) The dealer will supply a prop with your boat and motor package, and it's likely to be adequate for getting you started in boating. However, there's lots more you'll want to know about props as you become a more experienced skipper. This chapter takes a closer look at some of that information.

A prop functions in water like a screw passing through wood, drawing the boat forward as the engine, connected via the prop shaft, causes it to rotate. Also like a screw, the pitch determines the performance of the prop. (Get the wrong prop and it's you who will be screwed, however.)

In this chapter, you'll learn how a propeller functions, and how to select the best one for your particular combination of boat, motor, and preferred boating activity. We'll also take a look at some of the difficulties having the wrong prop can cause.

Gay Blades—And Serious Ones

The most obvious difference between one prop and another is the number of blades. The blades are the part that does the work, and the number, size, angle, and shape of the blades determine how the prop performs. The more blades a prop has, the less vibration there is. That's why a complete disc would be vibration-free—but it wouldn't move your boat an inch!

Here's a look at the characteristics of some popular designs:

- **Two-blade props** have the least resistance but the highest vibration. They are used mostly for smaller outboards and electric trolling motors.

Boat Bytes

Blades on performance props are usually "cupped," which means the tips and the back edges are slightly concave. This helps the blade grip the water, particularly on takeoff, at high trim, and in sharp turns.

- **Three-blade props** are the most popular design, offering good performance with moderate vibration at a reasonable price.

- **Four-blade props** have very low vibration, good takeoff, and good performance, at a higher price. They're a bit slower at top-end speed, too.

- **Five-blade props** have the lowest vibration, excellent takeoff, and some reduction on top-end speed, at a very high price.

Barrel Onward

The *barrel* or *hub* is the central structure of the prop, the cylinder to which the blades attach. Most props on outboards and sterndrives feature a "through-hub" design. The hub is large and hollow, and the exhaust from the motor passes through the center. It's a convenient spot to let the gases exit, and because they come out underwater, there's a considerable muffling effect.

Here's a closer look at the parts of the propeller, which are shown in the following figure:

- **Blade.** Thin, curved sections that grip the water as the prop rotates.

- **Hub.** The central barrel to which the blades attach.

- **Prop nut.** The nut that holds the prop to the prop shaft.

- **Prop shaft.** The stainless-steel rod that couples the prop to the drive shaft and gears.

- **Diameter.** The width, in inches, of a circle made by a blade tip in a complete rotation.

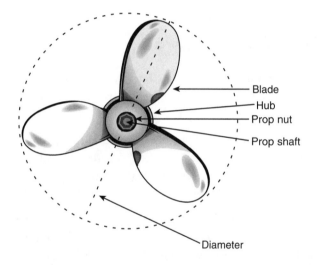

The typical three-blade propeller includes a tubular barrel or hub through which the engine exhaust passes.

Blade
Hub
Prop nut
Prop shaft

Diameter

An "over-the-hub" prop, shown in the following figure, is less common except on performance boats. The hub is much smaller and is solid steel in this design. Over-the-hub props create less drag and consequently can run faster. The motor makes more noise, but if you're after maximum speed, you don't care, do you?

Most props have a rubber or composite core pressed into the center of the hub that acts as a shock absorber should the prop strike bottom. It gives a bit and springs back into shape on light strikes, but tears in a hard strike—you have to get a new hub core pressed in, but you don't destroy the very expensive gears and shafts in the lower unit. The stripped hub will usually get you home at idle speed but won't move the boat at higher rpms.

Over-the-hub props are designed for high-speed boats. They feature a smaller, solid barrel compared to through-the-hub models.

Diameter and Prop Performance

Just as the diameter of your waist determines whether you are a fast or slow runner, the diameter of a prop determines its performance. The measure of prop diameter is the width, in inches, of the circle made by the blade tips.

In general, large-diameter props grip the water better and are particularly effective in low-speed maneuvering and in pushing heavy loads. Smaller-diameter props can "wind up" faster, and are often good choices for high-performance boats because they go through the water with less resistance.

Typical diameters on V6 outboard props range from 13 to 16 inches, with diameters for torque-rich four-strokes typically a bit larger than for quick-windup two-strokes. Typical diameters for 10-horse props are around 8 inches, while 20- to 40-horse motors carry props with diameters of 10 to 11 inches.

Salt Talk

Pitch is the term for the distance a propeller would move forward in one revolution if there were no slip. **Slippage** or **slip** is the term comparing the actual forward motion of a propeller through the water to the forward motion it would have if it were turning in a solid, like a screw moving through wood.

Here's the Pitch

Diameter is only one part of the prop equation. The other is *pitch*, which is the distance a prop would travel through water in one revolution if there were no *slippage*.

A prop is a water screw, remember: If it were screwing through wood, a 21-inch-pitch prop would travel forward 21 inches in one revolution due to the angle of the blades. In water, because of slippage, it might only go 19 inches due to the slip in the liquid medium. In this case there would be 2 inches of slip compared to 21 inches of pitch, or 9.5 percent slip. A slip of 4 to 15 percent is common in recreational powerboats.

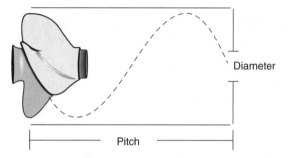

If there were no slip, a prop would move forward a distance equal to its pitch in one revolution.

Pitches for V6 outboard props typically range from 15 to 25 inches. Smaller motors will require lower pitches, down to as little as four inches for a 2-horse.

Putting It Together

The diameter is always listed first in prop designation. A 14 × 17–inch prop would have a 14-inch diameter and a 17-inch pitch. A prop of these dimensions is very common on runabouts in the 17- or 18-foot range, powered with a 120- to 150-horse outboard. The pitch, and sometimes the diameter, is stamped on the prop's barrel.

The higher the pitch, the faster the boat can travel for a given rpm if power is unlimited. But power is always limited, so the pitch must be matched to the weight and power of the boat/motor combination.

The right combo when the boat has five gallons of fuel and one passenger might be completely overwhelmed when there are 500 pounds of gasoline (gas weighs around 6 pounds per gallon), 800 pounds of people, and 500 pounds of ice, food, and gear added. The added weight will require a lower-pitch propeller to push it effectively. You want to select a prop that allows the motor to run in its peak horsepower range at full throttle, usually somewhere around 5,000 to 5,800 rpms for large and midsize outboards, 4,500 to 5,000 for sterndrives and inboards, with its typical load.

Boat Bytes

Larger-diameter props drop rpms and increase holding power and lift, but the diameters are limited by the space between the prop shaft and the anti-ventilation plate on outboards and sterndrives, so there's not much variety offered. In general, larger-diameter props are preferred on larger boats that travel at moderate speeds; smaller diameters are common on performance boats.

An inch of pitch increases or decreases rpms about 150 to 250 rpms. But props are offered by most manufacturers in only 2-inch increments, which vary rpms from 300 to 500.

So if your rig turns up 5,000 rpms with a 19-inch-pitch prop and the motor is rated for 5,500, you might drop down to a 17-inch to get it running at the max.

The lower pitch would also give better takeoffs, or "hole shots"—the hole being the hole left in the water when a planing boat takes off. The stern squats and there's a big hole pushed down for a moment before the hull squirts forward like a cake of soap to race along on top.

When One Goes Up, the Other Goes Down

For a given boat/motor package, the prop diameter and pitch are inversely related: The larger the diameter, the lower the pitch; the smaller the diameter, the higher the pitch needed for good performance.

This is also true in relation to the number of blades. A three-blade prop can be pitched a little higher than a four-blade prop used on the same boat/motor combination, because the four-blade has more gripping surface to "load" the motor.

 Boat Bytes _____

Boat props typically turn at only about half the speed of the engine rpms due to gears where the prop shaft meets the drive shaft. The gears, usually at a ratio of around 2:1, cut the prop rotation speed but increase the torque or twisting force. More powerful engines sometimes have lower gear ratios of around 1.85:1, and some racing engines have a direct 1:1 drive.

Propping is a science, and it's best left to a dealer who has plenty of props to play with and is willing to do the job right for you. Particularly in performance boats, the wrong prop can not only cut into speed, but also make a given boat difficult or even downright dangerous to drive, while the handling problems might go away completely with the right prop.

Four-blade props offer more lift for a quick takeoff, or hole shot, and run smoother than three-blade props. However, they're more expensive and a bit slower at top-end speeds.

(Stiletto Props)

Nautical Notes

How do you swap props? Props are held in place by a prop nut, which is sometimes secured by a cotter pin. To remove the prop, you first straighten the bent end of the cotter pin, and then remove it by inserting a flat screwdriver or punch into the rounded end and tapping lightly until it slides free.

When you try to take off the prop nut, you'll find that nut, prop, and prop shaft all turn happily together—there's no resistance to allow you to torque off the nut.

To secure things, place a pine 2 × 4 between one of the prop blades and the cavitation plate of the motor. This holds things in place so you can get the nut off. The nut secures a washer and a spacer—make sure to set them aside in the order they came off so you don't get confused later.

The prop should slide off easily once all the fasteners are removed. You might need to lightly tap the prop with a rubber hammer to get started, especially if it hasn't been removed in a long time. The prop can't be twisted off the shaft—it's splined in place, so you have to pull straight out.

Before you put on a new prop, rub a light coating of waterproof grease on the splines of the prop shaft. This will help the prop to come off more easily next time.

Replace the spacer and washer, grease the nut, and reinstall it to torque specifications, again using the 2 × 4 to hold the prop in place. And don't forget to use a *new* cotter pin, and only one made of stainless steel. Many a $400 prop has been lost due to use of an old 25¢ pin.

Right Hand or Left?

When the engine is in forward gear, single-engine props usually rotate clockwise, viewed from astern. This is called *right-hand rotation*. On dual-engine installations, it's standard procedure for the left or port engine to be geared so that it will rotate counterclockwise to balance the torque felt at the wheel and also acting on the stern, and thus it must be equipped with a counterclockwise-rotating prop. This is called *left-hand rotation*. A right-hand prop won't work on a left-hand rotating engine, and vice versa, unless the gearbox is designed for continuous full-power operation in either direction.

On dual-engine installations, it's common for the engines to rotate their props in opposite directions to counteract torque and make for easy steering.

Left-hand rotation

Right-hand rotation

The idea is that when you're going straight ahead, the opposite rotation of the blades helps to steady the boat and causes it to steer straight easily. If both blades rotated in the same direction, the back end of the boat would want to "walk" in that direction, forcing the bow in the opposite direction. (For more on how prop torque or rotating force affect handling, see Chapter 6.)

What Props Are Made Of

The materials used in making props are a compromise between durability, performance, and price. Props are usually made out of one of the following:

- ◆ Aluminum
- ◆ Stainless steel
- ◆ Bronze
- ◆ Plastic

Let's take a look at each of these materials in more detail.

Light, Cheap, and Bendable: Aluminum Props

Chances are that your first boat will come rigged with an aluminum prop. Aluminum is not the best prop material, but it is one of the cheapest, and that's the reason you see it on most package rigs designated "entry-level" or "value-priced."

But, as I must occasionally remind my wife, just because something is inexpensive doesn't mean it's bad. (She in turn reminds me that "cheap" is not a synonym for "good.") Prices range from as little as $45 for an aluminum prop fitted to 6- to 10-horse motors up to about $150 for props matched to the larger V6 outboards in sterndrives. For the right application, aluminum is just fine. Used on engines with moderate horsepower in areas where bottom contact is unlikely, it's the most common prop material, and survival can be good—as long as you don't hit bottom, an aluminum prop can last for as long as you keep your boat.

Where there's a chance you'll hit rocks, shell bars, or even hard sand, an aluminum prop will soon begin to look a bit worse for the wear. Those dings and bent blades greatly reduce performance and can also create vibration that can ruin the lower-unit seals or bearings. Also, aluminum props don't have the required stiffness in thinner castings to give maximum performance on large motors.

Stainless-Steel Reputation

Stainless steel is the material of choice for most seasoned boaters running outboards or sterndrives. It's extremely tough and rustproof, and the high strength allows it to be cast into very thin blades that slice through the water more efficiently than the thicker blades required in aluminum castings.

Steel also holds its shape at extreme speed and load, while aluminums tend to flex, slightly, but enough to lose efficiency at maximum rpms on big motors.

Fishermen like stainless steel because it can bounce off a submerged stump or oyster bar without turning into origami. And if the prop does get slightly bent, you can often straighten it out yourself with a hammer and pliers. Aluminums that get cobbled up have to make a trip to the heli-arc welding shop. However, because stainless is so tough, a hard strike on rocks can be transmitted to the prop shaft or gears of the lower unit and cause damage there, which is much more expensive to repair than the prop.

Stainless props ain't cheap. Prices start at around $300, and some of the high-performance models cost over $600. But one stainless prop will outlast a half-dozen aluminums in tough duty.

Stainless-steel props are relatively expensive but are so tough that they might outlast your motor. They're also best for high-performance boats.

(Mach Propellers)

Bronzed Warriors

Bronze props are rarely seen on small boats, but they're the choice for many large yachts with inboard power. Bronze offers good strength, but not so much that it will snap off the stainless drive shaft and make a hole in the bottom of an inboard boat, which is one of the reasons that it's a preferred material for big inboards.

Small bronze props cost about the same as stainless. Big-yacht props, usually four-bladers measuring up to 36 inches across, can cost thousands of dollars. Bronze props have an indefinite life span and in many cases will last as long as stainless.

Plastic Props

Plastic is … well, plastic. Plastic is a nice thing to make computer disks from. It's good for fishing lures, coolers, and a lot of other things. But plastic is not the best material to put on the end of the prop shaft of an internal combustion engine that can generate a couple hundred horsepower.

Boat Bytes

There are high-performance plastic props out there, but most never stack up to steel props in head-to-head performance tests, and when it comes to durability, the slightest touch on an oyster bar makes them vaporize.

Plastic props are very inexpensive, which is the only reason they have any chance at all in the market. They are like the little wheelbarrow-type tires put in modern cars as spares—adequate to get you home in an emergency, but not really up to the rigors of daily use in anything much beyond a 10-horse kicker. They are okay for motors of under 10 horses used as kickers, however.

Prices on typical plastic props for V6 motors run around $50 to $75, a good deal as insurance for the day your stainless-steel prop falls off (sob!) in deep water due to a loose prop nut.

Props for Electric Motors

The plastic, nylon, or Lexan props supplied with electric trolling motors do a good job due to their low speeds and modest horsepower. I've chewed several of them up pretty badly, but they still hold their blades and keep on functioning.

Trolling-motor props are available in three- or four-blade "weedless" models with large barrels and small blades, which are designed to cut through the thick weeds found where largemouth bass, pike, and other species live.

Weedless props are not quite as efficient as standard or "power" props in open water. Power props are usually two-bladed and have a smaller hub. They're a better choice for those who have to deal with strong currents or wind in open water.

Both weedless and power props for trollers are inexpensive, ranging from about $10 to $30.

Look Out!

When installing a plastic trolling-motor prop, tighten the lock nut with your fingers only. Tightening the nut with pliers might distort the hub or even cause it to crack.

Counter-Rotating In-Line Props

It sounds like Engineering 101, doesn't it? But two props on a single engine make sense for many boats. The concept, first perfected by Volvo Penta sterndrives in 1983, combines a right-hand and left-hand prop on the same shaft, one rotating each way. Mercruiser also markets a sterndrive version, and Yamaha has outboard models.

In-line systems provide a sort of "four-wheel drive" for boats, with amazing traction in hole shots, blazing acceleration, white-knuckle cornering, torque-free steering, and very positive reverse. With nearly twice the blade area of a single-prop unit, these systems do everything except top-end speed better.

The systems work via a prop shaft within a prop shaft, allowing the counter-rotation off a single main engine shaft. They cost more than conventional drive systems, but for those who can afford it, the advantages are well worth the price.

These Props Are Not Shiftless

Most props are shiftless, sitting there without ambition, mindlessly doing the job designated by their designers. But there are a few mechanical wonders that actually do show some unique capabilities to shift for themselves.

Boat Bytes

Which boats are most likely to benefit from shifting props? Usually those with a minimal power-to-weight ratio; that is, a small engine relative to the weight of the boat. Heavy sterndrives are the best candidates.

Shifting props use moveable blades that change position based on centrifugal force to adjust their pitch while underway. Why would you want this? Because boats, unlike cars, don't have shifting transmissions. The prop that starts you off well in low gear is somewhat of a compromise when it comes to top speed. Shifting props change pitch, through a system of cams and gears, and thus provide the right pitch for a variety of operating conditions. They're not needed on most boats, but they can help some underpowered rigs.

Problems of the Improper Prop

Problems with the prop are one of the primary woes of beginning boaters. Both initial selection and maintenance can cause difficulties.

If Your Prop Is Too Tall ...

If your boat doesn't want to take off, it probably has a prop that's pitched too "tall" or too high. The available power of the engine can't force the boat forward at the high rate of incline of this particular water screw, so it bogs down. This is to say, the motor might have only enough power to push the boat forward 17 inches per revolution of the prop (less slip), but you've got a 21-inch-pitch prop in place. It's like trying to start a stick-shift car in high gear; it doesn't work.

If you ever get this rig on plane, it might be very fast because resistance drops after the boat jumps up on top. But you probably won't ever get it on plane. Switch to a 17-inch pitch and things will go a lot smoother.

For the usual recreational user, a prop that provides a good takeoff with the typical load is much preferred, even if it's a couple miles per hour slower at full throttle.

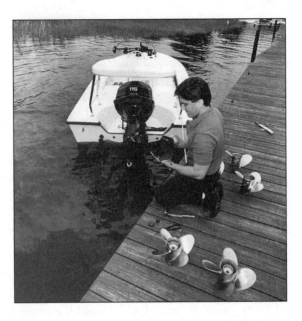

Some boat dealers will assist you in finding the best prop for your rig by swapping to achieve the best combination of hole shot and top-end speed.

(Frank Sargeant)

Boat Bytes

Some boats designed for top-end speed are purposely "overpropped" to squeeze out the last mile per hour at full throttle, even though this makes them real dogs at the takeoff. If you have to be the fastest skipper on the lake, you might want to select a prop that is "taller" than is best for all-around use. But in general, a do-it-all prop that gives good takeoff, good mid-range acceleration, and reasonable top-end is the best choice for the average boater.

If Your Prop Is Too Short ...

Props that are too "short" or pitched too low might just about smoke the tires on the hole shot, but they soon allow the engine to wind up into the stratosphere when the boat gets on top. It takes real care not to over-rev the motor and break something expensive inside with a prop that's several steps below the needed range. If this is happening, you might have to swap out a 17-pitch for a 19 or higher.

When Your Prop Is Just Right ...

The idea is to choose a prop that will take you and your entire crew and all their food, drinks, and diving gear up on plane quickly and without a lot of bow-rise, and then give an effortless performance in the cruising range of the engine, about 3,000 to 4,500 rpms for outboards and 2,500 to 3,500 for most inboards and I/Os. For boats that do not plane, including sailboats and electric-powered boats, a good all-around prop that has plenty of push is the target.

Bad Vibrations

Vibrations from a prop usually mean there is some sort of debris on the blades or barrel. An easy way to clear it is stop the boat, shift the engine into reverse, and let the boat slide backward for a boat-length or so. This often unwinds the plastic bags, weeds, or whatever has gotten into the prop. If this doesn't work, you might have to shut off the engine, tilt up the lower unit, and pull out the stuff by hand.

Boat Bytes

Vibrations can also mean that the prop is bent from hitting something. The prop will get you back to the dock, in most cases, but don't keep operating the motor with the gimpy prop because the vibration will soon ruin the seals and bearings, making the repair a whole lot more costly than it would be to simply fix the prop.

Used fishing line is a chronic problem these days on many waterways. If you run through a nest of this stuff, it will wrap around the prop hub and then work its way down around the prop shaft. On larger motors it's usually chopped up and spit out, but on smaller motors it often stays put and gradually cuts its way into the seal around the prop shaft. Water eventually gets in, and the first thing you know you're looking at a large repair bill.

The cure is to check your prop shaft after each trip to make sure there's nothing on it that shouldn't be. Line wrapped on the shaft can usually be unwound or cut away, but in extreme cases you might have to take off the prop to get it all cleared.

Care and Feeding of Your Prop

Props don't require much care. The paint that comes on many will wear away, but it has no effect on performance. However, over years of service the blade tips of aluminum props are sometimes worn away by "cavitation" or high-speed water vapor bubbles that form as the prop races through the water. These rough edges can reduce performance over time. Any chip in the blades or even the slightest bending away from the factory-set pitch can also cause a prop to lose performance or vibrate.

It's a good idea, every year or so, to drop your prop off at a prop shop and have the pitch checked and any nicks repaired by welding and/or sanding. Not only will your boat perform better, but you'll also ensure longer life from your lower unit with a vibration-free propeller.

The Least You Need to Know

- ◆ Props are selected for a particular combination of load and power.
- ◆ Variables including pitch, diameter, and number of blades determine prop performance.
- ◆ Stainless steel is the most dependable material for recreational boat props, although it's more costly than aluminum.
- ◆ Props need occasional care to maintain performance.

Chapter 4

It Follows You Anywhere: Trailering Your Boat

In This Chapter

- ◆ The right stuff for hauling your boat
- ◆ Getting hitched
- ◆ Trailer towing tips
- ◆ Loading and unloading your boat at the ramp
- ◆ Keeping your trailer in top shape

The great thing about putting wheels under your boat—whether power or sail—is that you no longer have to leave it in one particular body of water. Trailering your boat gives you access to lakes, rivers, and bays across the state and across the nation—you can even change oceans if you like!

Another plus is that you don't have to pay those monthly dock-rental fees. There are no worries about little creepy-crawlies clamping themselves to the bottom of your boat or boring through the hull as it sits week after week afloat. And when it storms, you know your boat is not going to sink, because it's sitting in your garage, as snug as the family cat.

In all states, boats up to 8 feet wide can be trailered without a special permit, and many allow trailer/boat widths up to 10 feet without requiring any flashing lights and wide-load signs. Thus, the size of boats that can be trailered reaches up to more than 30 feet long, although the larger boats require proportionately larger tow vehicles.

In this chapter, you'll learn how to select the proper trailer for your boat and what sort of hitch you'll need for your tow vehicle. I'll also offer some tips on driving while towing—it's different, but not that difficult. And we'll cover the most important part: launching and reloading.

Get Fit

It's important that trailers and boats fit together. A trailer designed for a 17-foot aluminum skiff will be flattened into twisted metal if you load it down with a twin-inboard cruiser, even if that cruiser is also exactly 17 feet long. On the other hand, you can spend a lot of money needlessly if you buy a trailer that's bigger than required for your boat. And the bottom of a deep vee boat won't fit a trailer designed for a flat bottom, nor will a catamaran fit on a trailer designed for a monohull.

Your boat dealer will usually fix you up with a matched boat and trailer, but not always—trailers come in a variety of quality levels, and some fly-by-night operations occasionally try to get away with a light-duty trailer under a heavy boat to put a little extra profit in their pocket.

The following figure gives you a look at the parts of a trailer. Note that the one shown is for a typical monohull powerboat. Those made for catamarans and keeled sailboats look quite a bit different.

Boat trailers make it possible to visit distant lakes, bays, and rivers with ease, and also enable you to store your boat in your garage rather than at a marina.

Like everything else in boating, the parts of a trailer have specialized names. Here are some of them:

- **Coupler.** The fitting that attaches to the hitch ball to secure the trailer to the towing vehicle.

- **Tongue.** The extension from the main frame members forward to the coupling.

- **Tongue jack.** A lifting device used to raise and lower the tongue so it fits easily on the hitch ball.

- **Winch.** A winding device used to pull the boat into place.

- **Winch stand.** The supporting frame for the winch.

- **Frame.** The main support members of the trailer.

- **Axle.** The steel member on which the wheels turn.

- **Roller.** A rubber cylinder that allows the boat keel or hull to roll into place on the trailer.

- **Bearings.** The friction-eliminating devices between the axle and the wheel hub.

- **Taillights.** Red lights mounted on the rear of the trailer so that it can be seen by other drivers after dark. Wiring couples these lights to the lighting system of the tow vehicle, allowing them to signal stops and turns.

- **Bunks.** The boards on which the boat bottom rests.

> **Boat Bytes**
>
> It's a good idea to get a trailer with full-sized tires, 14- to 15-inchers. These run cooler than smaller tires, roll over potholes better, and give your boat a smoother ride. They also last a lot longer—the little donut jobs get hot and blow out at a distressingly high rate.

Keep in mind that trailers have both length and load ratings listed on the tag on the tongue. The length of the trailer must match the length of your boat—and in outboard-powered boats, it must fit so that the transom is fully supported, not hanging over the back of the bunks even a half-inch. A trailer that's too big is better than one that's too small.

Weight Wisdom

It's wise to buy more load capacity than you think you need. That rig that weighs 2,500 pounds on the day you buy it will, like most of us, tend to get a bit more portly with age. Add anchors, ice chests, fuel, water, sails, lines, fishing, skiing, and diving gear you might accumulate aboard, and you can boost the load by 50 percent. Allow enough capacity for the add-ons.

Two Wheels or Four?

Trailer tires are not car tires. Trailer tires are made of more layers, called plies, and have a higher load rating, which is why you can often carry a fairly large boat on two tires instead of four.

Two-wheel trailers are easier to back and maneuver than four-wheelers—that is to say, two axles, two wheels per axle—also known as "tandem" trailers. However, if you have a flat tire on a two-wheeler, you must stop immediately and fix the problem. With a four-wheel trailer, you can continue to a station at reduced speed (*very* reduced—no more than 20 mph) if you have a flat, because the second tire on that side will support the load.

With bigger boats, there's no choice—big weights require two-axle or "tandem" trailers, period. A few of the largest boats even need three-axle trailers. However, the more axles, wheels, and tires, the higher the price, and the heavier the weight. The more weight, the larger tow vehicle you'll need. There are always trade-offs.

Four-wheel trailers like this ShoreLand'r are a must for hauling big, heavy rigs with V6 outboards. Submersible trailers like this one have pressurized grease fittings to keep water out of the bearings.

(Lund Boats)

The Right Stuff

Painted steel trailers are inexpensive and have reasonable durability if always used in freshwater. Baked enamel finishes that match the boat make them the best-looking of all trailers. Put them in saltwater even once, though, and you'll soon see the rust streaks start to form. If you plan to use your boat in coastal areas, don't buy a painted steel trailer.

Trailers made of galvanized steel are rustproof, tough, and probably the best value on the market, although they're more expensive than painted steel. They also don't look as slick as a painted model.

Aluminum might be the best of all trailer materials. It's light but strong, corrosion-resistant, and looks good without paint for years. Aluminum trailers are somewhat more costly than galvanized but are worth the price in easy towing and years of service. (Some aluminum trailers are so light that the air in the tires will cause them to float once the boat is unloaded!)

Stainless steel is the most expensive trailer material, but it's exceptionally strong and durable. Stainless trailers are made by only a few companies nationwide—you're much more likely to find galvanized or aluminum.

Some trailers are "drive-on" designs, which means you submerge part of the bunks and literally drive the boat on. Others are "break-frame" or "tilt" models, with a hinge in the frame that allows the bunks to tip up for easier launching and loading while most of the trailer stays dry—you winch the boat into place. The drive-ons are easier to use, but might have more maintenance problems due to constant exposure to water, particularly in salty environments. A third type of trailer, used mostly for sailboats, is designed strictly for use with a hoist; you can't launch directly from a boat ramp with these models.

How Trailer Winches Work

Winches multiply rotary force and enable you to crank a 3,000-pound boat into place with only enough effort to start a couple of hernias. The winch sits on a winch stand, a stout brace that elevates it to about the height of the bow eye on the boat. The assembly can be adjusted up or down by loosening the U-bolts that hold it in place, and the entire stand can be moved forward or backward to make the boat balance and fit properly on the trailer.

The winch works because you're turning a long handle attached to a tiny gear, which meshes with a gear about the size of a CD. The ratio, or mechanical advantage, gives you the power to move the load. Some winches are two-speed, with a lower (but slower) gear you can shift to for the heaviest strain, and a higher (but faster) gear for taking up slack.

There's a three-way ratchet on the winch gear that allows it to go only forward, only backward, or to freewheel. A small lever next to the gears controls it.

You back off on tension on the gears slightly with the handle, and you can move this lever where you want it, to allow the cable or strap to pay out to launch the boat, or only to wind on when you're retrieving it.

The gears in winches multiply effort, making it possible to crank heavy boats into place with ease. Note the spare tire bolted to the frame.

(Frank Sargeant)

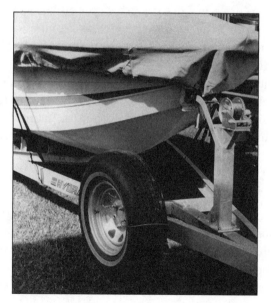

Tongue Jacks

The jack is the assembly that allows you to raise or lower the trailer tongue to fit the height of the hitch ball on your tow vehicle. It's bolted to the tongue a foot or two behind the hitch coupling. Most have a caster or wheel on the bottom that enables you to roll the trailer around manually when it's unhitched. If your trailer doesn't come with a caster wheel, you can buy an add-on from marine supply stores.

After the trailer coupling is attached to the hitch, the jack is cranked to the "up" position so the wheel doesn't hit the roadway. This usually takes a lot of cranking—the gear ratios are low. A much handier type of jack is the "swing-away" model. After the weight is off this jack, the design enables you to pull a pin on the shaft and swing the jack up to lock parallel with the tongue, rather than cranking and cranking to get the thing up out of the way.

Look Out!

Failing to raise the jack wheel is a common oversight. Always double-check that the wheel is well clear of the ground before you take off, or the jack assembly will be bent into a paper clip as the rig moves forward.

Do You Need Brakes?

If the rig weighs more than 1,500 pounds, trailer brakes are a good idea. They're particularly important if you tow with a small or midsize vehicle, because the weight of the boat pushing against the hitch can actually overpower the stopping capabilities of the tow rig.

Some states require trailer brakes if the towed weight is above a certain level. Nearly all rigs big enough to require two-axle trailers are equipped with brakes. However, brakes are a real headache around saltwater and might have to be reworked as often as once a year to keep the actuating mechanisms inside the wheel from rusting solid.

Washing your brakes with soapy freshwater after each trip to a saltwater ramp will significantly improve their longevity. If possible, order your trailer with a built-in hose coupling and wash-down tubes, which pipe freshwater to the inside of the brake drums when a garden hose is attached.

Trailers with brakes have a special coupling that includes a manual brake cable. If the coupling fails, the cable activates the brakes.

(Frank Sargeant)

Getting Hitched

The hitch is the connection between the trailer and your tow vehicle. The best place to buy a hitch is at a trailer rental company such as U-Haul or a shop that specializes in hitches. Hitches are very particular about which cars and trucks they're fitted to, and sometimes the hitch for a 1994 model won't fit a 1995 model of the same vehicle. The specialized shops have hitches on hand to fit all makes, models, and years.

Have the shop do the wire hookups, too. Trailer wiring is notorious for causing problems because it can be difficult to sort out where the yellow and green and brown and striped wires go.

U-Haul, Reese, and Draw-Tite are probably the best-known national hitch makers, and all have franchised shops nationwide. It takes only 30 minutes to an hour for most installations by the dealer, including taillight hookup. Prices vary from around $100 to $250, including installation, depending on the load capacity and design.

Matching the Load—Hitch Ratings

Hitches have load ratings, just as trailers do. One size does not fit all. Standard hitches put all the weight on the point of contact with the tow vehicle. Weight-distributing hitches use spring-tension bars to put some of the tongue weight onto the suspension of the tow vehicle; therefore, they're more suitable for very heavy loads, but they cost more and are more troublesome to hook up.

Here are the hitch ratings:

- ◆ **Class I.** This is the standard bumper hitch, cheap and easy to install. However, the load limit is 2,000 pounds and the tongue weight a maximum of 200 pounds, so it's suitable only for lightweight rigs.

- ◆ **Class II.** These can be either bumper hitches or frame hitches, rated for up to 3,500 pounds and a tongue weight of 300 pounds.

- ◆ **Class III.** This includes frame hitches that can handle up to 7,500 pounds and that distribute some of the tongue weight to the tow-vehicle frame.

- ◆ **Class IV.** This includes frame hitches that can handle up to 10,000 pounds and that distribute some of the tongue weight to the tow-vehicle frame.

Have a Ball: Hitch Balls

Hitch balls come in several sizes, and the ball has to fit the coupler on your particular trailer. The most common are $1^7/_8$ inches in diameter, which is suitable for weights up to 2,000 pounds; and 2 inches, which is used for boats up to about 3,500 pounds.

If you pull a really big boat, you might go to a $2^5/_{16}$-inch ball, which is rated for 10,000 pounds. You won't find these big babies at Wal-Mart, but hitch dealerships like U-Haul have them.

It's a good idea to select a hitch ball with a predrilled hole in the shaft for a cotter pin. Because the trailer puts a lot of twisting force on the ball during turns, it's very common for the nut to work loose. Without a cotter pin, it can actually come off, and as a result the ball pops out, leading to potential disaster.

Keeping Your Trailer on the Trail: Maintenance

Your trailer must be washed after use in saltwater, even if it's galvanized, aluminum, or stainless. The wheels, nuts, and other parts might be carbon steel and subject to rust. Spray the trailer with a dish-soap solution and then rinse with fresh water. After it's rinsed clean, coat the springs and bolts with a rustproofer like Corrosion-X or WD-40.

If you have trailer brakes, make sure you don't get spray oil anywhere near the brake shoes or pads. Even a trace of oil on the brake pads can ruin them permanently—and you might only find out you have a problem when you really, really need to stop quickly.

Wheel and Tire Maintenance

The bearings, which cut friction between the wheel and the axle, must be greased before and after each long trip. Bearing Buddies are spring-loaded grease fittings that hold grease inside the wheel hubs. They're cheap and easy to install and eliminate lots of bearing headaches. You simply tap them into the wheel hub. Grease can then be added through a fitting in the center of each Buddy. When filled, the devices keep pressure on the grease, forcing it into both inner and outer bearings. The fittings are available at most dealers.

Boat Bytes

The best way to get waterproof grease off your hands is to wipe them thoroughly with paper towels, and then use hand cream and more towels to remove the residue. Soap and water alone won't do a good job.

To get grease into the hub at the bearing fittings, use a grease gun and waterproof grease. It's messy (stow the gun in double-Ziploc bags) but essential. Make sure you wipe off excess grease from the fitting, or centrifugal force will toss it all over the wheel, trailer, and boat. (You can get a plastic snap-on "bra" to keep this grease from making a mess—they're around $5 at discount marine supply stores.)

Let There Be Lights

Functioning trailer taillights are critical because cars behind you can't see the stop or turn lights on your tow vehicle when you're pulling a boat and trailer.

When trailer lights don't light, it's due to either a bad wire, a short, or a burned-out bulb. Check the bulb first. Remove it from the socket and check it for corrosion. Coat the socket with Corrosion-X before putting the bulb back—the stuff conducts electricity, so it won't interfere with the current.

If the bulb is okay but the lights still don't work, there's a problem in the wiring. You'll need a circuit tester to check this. These are available at Radio Shack and other electronics stores for less than $20 and worth hundreds in the money they'll save you over a few years.

Getting Wired

The trailer connection to the hitch ball forms the ground or negative connection on many hookups, so you can't test trailer wiring unless you actually couple the ball to the tow vehicle, or unless your harness has an extra ground wire running back to the tow-vehicle battery.

> **Boat Bytes**
>
> Dirt or rust in the coupler can cause electrical shorts—keep the inside of the coupler clean by wiping it out with oil every now and then, and wire-brush it yearly.

One wire controls the lights, one the left signal and brake light, and one the right signal and brake light. So if the turn signal works, you know the brake light also works—you don't need somebody stepping on the brake to check.

Avoid any breaks in the wire run. If you get a nick in the insulation, you can be sure the wire will soon corrode there and quit working. Cut it and clean it immediately.

Take special care when repairing wire that will be submerged in water. Follow these steps:

1. Cut back bad wire until you see bright, uncorroded wire.

2. Bare about one-half inch of wire on each end.

3. Securely wrap the wires over each other.

4. Solder the junction.

5. Place a "heat-shrink" plastic fitting over the junction and heat it to seal the wires, and then follow up with silicone sealer or electrical tape.

Look Out!

Many galvanized trailers attach the wiring with unpainted raw steel clips. These last about as long as paper clips would around saltwater. Replace them with nylon tie-wraps or other nonrusting clips.

Inflation Is Good

Check the side of trailer tires carefully for the recommended inflation and top them off once a month. If you don't, the tires will inevitably overheat during a long pull and blow out. Underinflation allows the sidewalls to flex, which builds up heat. You've seen the sad trailer waifs along the side of the road, waiting until Dad comes back with a spare. Don't put your kids among them.

Boat Bytes

If you have a four-wheel or six-wheel trailer, carry a "jack-ramp." This can be three 2 × 6s that are nailed together to form a small stairsteps. You pull either the front or back wheel on these ramps and it raises the other one on the same side, without a jack or without any work on your part. It's safer than a jack, too, because it can't slip out and let the trailer crash down.

Winch Maintenance

Check the cable hook, eye, and winch regularly and tighten the nuts on the gear mechanism. The nut on the winch handle is notorious for coming off, causing the handle to be lost. Put a second nut on behind the first to act as a locknut, or coat the threads with a silicone sealer—it's firm enough to keep the nut in place, but can be stripped off if you ever need to replace the handle.

Get Tight and Load It Right

Make sure the hitch is locked to the ball and that the ball nut is securely tightened in place—it will work loose with some frequency due to turning forces from the trailer.

How to Avoid Wandering Trailers

Having a mind of your own is good if you're a human but bad if you're a boat trailer. Less weight on the hitch makes the trailer pull up on the back wheels of the car, making it hard to steer. Put some weight on the hitch by loading ice chests or other heavy gear forward in the boat or, more permanently, by moving the winch stand forward. Don't overdo it—just a couple of inches at a time will do it. Secure all bolts after this change.

Conversely, if the back of your tow vehicle squats and the front tires barely touch the ground, either you are driving a low-rider or you have too much weight on the hitch. Move the winch stand aft an inch or two at a time so that the weight of the boat is better balanced.

The fore and aft adjustment of the boat is controlled by the location of the winch stand. The transom should just fit onto the bunk—don't let it hang over even a half-inch or you're headed for trouble. The stress on the transom created by the lever action of the motor will eventually cause damage.

> **Nautical Notes**
>
> Trailer loading can be a factor in handling and safety. You need about 10 percent of the weight of the load on the hitch, or up to the limit of the tow vehicle. This can be anywhere from 100 to 300 pounds.

Tie Downs

It's a good idea to use transom tie-downs so that the boat doesn't hammer itself against the trailer on rough roads or railroad crossings. The ratchet type are best, with strong nylon straps for security. These can even keep the boat on the trailer in an accident.

Put a piece of toweling under the strap where it crosses the gunnels to prevent friction wear on both the straps and your shiny gel coat.

Motor Supports

A motor support for outboard motors is another good idea. Most newer motors have a trailering brace that flips into place and is secured by the weight of the engine. If your rig doesn't, use a "Transom Saver," a removable metal bar that fastens to the lower unit and to the aft member of the trailer frame, to support your motor. They're available at most marine dealers.

The Chain Gang

Trailer chains are used as a security factor should the hitch ball or the hitch itself break or come loose. They won't do much good, though, if they're not big and stout. Welded chain is best.

The chains should be crossed several times to help them catch the trailer tongue before it can hit the ground. Leave just enough slack so that you can make a sharp turn without binding with the chains.

Towing Tips

Towing a big rig at highway speeds looks scary, but with a properly matched rig and a little practice, there's nothing to it. Just remember that it takes longer to stop, and that you have a "tail" hanging behind the car that's longer than the car.

Some people advise that you shouldn't tow in overdrive, but according to Chevrolet Trucks, there's no problem with using overdrive with automatic transmissions as long as the weight of your rig doesn't cause continual shifting at highway speeds. If it does, it's better to drop down to third gear or even lower on a long mountain grade. (Some other companies do advise against towing in overdrive—it's best to follow the manual for your specific rig.)

Watch Where You Tow

There are some places that even the most experienced trailer-boater will not take his rig. There's no sense causing yourself problems by trying to fit the rig into a tight, 90-degree parking spot when you can pull straight ahead into several empty slots. Watch out for these potentially hazardous situations:

- **Using a drive-thru.** Never go through the drive-thru of a fast-food restaurant or store unless you're sure the boat is not much wider or taller than your towing vehicle. The overheads are particularly hazardous because we tend to forget about them.

- **Making a U-turn.** If you need to make a U-turn in heavy traffic, the best advice is *don't make the U-turn*. Choose a light with a turning lane if possible, turn left into the cross street, make another left into the alley, and then another to bring you back to the highway—and now you've got an easy right to get back where you need to go. That's better than risking an accident—or these days, a gunshot— by pulling across traffic.

Secure It All

Sargeant's Law says that anything that can blow out of a boat will blow out of a boat when it is being trailered. The last step before you head down the driveway should be to climb aboard the boat and look things over.

Hatch lids are notorious for disappearing if they're not hinged in place. Loose cushions also take wing, never to be seen again. Life jackets and cooler tops, or even whole coolers if empty, also disappear regularly.

Tie everything down or stow it in a secured box to avoid any problems. (Bungee cords are great for this—buy a dozen of them and keep them onboard your boat.) Even heavy objects like anchors can leap right out of the boat on a rough road. Don't give things a chance to go wrong—make sure everything is secure before starting out.

Maneuvering Your Trailer

Backing a trailer is a challenge almost equivalent to docking a boat. The way to learn it is to practice—at home, not at a crowded boat ramp late on a Sunday afternoon.

The basic thing to remember about backing a trailer is that the trailer goes in the *opposite direction* of the back end of the tow vehicle. The no-brainer way to remember this is to grip the bottom of the steering wheel with one hand. (Not that hard! No need for white knuckles here.)

To make the trailer back left, move your hand left. To make it back right, move your hand right. Make these movements small unless you're trying to back around a corner (not recommended for beginners).

If things get completely out of whack, simply pull forward, get the trailer and the tow vehicle in a straight line again, and try once more. You can also make small adjustments by stopping, pulling forward a bit, and then backing up again during your approach to the ramp or garage.

With practice, you'll be able to back the rig around sharp corners, but beware of getting "jack-knifed," which is when the angle between the trailer tongue and the car becomes so sharp that the vehicle bumper starts to push the trailer sideways. Keep an eye on how close you're getting through the side-view mirrors (if your vehicle doesn't have them and you trailer your boat frequently, invest in a pair of large ones).

Highway Trailering

Pulling a trailer down a highway is fairly straightforward except you have to remember you have less acceleration than normal, so taking off takes longer. You also have more weight to stop, particularly if the trailer doesn't have brakes, so it will take longer to stop.

Air blast from passing trucks can make a trailer swerve. If this happens, hold your course and speed and don't hit the brakes, and the trailer will straighten out. Sometimes, severe swerving can be corrected by a short burst of acceleration, but as soon as the rig straightens out, let the vehicle slow down—you are probably going too fast for the way your trailer is loaded.

When trailering a boat, you also have to change lanes more gradually and allow twice as much room when passing before you pull back in. Getting up to passing speed might take three times longer, too. Remember not to cut corners too close. The trailer will go over the curb or hit the fire hydrant on the corner if you don't go around the corner wide.

Look Out!

If you can't keep up with traffic and it's stacking up behind you, do other motorists a favor and pull over to let them pass!

Keeping Your Cool

The added load of trailering can be hard on your tow vehicle. Make sure the cooling system is full and working properly before you start a long tow. If the system starts to overheat, turn off the air conditioning. In a worst case, turn on the heater until the engine cools—it makes it miserable inside the vehicle in the summer, but the heater acts as a mini-radiator that helps throw off heat in a hurry.

If you tow a big boat, you'll need a transmission cooler. It's a radiator for the transmission and sits in front of the regular radiator. Without it, you can boil the transmission fluid or fry it—neither is good for your transmission, and I speak as one who spent $1,400 a few years back for a rebuild on my Explorer tranny.

If you're buying a new tow vehicle, opt for the tow package—transmission cooler, larger cooling system, larger battery, trailer harness and

Look Out!

Inflate the tires on your tow vehicle to the max. The added weight will otherwise build up heat, particularly in the rear tires. A hard, skinny shape builds less heat than a soft, flabby one.

sometimes a hitch, and a lower gear in the rear end. You won't have any towing problems and you'll be glad you spent the extra bucks.

Pushing Off

It's wise to tow the first 10 miles, and then stop and check out the rig. Touch the bearing housing and the trailer tires to check for excessive heat. (They're dirty, so have a paper towel handy to wipe your hands afterward.) Both will be warm, but if they're hot to the point that they're uncomfortable to touch, something is wrong—check the bearing grease and tire pressure.

Make absolutely sure that your hitch is secured and the ball is tight. A friend of mine had his hitch ball come loose while he was traveling a four-lane highway in south Florida. The trailer tongue dropped on the pavement and sent out a mighty shower of sparks as the rig swerved into the left lane and passed the slowing truck at flank speed. It then went across the median, dodged two lanes of traffic coming south, and ran down an embankment to neatly deposit the boat into a river. The trailer was ruined, but the boat was miraculously unscathed!

Had my buddy used safety chains, properly wound around each other to snub the tongue in the event of hitch failure, he wouldn't have lost his rig.

If your trailer has brakes, don't forget to attach the trailer's brake cable—it's a small cable with a hook, coming out of the trailer brake mechanism on the tongue to the hitch. If things come apart, pressure on the cable will apply the trailer brakes.

Let's Do Launch

After you've arrived safely at the ramp, get the boat ready to launch in a parking area away from the actual launching zone. This saves time and avoids jamming the ramp for those who are ready to go.

Get your lines untangled and secured to a *cleat*, remove the tie-downs on the boat and the motor support, make sure the boat key is in the ignition, and *be sure the drain plug is in place*. This is a biggie that's often forgotten. Many a boat has sunk because the intrepid skipper didn't put that little $2 plug in place. Put it in, and then check it again just before you put the boat in the water. (It's always a good idea to carry a spare plug—or buy one of the "tethered" plugs that secure themselves to the plug hole, so that they can't be lost.)

Salt Talk _____

A **cleat** is a clever but simple device that eliminates the need to tie a knot in securing a boat. The two-horned prongs, usually metal but sometimes fiber-filled plastic for smaller boats, allow quick tie-ups and avoid the jamming of knots common under stress. To use a cleat, you take a full wrap around the base, make a half-hitch over one of the horns, and then another couple wraps around the horns.

Then it's time to back down the incline of the ramp, utilizing the lessons practiced at home. Have a crewperson stand on the dock, holding a bow line attached to the boat.

If your trailer has Bearing Buddies to keep water out of the bearings, you can back right in until the boat floats free. The crewperson then pulls it in and ties it to the dock while you go park the car. Some experienced boaters simply put a driver at the boat wheel and have him or her back it off and move it to the dock under power.

With break-frame trailers or trailers without sealed bearings, you back in until you're just short of sinking the wheel bearings, and then pull the pin on the trailer frame and push upward on the boat bow. This causes the trailer to tilt backward and allows the boat to slide free.

Look Out! _____

Don't forget to attach a bow line before you push the boat off the trailer, or you'll have to swim to recapture it!

Up-Loading

When your day on the water ends, don't make the mistake of sinking the trailer out of sight as you try to reload the boat. Back in just far enough to wet the bunks completely, then pull forward so that only the last foot or two of the bunks is underwater. Even though this looks like the trailer is too far from the water to ever load the boat, this is the way to do it. Resist the temptation to sink the bunks. If you do, the boat can't possibly center itself on them because it won't even touch them!

Place wheel chocks made of foot-long 4 × 4s behind your tow vehicle's back wheels—this prevents turning your car into a boat—and you're ready to load.

Power Loading

Power loading is using the boat motor to push the boat onto the trailer. It's fast and easy: Get the boat lined up squarely with the trailer, ease forward until the keel makes

Look Out!

Some launching ramps have a ban on power-loading because it tends to blow out the bottom strata at the end of the ramp, creating a drop-off that has to be repaired. Always check for "no power-loading" signs before you motor onto your trailer.

contact with the center roller, and then advance the throttle a little so that the boat climbs right up onto the trailer bunks. It should stop a few inches from the winch hook.

Hook up the winch and use the ratchet to snug up the boat against the bow roller. Shift the winch lock to the "on" position, add a safety chain from bow to trailer, and you're ready to pull out.

Break-Frame Loading

If you don't have a drive-on trailer, you probably have a "break-frame" that tilts up when you pull a pin on the tongue. These are suitable for light, small- to medium-size boats, up to about 17 feet. Your partner slides the boat bow onto the back roller of the trailer (What, you don't have a partner? Then get a drive-on trailer!), then you walk the plank, teetering your way along the frame as you pull out the winch cable to hook onto the bow eye. Then you teeter back and crank the boat into place.

You might have to use a stern line to keep the back end of the boat aligned with the trailer in the early going, particularly if there are winds or a current from the side.

After the boat is in place, secure the break-frame pin and bow chain as described previously.

Boat Bytes

Although you don't want to release the emergency brake before putting the car in gear, you *must* take it off before trying to pull forward. Sounds too obvious for you to possibly ever forget, doesn't it? I do it about once a year and usually can't figure out why my truck suddenly has lost power.

Pulling Out

Remove wheel chocks, put the car in low gear, take off the emergency brake *only then*, and pull out steadily. If you take off the emergency brake first, the car will rock back against the transmission park pin, making it difficult to shift into drive. Or, even worse, it might rock back and break the pin and proceed rapidly down the ramp into the water.

Trouble at the Ramp

There are times when you can't pull out. Slippery, steep, or potholed ramps or dirt or gravel can make it difficult. So can a boat that's too big for your tow vehicle. The best thing to do in a situation like this is get a tow from a nearby vehicle, if possible.

You can also try to improve traction by scraping away moss or loose gravel in front of the drive wheels. Mats laid in front of the drive wheels might help—carpet, plywood, or anything that will provide traction can work.

Sometimes, you might have to offload the boat, pull the trailer out, and put it in again at another location on the ramp where traction is better.

In an emergency, you can use your boat engine's power to give you a push those first few critical feet. You need a helper for this—one person drives the tow vehicle, the other the boat. Make sure the boat is completely tied down with both winch strap and safety chain. Lower the lower unit, make sure the propeller and water pickup are underwater and that the prop clears bottom, and start it up.

As the vehicle driver applies power, you put the boat in gear and give a power assist. Sometimes it only takes a nudge, sometimes a more authoritative push. In either case, a quick hand is required to cut back power as soon as the vehicle wheels begin to grab. The quickest way to shut it down is pull the kill switch lanyard, which cuts off the ignition.

A word of warning: You *must* shut off the motor before the water intake clears the water or you might wind up with a fried engine. Over-revving is also possible if the propeller clears the water. And of course, if you apply too much power and the hold-downs are not adequate, you could wind up turning your car into a boat trailer. Clearly, this is no remedy for the faint of heart, but it's highly effective and one that the experts use when necessary.

A Taillight Cure

Trailer taillights are chronically ill because they're so often submerged. One cure is to put the taillights atop PVC plastic tubing made into guide poles. These poles help steer the boat onto the trailer during reloading, but they also keep the lights out of the water. U-clamp brackets will hold them in place.

Run the wires through the hollow interior of the pipes. The pipes are also a good place to mount your trailer license—the low mounts on the trailer expose the license to being scraped off on rough ramps.

Trailering seems daunting the first time you pull up to a ramp, but after a few successful launches and retrievals, you'll find it's the easiest part of boating.

The Least You Need to Know

- ◆ It's important to buy the right trailer for your boat.

- ◆ Hitches are load-rated and must be matched to the towed package.

- ◆ Practice maneuvering a trailer at home before you try it at the launch ramp.

- ◆ Maintenance is critical to extending trailer life.

Part 2

The Basics of Operation

Okay, now you've got a boat, so how do you run it? Part 2 gives you the nitty-gritty on powerboats—getting the crew aboard, starting the engine, handling the boat around the harbor, and keeping your crew happy.

Not only do you learn how to make your boat move in this part, but also how to make it stay put. There's a surprising amount to know about anchoring, which we'll explore in Chapter 8. The use of ropes aboard—don't forget that boaters call them "lines"—is also covered in this section.

And if you're into pollution-free propulsion that's good for the cardiovascular system as well as the soul, don't bypass the chapter on "alternative boats." Or, if paddling is a bit slow for you, there's also a section on fast, sexy personal watercraft in this chapter.

Chapter 5

Getting Underway for the First Time

In This Chapter

- ◆ Boarding your boat
- ◆ Starting the engine
- ◆ Keeping trim
- ◆ Getting gassed

You don't have to know much to make a powerboat move. A sailboat requires a little more training, but at the dock, under power, both boats have one thing in common: turn the key (or pull the starter cord, in manual start motors), shift into forward, and away you go. However, there are a few basics of operation every boater should know before pushing off.

It starts with getting yourself and your crew safely from the dock into the boat.

In this chapter, we'll cover the safe way to get aboard, how to get even a temperamental engine started, how to get underway, and how to get the boat trimmed out for the best ride. We'll also look at a very important safety topic: refueling the tanks.

Plan Ahead

Before you leave home, of course, you'll make sure all the required safety gear is aboard (see Chapter 7), check the weather and the tides (see Chapters 15 and 16), and let a neighbor or friend know where you'll be boating and when you plan to return.

This becomes automatic after you've been boating for a while, but when you're getting started, it's not a bad idea to make a simple checklist to make sure you're not forgetting some of those extras—like sunscreen and sunglasses—that make life afloat more comfortable and fun.

All Aboard!

Getting aboard the boat is usually pretty straightforward, but it's not quite as simple as stepping into your car. There is a delicate moment when going aboard that invites disaster. Getting into a small boat requires a positive but not hurried motion. He who hesitates with one foot on the bank and one in the boat is assuredly lost—the boat moves seaward due to the push from the foot, and the boarder falls between boat and dock. I know this to be true because I have done it in moments of inattention, several times. Avoid doing as I have done, and do as I say.

With a small boat, step as nearly amidships as possible, near the center rather than on the gunnels. Stepping on the gunnels of small, light boats leads to rather spectacular reverse flips. You may earn a 9.9 from the judges, but you won't be happy.

A small sailboat with no keel—known as a dinghy—operates on the same principle. Step in the center of the boat (don't hesitate!) and keep your weight low. On a larger sailboat with a keel, although it's more stable, you might have to step over cables strung along the topsides. These are called "lifelines" and although they're designed to keep you on the boat when it's underway, they can be tricky to step over. The best way to board a sailboat with lifelines is to step up onto the edge of the boat while hanging on to part of the rig, and then step over the lifelines, one foot at a time.

Small children often find it easier to duck under the lifelines as they climb aboard, especially if the boat is tied so that it is very close to the dock. It is often worth adjusting the dock lines to make this possible. Apprehensive kids will have a lot more confidence from the start if they can climb on and off the boat by themselves.

Look Out!

Particularly early in the morning, all walking surfaces aboard a boat are likely to be covered with dew. Be very cautious when stepping onto a wet surface—it can be as slippery as ice.

But be very attentive to children on the dock. After you're underway, it is very unlikely that anyone will fall overboard without being noticed, and if a small child goes in, a parent is almost guaranteed to follow within a fraction of a second. But on the dock, it's very easy for children to run out of sight, and if they fall in, it could be a while before anyone realizes that they are missing. For this reason it is very important for kids to wear PFDs (personal flotation devices) from the first moment they set foot on the dock. If the life jackets are stored on the boat, keep a very, very careful watch on the kids until they have their flotation gear properly fitted.

In some larger powerboats, things stay put much better, and there's usually a broad step on the transom or aft gunnel to make things fairly easy. Don't expect a boarding ramp like they have on the *Love Boat* unless the boat you are boarding is more than 50 feet long.

Boat Bytes

Tired of hearing kids complain about those life jackets? They won't complain if they see all the grownups wearing them, too. You might not like it either, but it's not nearly as bad as a whiney kid.

Keep Your Hands Handy

Always step aboard with a free hand—if you step on the boat with your hands full and the boat shifts, you might fall, hard. (Even if you intend to honeymoon aboard, don't try to carry your bride over that nautical threshold.) Instead, lay your gear on the dock and then step aboard the boat, ready to lower your weight and grab on to something so you don't fall. After both feet are securely on deck, reach back up for the gear or have someone hand it to you. A good way to remember this caution is the old seaman's saying, "one hand for yourself, one hand for the boat."

It's a good idea to pull the boat in close to the dock before trying to board. Cleat the lines short and then step aboard. However, make sure you don't start to go out, change your mind, and leave the boat with the lines tied short. In coastal waters, the tides might drop and leave your boat suspended in midair!

Starting the Engines

Starting the engine is supposed to be very simple—turn the key and the boat runs. But some engines are temperamental—far fewer these days than a decade ago, thanks to fuel-injection, but there are still occasional problems. Here's a basic procedure that will get most engines going—you might have to customize it a little to suit your particular motor:

1. Turn on the blower, if your boat has one—this is an exhaust fan down in the bilge. This helps remove any fuel fumes that might have accumulated in the bilge area since last time you used the boat. It's an essential safety measure, particularly in inboard and sterndrive boats where batteries might be in the same below-decks areas where fuel tanks and lines are located. Allow the blower to run at least five minutes before you move on to step 2. Be aware, however, that sometimes even five minutes of bilge blowing can change an over-rich mixture of fuel vapor and air (flammable, but not explosive) into just the right fuel-air mix for a big bang! If you don't have an electronic vapor detector, your nose is your best friend. Always sniff the exhaust from the blower—gasoline fumes are not that hard to detect. If you smell gas, don't try to start the boat! Instead, seek out the leak.

Salt Talk

A **kill switch** is a safety switch attached to a lanyard that shuts off the motor if the driver leaves his or her seat.

Provided you're fume-free, turn on the key or the electrical power switch to make sure there's fuel in the tank according to the fuel gauge. If there's a *kill switch*, make sure it's in the "run" position.

2. Pump up the fuel bulb (shown in the following figure), if there is one. Most outboards have fuel bulbs about the size of an oblong tennis ball placed in the fuel line, either in the motor well or in a compartment near the stern. Just follow the fuel line and you'll find it. Squeeze the bulb until it's firm. This means that there's a solid charge of fuel from the bulb into the engine.

The primer or fuel bulb is a small pumping device that pushes fuel into the carburetor when squeezed. It's usually found within a foot or two of the motor.

3. Make sure the drive gears are in neutral. On single-lever systems like most outboards and sterndrives, this will be when the shifting lever is straight up. There's a detent or slot in the shifter housing so that the throttle lever clicks as it goes into neutral. Wiggle the lever around until you feel this click. Most motors will not crank unless the gears are in the neutral position.

On inboards and some performance boats, the throttle or fuel lever is separate from the shifting lever. The fuel lever has a red knob, the shifting lever a black knob. Advance the red knob slightly to start, but keep the black one centered for neutral.

4. Prime or choke the motor if needed. On fuel-injected motors this won't be necessary. Otherwise, push the choke or prime button. Sometimes it's built into the ignition key and you prime by pushing in on the key as you turn it. Choke or prime as you crank the engine for about 5 to 10 seconds.

5. Some motors start best if the throttle is advanced slightly. On single-lever controls, you do this without putting the motor into gear by pushing a lockout button on the throttle base and then advancing the throttle. Move it only an inch or so—don't push it all the way forward or the motor will start at 5,000 rpms!

6. Normally, the motor starts, or at least coughs, within the first 10 seconds. After it coughs, there's fuel in the cylinders—don't prime or choke it again right away or you'll flood it (that is, you'll get an excessive amount of liquid fuel into the firing chamber and make it tough for the spark plugs to touch it off).

7. After the motor starts, you might have to give several short bursts of choke to keep it running, particularly on chilly mornings.

8. After about 20 seconds, you can pull the throttle back to idle speed. The motor should now run normally. If it stumbles and quits after it's been running a minute or two, don't choke it again. Simply put it in neutral and restart it.

The throttle lever and shift controls are combined in one handle on most outboards and sterndrives. The rocker switch on the handle controls the trim of the lower unit, which adjusts the running attitude of the boat.

In twin-engine boats, follow the same routine for the second engine. However, if one of the engines is hard to start, start that one first. It's difficult to hear what the second engine is doing when the first one is running, so get the troublemaker out of the way first. Keep an eye on the tachometer of the first engine to make sure it keeps running after the second one fires up—it's not uncommon for one to go back to sleep, and you can't hear that it has because of the noise from the second engine.

Leaving the Dock

Getting away from a dock is usually less challenging than returning to it, but there are a few tricks. First of all, make sure everybody is seated or at least in a safe spot. Kids, in particular, have a way of getting their hands between the dock and the boat at just the wrong moment.

Boat Bytes

In many states, children age 12 and under are required by law to wear PFDs anytime they're in a boat. And the jackets must be child-sized, so that they fit snugly and will stay in place in the water.

In small boats, PFDs should be worn by all aboard, and *must* be worn by nonswimmers and children. In cold weather or when facing rough water, or when preparing for high-speed operation, everyone should automatically put on a life jacket. As skipper, you are responsible for making sure there's a PFD of the right size for every person aboard your boat—it's a legal requirement.

In larger craft, tell everyone where the jackets are, and show novices how to put one on.

If the boat has been attached to shore electrical power to recharge batteries or to operate accessories, make sure the power cord is disconnected and stowed. Ditto for water hoses. The dock fenders—plastic bumpers you hang over the side of your boat—can also be put away at this time.

Normally, you simply cast off the dock lines and put the boat into gear to leave the dock. But sometimes it can be more complicated—see Chapter 6 for details.

Keeping Trim Afloat

The trim system on a sterndrive or outboard controls the angle of attack of the prop to the water and also affects the running angle of the boat. Small motors have manual trim, adjustable only when the engine is stopped by moving a pin on the mounting bracket to shift the lower unit in or out relative to the transom.

But most motors larger than 50 horsepower have power trim, an electrical/hydraulic system controlled most often by a rocker switch on the throttle lever or sometimes by a separate rocker switch on the dash. You push the button to activate a pump in the hydraulic tube, causing the lower unit to tilt in or out relative to the transom. A few performance boats have the trim switch on the steering wheel, allowing the driver to keep both hands in place while he adjusts for top speeds.

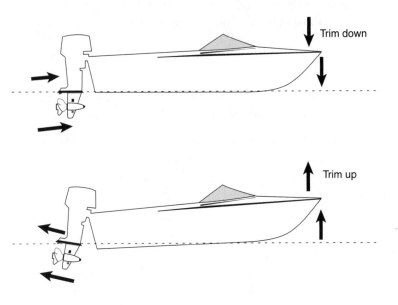

Trimming the motor closer to the transom forces the bow down, while trimming it away from the transom pushes the bow up.

Time to Trim In

Push the bottom of the trim button when you want to take off or begin planing. This is called "trimming in" or sometimes "trimming down." This tilts the bottom of the lower unit closer to the transom. Most lower units will trim to a negative angle, which means the lower section tilts beyond vertical toward the transom. When power is applied, this boosts the transom up and pushes the bow down, which is what you want for a quick takeoff or hole shot.

You also trim in to make a series of tight turns at speed. This holds the stern better, preventing it from sliding sideways.

Those Are the Brakes

Trimming in can help you slow down quickly as well. Rapidly dropping the lower unit creates drag to slow the boat and also drops the boat off the optimal running angle, further reducing speed. Reducing throttle and trim act as the high-speed "brakes" on a boat.

Look Out!

Never shift the motor into reverse at high speed—it can damage the gears.

When your boat is at a speed of under 5 miles per hour, the reverse gear becomes your brake. Just like reversing the engines on a landing jet, kicking the gears into reverse quickly pulls the boat to a halt. This doesn't work at higher speeds—the prop simply ventilates or grabs air and makes a lot of noise, but the boat keeps on going.

Softening the Waves

Because it drops the bow, trimming in brings the sharp forward vee of the keel (the "entry") into first contact with the waves, splitting them and softening the ride.

All vee and semi-vee boats have a sharper bottom at the bow than they do near the stern. If you get this sharp vee into the water, the ride is improved, like a knife going through the water instead of a rounded spoon slapping down on the surface. This slows the boat a bit, but it greatly improves passenger comfort.

Trimming down too much at high speed might cause the boat to "bow steer," meaning the bow digs in while the transom slides around on turns. You can tell if you've trimmed down too far because the steering starts to feel heavy and the white water rushing out the sides of the boat moves forward beyond amidships. Trimming down too much also lowers freeboard at the bow, decreasing the distance from the water to the gunnels, which you want to avoid in high waves.

Time to Trim Out

Trim out (push the top of the trim button) when the boat is on plane and you want to go faster. This causes the lower unit to tilt away from the transom. It's also known as "trimming up." Trimming out raises the bow and rocks the boat back onto the aft third of the bottom, the surface designed for most efficient high-speed running in a planing hull.

Salt Talk

Negative trim is when the lower unit of an outdrive is tilted in toward the transom. **Positive trim** is when the lower unit of an outdrive is tilted away from the transom.

This reduces what engineers call the wetted surface, the section of bottom in contact with the water, and consequently cuts drag and improves speed and fuel economy.

In the extremes, as in high-performance bass boats and racing boats, the front half of the boat is actually out of the water when the boat is fully trimmed up. On family boats, the front might just touch the surface, but it's not plowing along as it would under zero or *negative trim*.

With the bow forced upward by trimming out the twin outboards, this Triton can get anglers offshore in a hurry.

(Triton Boats)

It Ain't Flipper: Stop Your Boat from Porpoising

The higher you trim the bow, the faster the boat will go until you overtrim, at which point the prop and speed can't support the bow and it falls off, or drops the bow back to the surface.

This creates fore-and-aft rocking called porpoising. In the extremes, it's a bit like riding a bucking horse. You stop it by trimming in a bit, or by giving more throttle, because the faster you go, the more weight the combination of engine power, prop, and hull design can support.

Boat Bytes _____

What if your boat porpoises all the time? Chances are you have too much weight forward, making it impossible for the prop to adequately lift the bow. A quick fix is to move passengers, ice chests, or other heavy gear aft. Or you might want to switch from a three-blade prop to a four-blade—the added blade area sometimes helps in giving more lift.

The Art of Cornering

Lots of trim makes steering light and easy and adds speed, but it also makes the boat more inclined to skid in sharp turns. So if you're faced with running through a narrow, winding creek or making sharp turns, the lower unit needs to be trimmed down. Otherwise, you could wind up boating on dry land.

Don't trim in too much or the boat might "bow steer," with the front section of the keel grabbing the water and pivoting the aft section so sharply that gear and passengers might be endangered.

Ventilation: Good in Motel Rooms, Bad in Props

Excess trim can lead to "blow out" or prop ventilation, in which the prop sucks in surface air as it breaks the surface. This is most likely to occur on turns as the boat heels or leans into the turn. The prop loses its grip on the water and the motor howls, winding up very fast while the boat slows quickly. Ventilation sometimes occurs when a fast boat jumps over a large wave as well.

You know you're at maximum trim when rpms go up but speed does not. On most performance boats, this can be quite high, to the point where the motor howls and there's a healthy "rooster tail" or white-water spray upward from the prop. (This looks cool, but it wastes fuel.)

Some performance props are what are called surface piercing, which means that at the top part of the stroke, each blade pops free of the water. Because it takes less power to turn out of the water than in, the prop load decreases and the engine winds higher.

Nautical Notes

The redline is the upper limit in revolutions per minute (rpms) recommended by the engine manufacturer. It's indicated on the tachometer, the dash instrument that shows rpms. Most motors are redlined at well below the rpm that will destroy them, but exceeding the redline regularly or for prolonged periods will definitely cause the powerhead to start making ugly noise—or even worse, no noise at all.

Most two-stroke outboards are redlined between 5,000 and 5,800 rpms, and many four-strokes redline at 6,000. A few high-performance versions are designed for sustained speeds in excess of 6,000 rpms, and motors used in racing sometimes rev up to 10,000 (but they don't have to live very long between rebuilds). There is actually a red line on many tachometers indicating the line beyond which you should not go if you don't like spending time and money in the company of mechanics.

Surface-piercing propellers use ventilation to advantage. Each blade carries an air cavity into the water with it so that cavitation—a much more damaging condition than ventilation—is completely suppressed. Also, surface-piercing installations can be designed to keep most of the lower unit out of the water, significantly reducing drag on very fast boats.

Heavy displacement boats can benefit from surface-piercing propellers, too, especially when operation in shallow water is required. But the propulsion system—if not the entire boat—should be designed from the keel up for surface-piercing operation.

Shallow-Water Trim

You also trim up at idle speeds when crossing shallows or grassy areas—it gets the prop higher and avoids bottom contact. Many times, when you think you're stuck on a shoal, you can get off by trimming up the lower unit of an outboard or sterndrive to the point where the water pickup is barely below the surface and the prop is actually breaking the surface.

You lose a good bit of your propulsion with the prop in this position and you can hardly back up at all, but the blades grab enough to ease you off the obstruction—usually. If not, it's time to shut off the motor, step over the side, and put your shoulder to things.

Avoid trimming up much at speeds between 1,000 and 2,000 rpms in the shallows because this pushes the stern down. The boat actually runs deeper in the water than if you had the motor in the full down position.

Remember that at about 1,500 to 2,500 rpms on outboards, many boats will "plow" or bog severely. You'll go slow, but you'll actually make a much larger wake and burn more fuel than if you went fast.

> **Boat Bytes** _____
>
> Don't make the amateur's mistake of trimming up at low speeds and then trying to put the boat on plane. The motor will roar and the water will fly, but you'll go nowhere fast.

This sort of slow-down infuriates skippers tied to the docks when you pass, and marks you as a real amateur. (You're legally responsible for any damage your wake does!)

The boat's running angle or attitude also makes it very difficult to see over the bow in some models. You're driving blind! Avoid the plow!

Refueling Your Boat

Gasoline is very dangerous in boats because the bowl shape of the hull interior traps any spilled or leaking fuel. The closed decks and compartments can hold in leaking vapors, creating a fuel-air bomb that is only lacking a spark to turn your boat into a Roman candle.

Diesel fuel is less explosive than gasoline but still highly flammable. Thus, fueling is a business that requires your undivided attention.

Most trailer boats get gassed up at a filling station on the way to the ramp, and this is a good idea because it saves you big on fuel costs. Buying fuel from a marina is usually 15 to 20 percent more expensive than buying it from a filling station. However, at times you will need to refuel on the water, even with a trailered boat. With larger boats stored at the marina or in the water, this is always standard operating procedure. Follow these steps to do it right:

1. Make sure your boat is properly tied to the fuel dock. Nothing is more distracting than having the boat begin to leave the docks with the fuel hose in the filler! Incompetent cleating can make it happen, so if you let Uncle George handle the lines, make sure he knows how to make things stay put.

2. Make sure you put fuel only into the fuel tank. Where else could you possibly put it? On some boats, the water filler cap looks exactly like the fuel filler cap—gasoline shower, anyone? There have even been instances of people pumping fuel into trolling rod holders! How do you know which cap leads to the fuel tank? It has a code on the cap. It says "F-U-E-L."

3. Avoid careless spills, which are both dangerous and bad for the watery environment. Any spilled gas aboard should be wiped up with paper towels, which should then be disposed of at the marina in a metal barrel, *not* in the nearest plastic trash can.

4. It goes without saying neither you nor anyone aboard should smoke during fueling. That is, it goes without saying unless someone tries it. Better to warn everyone ahead of time. Even if it means putting out that freshly lighted $10 Macanudo.

5. Have someone keep an eye on your gallonage, and slow down the flow rate on the fuel as you get near what you think should be full. Some marina hoses have an extremely high flow rate so that they can fill yacht tanks quickly, but this can mean your smaller tank fills a lot faster than you think it will. Fuel can come shooting back up the fill pipe and drench you.

6. Open all hatches, particularly the engine compartment on inboards and I/Os, after fueling. This is also a good time to check your fuel hoses for tight connections and for deterioration. The slightest seepage should be investigated and corrected immediately.

7. Turn on the blower and let it operate for several minutes. This little exhaust fan down in the bilge sucks out any fumes, pushing them out vents usually located near the transom.

8. Secure the fuel cap. Make sure it's tight enough so that rain and spray won't get into the tank. Some fuel fill caps require a "key" (shown in the following figure), which is a tool that fits into detents in the cap, allowing you to open or close the cap. Can't find the key? Often, the back of the blade of a closed folding knife will fit into the slot and allow you to turn the cap. A quarter can also be substituted on some caps.

9. Sniff for fumes. You can buy $200 fuel fume detectors, but they don't work as well as your own nose. (Just don't do this too much, or it will lower the SAT scores of any potential offspring.)

10. Start the engine only when the cap is secured and you're sure there are no fumes should you touch the ignition key.

Gunnel of boat

The fuel key helps in opening fuel caps that are too tight to open with your fingers alone. Caps must be tightened securely to prevent water from getting into the fuel.

All of this is not to say that your boat is likely to explode at any moment. Fuel fires afloat are extremely rare. But they do happen, and the results can be catastrophic. You can't simply run out in the street and wait for the fire department.

All powerboats with enclosed fuel tanks are required to carry one of the various classes of fire extinguishers at all times. See Chapter 17 for details on selection and use.

The Least You Need to Know

- Boarding a boat can be tricky—make sure your passengers use care.
- Starting the motor is easy if you follow the proper procedure every time.
- The trim button is the key to efficient boat operation.
- Use special care when refueling, and ventilate the boat afterward.

Chapter 6

The Art and Science of Docking

In This Chapter

- ◆ Undocking your boat
- ◆ Landing your boat
- ◆ Picking up a mooring
- ◆ Securing your boat in a slip

Handling your boat in and around a marina or boat ramp is not all that difficult. (Of course, neither is calculus after you learn it—just kidding!) In fact, after a few months afloat, you'll find there's nothing to docking. But first learning how to handle a boat around a marina or ramp can be a challenge, not because it's really difficult or dangerous, but because it's potentially embarrassing if you goof. And you can also do some damage to your boat if you're really careless.

There are "ramp ghouls" who entertain themselves on Sunday afternoons at the marina by sitting in lawn chairs, sipping a cold one, and laughing at the errors of boaters allegedly less skilled than themselves.

The good news is that with a bit of practice, you won't give them anything to laugh about.

In this chapter, you'll learn how to leave the docks and how to return smoothly. I'll also cover the art of picking up a mooring and how to tie up the boat in a slip—a special art where tides can vary the water height several feet.

Maneuvering Out of a Slip

Like everything else in boating, the ropes used to tie up and maneuver a boat around a dock, which are always referred to as *lines*, have special names. A *bow line* is attached to a cleat or ring on the front of the boat. A *stern line* is attached to a cleat on the back end of the boat. A *spring line* is attached to a forward cleat and run aft to the dock, or attached to an aft cleat and run forward to the dock. It keeps the boat from moving forward or backward at the dock.

A *slip* is a boat's home, a spot where docks and pilings allow the boat to be tied securely. Leaving a slip in still water when the boat is backed in is simply a matter of putting the boat into gear and going straight forward at idle speed until the stern clears the outside piling or the end of the dock.

Look Out!

When parked parallel, don't turn the wheel away from the dock and go forward. If you do, the stern will be pivoted into the dock—the stern does the steering in powerboats, remember?

With a single-engine boat, prop torque (assuming you have a single-engine boat fitted with the more common right-handed propeller) might walk or edge the back end of the boat very slightly to starboard, which can bring your port bow too close to the pilings. You might have to give a bit of right rudder to compensate.

Keep the boat moving straight ahead until the stern is clear of the slip and the pilings. If you start to turn too soon, the stern will pivot into the pilings.

If the boat is bow-on, or pointed into the slip, back out straight until the bow is clear of the last piling, and then turn. The stern might work slightly left—a crewperson might have to fend off the starboard bow. (The rudder doesn't help much at extremely low speeds in reverse with inboard boats. Reverse steering is more positive with outboards and I/Os.)

Pulling Away from a Dock

If your small boat is tied parallel to a dock and pointed toward the channel, and there's no wind or strong current, all you have to do is push off the bow and go. Keep the wheel dead ahead and put the boat into gear at idle speed. Hey, you're boating!

With twin-engined boats too big to push around, the standard technique is to put the outside engine into reverse for a moment, and then pop it back to neutral. The burst of thrust pulls the bow away from the dock, and you can then go straight ahead to get clear. After the bow has swung well out, you might give a short burst of forward thrust to the inside engine to help it. All this is done with the rudder dead ahead, so don't touch the steering wheel.

If there's another boat or an L-section of dock behind your boat, you add a "spring line" running from an aft cleat well forward to a dock cleat. (Springs are lines used to control a boat's lateral movement along a dock. The lines are run from aft cleats forward to the dock, and from forward cleats aft to the dock.) Then, that same burst of reverse works to pivot the stern in place with no backward movement at all, and thus no unkind words from your neighbor to the rear.

When the Wind Is Blowing Away from the Dock

If there's wind or a current moving away from the dock, pushing off is even simpler—just untie the lines and wait until the natural forces carry you a couple yards away from the pilings before going ahead. Again, don't turn the wheel sharply away from the dock or you might force the stern right back against the pilings. Wait until you're well clear before turning.

Boat Bytes _____

Don't use a short line direct from an aft cleat to a cleat on the dock because this might hold the stern in too close. Running a line forward as a spring gives the boat room to pivot away from the dock. Be sure to put fenders off the stern area to protect against scrapes.

Look Out! _____

If you have inexperienced crew helping out, make sure that all the lines are actually untied and stowed before you try to leave the docks. It's not uncommon for a spring line to be overlooked, and this definitely puts a crimp in your style when you try to pull out. Don't forget the power, water, and phone lines, too, if you have those hookups.

When the Wind Is Blowing Toward the Dock

When a strong wind or current is blowing into the dock, it can be a handful. I once saw a 40-foot cruiser pinned against a dock by a 20-knot wind, and the inexperienced skipper couldn't figure out how to get clear. The shouts and conflicting advice of a half-dozen bystanders didn't help, even though they upped the volume each time he crashed back into the pilings.

You can't get away from a dock by turning away and going forward in this situation, because the back end of the boat will swing away from the direction of the turn first, locking itself against the dock. No matter how much power you apply, you can't force the bow out. (You might knock down the dock if you work at it, though.)

The trick here is to get the stern of the boat into the wind and back away. Tie a long spring line to the bow cleat. Then run the spring line aft on the dock to somewhere near the stern (see part A of the following figure). Hang a couple of fenders off the bow quarter to protect it from scrapes as you pivot.

Now, when you put the outside engine into forward, the rudder dead ahead, it walks the stern away from the pier, pivoting on the spring (see part B of the following figure). The same thing works with a single outboard or sterndrive, but you might want to turn the wheel slightly toward the dock to give the stern an assist. (This works best if you're docked port-side to, because the clockwise rotation of the prop when going ahead will want to walk the stern to the right or starboard.)

Boat Bytes

A boat likes to keep spinning the way it's backing. If you're backing to starboard, spin the wheel to port before putting it into forward. This encourages bow and stern to keep doing what they're doing, and thus will spin the boat smartly.

When the stern is straight into the wind, cast off the bow spring line from the dock and back up the boat far enough to give *plenty* of working room to turn around. It's not a problem with twin engines, but with a single, you might be blown right back to the dock by the time you can spin unless you give yourself *many* boat lengths. Go out twice as far as you think you could possibly need, and then double that, until you get more salt in your hair.

When the Wind Is Blowing Parallel to the Dock

With the wind blowing parallel to the dock, all you have to do is cast off the upwind end of the boat first, give it a push, and the wind will quickly get either the bow or the stern pointed where you need to go. If the wind is off the bow, take in that line first, let the bow swing completely clear, and then go ahead slowly.

If there's another boat behind you, you'll have to put out an aft spring line (see part A of the following figure), running from a stern cleat forward to the dock, so that the boat doesn't slide back and bump into it as the wind pushes on the bow. Don't forget to position a fender between the dock and the boat.

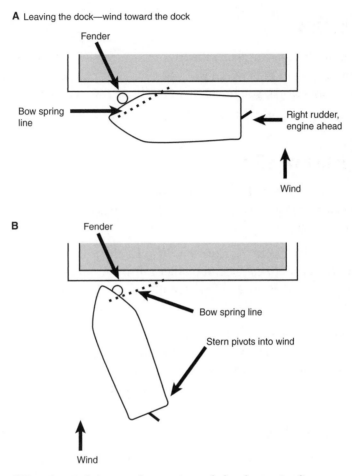

A Leaving the dock—wind toward the dock

Fender

Bow spring line

Right rudder, engine ahead

Wind

B

Fender

Bow spring line

Stern pivots into wind

Wind

When the wind pins your boat against a dock, a bow spring line can help get the stern out into the wind so that you can back away.

A

Leaving the dock—wind from the bow

Aft spring line

Wind

B

With the wind parallel to the dock and another boat close behind you, it's best to put out an aft spring line, then push off the bow and let the wind swing the front of the boat clear.

Docking Tactics

In boating, as in flying an airplane, the landing is everything. Whatever mistakes you make out on the water are between you and your crew and the seagulls, but when you come in to a busy marina, you'll feel that everybody is watching you.

The bad news is they will be, if you start banging into things.

The Best Plan Is to Have a Plan

Go over with the crew exactly what you want to do, and exactly what you want them to do, long before you get near the docks. Then things can proceed step by step as you instruct in a calm voice.

Before you begin, look over the situation. What is the wind doing? Is the tide high or low? Is there any current? Is there any other traffic? Are there any unusual problems, tight squeezes, or shallow areas? Consider all these things before you speak to the crew.

Every docking situation can be different, but in general it's best to work *into* the wind when possible—that gives you a natural brake if things don't line up just right. Going with a strong wind can make the job twice as difficult because the boat will move toward the dock—and other boats—even when you don't do anything.

Practice, Practice, Practice

It's best to learn the basics in a quiet backwater where forces of wind and tide are minimal. Go slowly at first as you study what happens when you apply a short burst of power in forward, and then reverse.

As you'll notice, a single-engined boat does not simply go straight ahead or straight back in this situation. The torque of the prop makes it walk sideways a little, the stern kicking slightly right (with right-hand or clockwise rotation, as most motors have) and the bow left when you go ahead. It's exactly the opposite when you put it in reverse.

You can use this tendency in your favor. If you need to ease the bow left, giving a quick burst of forward *without turning the wheel* will often be all that's needed. If you need to make the bow go right, a burst of reverse might accomplish it—again, without turning the wheel at all. (This is particularly true on large props with cupped blades, which tend to "paddlewheel" sideways more than other prop designs.)

However, if you want to back up straight with a single-engine rig, the paddlewheel effect can be a problem, particularly in reverse where the rudder doesn't help much. You might have to give lots of starboard rudder—or in outboards and sterndrives, turn the lower unit a bit to starboard—to make the boat back straight.

Nautical Notes

Thrusters are sort of like giant trolling motors for yachts and other large boats. Basically, a thruster includes a prop mounted inside a tube near the bow, driven by an electric motor inside the hull just above the prop. When you need them, thrusters provide a bit of added low-speed steering that makes it very simple to ease a boat into an otherwise tough slip. Steering is usually through a "joy stick" near the helm. Prices range from $1,500 to as much as $10,000, depending on size.

Backing Into a Slip

Twin-engine steering around the docks is usually accomplished with the wheel straight ahead—if you want to go ahead left, you put the starboard motor into gear for a few seconds, and right, the port motor. It's much more effective than using the wheel or rudder.

With one engine, it's more difficult—you have to turn the wheel and be quick with the gear shifting. Again, be aware that the prop can walk your stern sideways a little if you use short bursts in either forward or reverse.

When going into a slip, you should have one crewperson on the bow and one at the stern. If you only have one other person aboard, put him on the stern to start. As you back in, the crewperson should pick up one of the bow lines off the post (a boathook helps!) and walk forward.

For example, let's say you've got twin engines, and your helper grabs the port line first. You stop the boat with a short burst of forward as the bow comes even with the bow post, and the crew ties off that side, allowing some slack for maneuvering. Now you bump the port engine into gear for a second or two, and it will magically walk the bow over to the starboard post, where your crew can pick up that line and tie it fast. Then you apply a bit more reverse on both engines. The boat backs up, and you stop it within a foot or two of the docks with a short burst of forward. The aft crew person then jumps up on the dock and completes the securing process.

Making use of the thrust of two engines rather than one eases handling around the docks, often without turning the wheel at all.

(Frank Sargeant)

Parallel Parking at a Dock

Arriving at a parallel dock is usually less challenging, unless other boats are blocking the ends of the parking spot. If there are no complications, you simply motor toward the dock at a 30-degree angle at idle speed, then take the prop out of gear, turn the wheel away from the dock, and let the momentum start to carry the stern toward the pilings.

This is easiest with a single, clockwise-rotating engine if you go in port-side to. Straighten the wheel and give a burst of reverse and the boat stops, but also magically crawls sideways to barely touch the dock—man, you look cool!

You can do the same thing with twin engines, leaving the port engine in neutral and giving the starboard engine a shot of reverse. Because the starboard engine has more leverage to turn the stern to port in reverse (assuming the more usual "outward rotating" configuration in which the starboard prop is right-handed and the port prop is left-handed), you only need a second or two of power to do the job. Is this easy or what?

Of course, there are often complications. One more little test life puts in your way.

When the Wind Is Blowing Away from the Dock

If there's a strong wind or current pushing off the dock, you might have to ease the bow in and get a bow line on a cleat either with a helper ashore or by having a crewperson step down on the dock (see part A of the following figure). Then you would dock by going ahead slowly, the wheel turned away from the dock, as the bow line acts as a bow spring to walk the stern right to the dock (see part B of the following figure). This is also the tactic for getting in between two other boats against the docks.

Again, with a single engine, it's easier if you go port-side to. With twin engines, use the inside engine in forward to do the job. In either case, have a crewperson on the stern ready to get the line ashore as soon as you touch or you'll have to go through the procedure all over again.

Look Out! _____

With a big boat and a strong wind, docking this way can generate a lot of force—make sure none of your crew has a foot or arm between the boat and the dock!

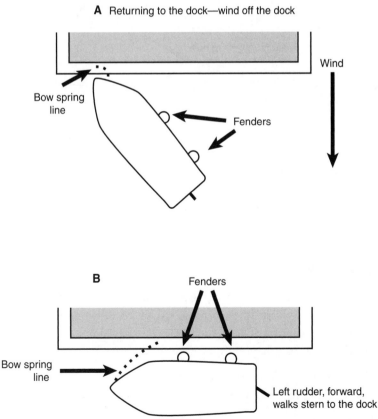

A Returning to the dock—wind off the dock

Wind

Bow spring line

Fenders

B

Fenders

Bow spring line

Left rudder, forward, walks stern to the dock

When the wind or current is off a parallel dock, a bow spring line is used to pivot the boat close to the pilings. The wheel is turned away from the dock and the engine put in forward idle.

When the Wind Is Blowing Toward the Dock

If the current or wind is toward the dock, it's easier—you simply pull up parallel to the spot where you want to land and put the engines in neutral. Let nature dock you, shifting in and out of gear briefly if you need to adjust by a foot or two. Get your dock fenders over the side in advance.

When the Wind Is Blowing Parallel to the Dock

Currents or winds parallel to the dock are usually less problematic. The only trick, if you come in bow-on to a current, is to get a bow line on the dock quickly (see part A of the following figure). The force of wind or current will then cozy you up to the planks (see part B of the following figure).

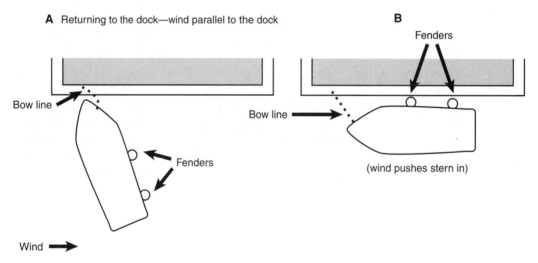

The wind does the work when blowing parallel to the docks if you simply drop a bow line on a cleat and slip the fenders over the gunnels.

Shoehorn Maneuvering

If there are boats ahead of and behind the spot you need to fit into, the best plan is to pull up parallel to the dock and toss your lines to somebody ashore. If there's no one there, nose the bow in and put a crewperson on the dock. With a small boat 25 feet and under, the crew can then manhandle you in, even in moderate winds or currents.

With larger boats, fitting into a spot like this requires using spring lines and judicious maneuvering—it's not something to try until you've seen a lot of water pass under the hull.

Slow Is Good

Things can go badly wrong when docking at anything other than dead slow. A few years ago I was standing on the dock at Southwest Pass, Louisiana, as a brand-new 50-footer was being brought briskly to its slip by a seasoned skipper. All went well until one of the hydraulic lines on the gear box let go just as the captain needed reverse, and lots of it, to stop the boat's momentum. The bow plowed about three feet through the railroad-tie dock. Damage to the boat was about five grand!

That sort of accident is rare, but it's not at all uncommon for an engine to die just when you're depending on it to brake your hull. Keep that in mind, be cautious, and go slowly. It's not a bad idea to slip the boat into reverse briefly while you're a good distance out, just to slow momentum and make sure the motor won't die when you need it most.

Nautical Notes

There might be a time when you have to turn around in an area that's too small for your boat to turn in while underway—for example, the space between main piers. Managing this with a twin-engine boat is easy—with the engines idling, put one in forward and one in reverse, steering dead ahead, and the boat rotates like it has eyes.

That is, it rotates if there's not a strong wind or tide ruining your act. You might have to apply more forward or more reverse on one engine to overcome these forces.

But how about with one motor? With an outboard or sterndrive, you do it much as you would with a car, spinning the wheel hard to port as you go forward a few feet, and then back to starboard as you reverse a few feet, until the turn is complete.

With single inboards, though, it's a different deal. The best procedure to rotate to the right is to put the wheel over hard right and then leave it there as you alternately shift the engine into forward and reverse.

The boat will slowly swing around, backing slightly left in reverse even though the rudder should make it back to the right. The reason is that the paddlewheel or torque effect of the prop in reverse is stronger than the steering effect of the rudder. It takes some time but it works—as long as a strong wind or tide doesn't interfere!

Picking Up a Mooring

Moorings are large permanent anchors secured well out from the docks in a harbor. They allow large boats to avoid the hassles of docking and also increase the usable overnight space in a harbor.

Picking up a mooring is an "easy" job: It's easy to miss it, easy to drop it, and easy to have a crewperson jerked overboard. So everyone has to pay attention for the few moments this "easy" job takes until the bow line is secured to the mooring.

The mooring is marked by a large buoy, which is attached to the heavy line or chain below. Also usually attached to the buoy is a smaller pick-up float with a ring in the top, making it easy to hook with a boat hook or gaff. To moor, you pick up the small float with a boat hook, and then attach the pendant to a bow cleat.

Some moorings don't have the smaller float, just the main float attached to the anchor chain. Use your anchor line to attach to the bottom of the main buoy if you're going to be at the mooring overnight and heavy weather is a possibility—otherwise, just use a mooring line. (Be careful about attaching your anchor line to the ring on top of the pendant buoy, though—some are not designed for heavy loads.)

One problem that might arise is that the skipper sometimes can't see the float as it comes "under" the bow, particularly in larger boats with lots of freeboard. So a crewperson stands up front and guides him in—hand signals are easier than shouting.

Provided the approach is accurate, the crewperson simply plucks up the mooring float, the boat is put into reverse to bring it to a halt, and then the pendant is brought aboard and cleated off. If you miss the float, just go around again—it's not going anywhere, and probably nobody is watching. Just don't ask the crewperson to lunge at it, because everybody *will* watch a guy falling overboard.

Be careful, though. If you see that the boat won't stop quickly enough to prevent the crewperson from being pulled overboard if he hangs on to the mooring line, have him cast it off and try again. This can go from funny to dangerous very quickly because you're traveling forward and the props are close to where the swimmer will fall.

Tidal Tie-Ups

Tides vary from a few inches in south Florida to more than 40 feet in Canada. If you tie your boat up close in an area that has a lot of drop between high and low tide, you might have it swinging in the air when the tide goes out.

No kidding, I've seen it happen with rowboats and skiffs. They often turn over when the water leaves, dumping out life jackets, paddles, and whatever else is left aboard.

Even worse, tying up too loosely might allow your boat to drift *under* the dock. When the tide comes back, the boat gets a hydraulic crush. The lifting force of water is amazing—it can crack the cowling of an outboard, smash a windshield, even crumple a cabin top.

Obviously, tying up properly is critical for coastal boaters. (I'll tell you more about how tides affect coastal boating in Chapter 16.)

Dock Lines

You need at least four dock lines twice the length of the boat if you live in an area with maximum tides, while in moderate tide zones like south Florida the four lines should be about the length of the boat. You don't use all this length very often, but you will need it sooner or later if you cruise a lot.

The best dock lines are woven nylon, $\frac{3}{8}$-inch or better. The larger the line, the stronger it is and the longer it lasts—and the easier it is on your hands. But line that's too big won't fit the cleats of a smaller boat, and it costs a lot more than smaller stuff.

Securing Your Boat

The best tie is a four-point suspension—two lines on the bow, two on the stern. The longer the line run, the less it restricts the rise and fall of the boat, which is why the lines are run to opposite cleats on the transom—that is, the line from the port side of the dock goes to the starboard cleat, and vice versa.

With a long run, it's possible to tighten down the lines securely, holding the boat in the slip so it doesn't touch the pilings at any point, yet still has enough vertical movement to ride the tides.

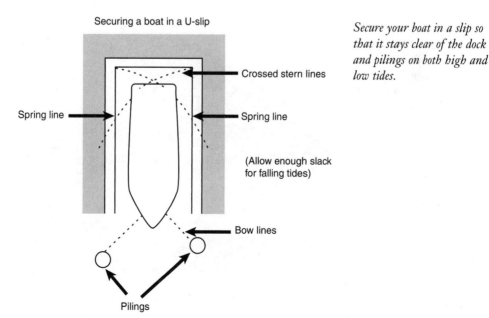

Securing a boat in a U-slip

Crossed stern lines

Spring line

Spring line

(Allow enough slack for falling tides)

Bow lines

Pilings

Secure your boat in a slip so that it stays clear of the dock and pilings on both high and low tides.

A single aft spring line is often added in U-slips to keep the transom from getting under the dock. For long-term storage, most add a pair of spring lines amidships, running fore or aft, to hold the position longitudinally.

Chafing Gear for Your Lines

If the boat is to be left in the slip long-term (more than a week), and if it's more than 20 feet long, it's a good idea to add chafing gear to the lines anywhere they pass through a metal chock or scrape across a dock edge.

These are simply split lengths of old garden hose, or they can be the ubiquitous duct tape—anything to prevent the friction from weakening the line. (The best tape for this is a thick vinyl that won't give out when exposed to rain and salt.)

Fenders Are Meant to Be Squashed

Fenders in boats are not quite the same thing as fenders in cars. If your teenager squashes the fender of your BMW, you'll be exceedingly unhappy. If he squashes the fenders of the boat, you'll note that he's learning to be a competent skipper.

Boat fenders are meant to be squashed, squeezed, and crushed. They're made of tough but pliable vinyl or other materials that absorb shock, and they're designed to fit between a boat and a dock, pier, or other solid structure, or sometimes between two boats.

Heavy vinyl fenders inflated with air act as cushions or bumpers to keep the gunnels and sides of your boat from being damaged by docks and other boats.

(Polyform Fenders)

Fenders can be anything from a piece of Styrofoam to a boat cushion, but the best fenders are the commercial models, usually inflatable, that are made of thick vinyl. Cylindrical fenders are most common, although spheres are also sometimes used. They range in size from a foot to three feet long, with diameters from six inches to a foot or more.

The bigger your boat, the bigger the fenders you need, because a 20-ton yacht can generate enormous crushing force when rocked by a wave. And a boat docked in an open area subject to wave action will require bigger fenders than one docked in a well-protected harbor.

The fenders have to be fitted to the boat, and hung over the side where contact with the fixed object is most likely. This might not be where there's a convenient cleat or rail stanchion—if not, run a stout line between two cleats and hang the fender from that.

The usual arrangement is to put one fender in the center of the boat and one on each end, so that however the boat works back and forth on the dock lines, it will be protected.

A dock board is sometimes hung on the docks outside of the fenders if the dock is particularly rough or covered with barnacles. This prevents the sharp edges from puncturing the fenders.

Fenders take a lot of abuse, and when used properly, will show some well-earned scratches. Some boat owners buy fender covers to dress up the boat!

The Least You Need to Know

- Always consider wind and current when leaving or approaching a dock.
- Inform your crew of your docking plan.
- When learning how to maneuver in and out of a slip, remember that practice makes perfect.
- Consider tides when tying up your boat for the night.
- Fenders are your boat's best friend.

Chapter 7

People Management and Safety Aboard

In This Chapter

- ◆ Captaining a boat with authority
- ◆ Helping your passengers help themselves
- ◆ Coping with seasickness
- ◆ Protecting your crew from the elements
- ◆ Keeping bugs at bay

In the pages that follow, we'll review some of the ways that the skipper can help all aboard stay safe, happy, and healthy. Your boat is much like your home, both in that you want your guests to enjoy themselves, and that you want them to follow some basic rules so that everyone else can stay happy as well.

As any business leader these days knows, you don't just manage a business, you manage people. It's like that aboard nearly every boat, too—except maybe a one-person kayak (and even there you might have to manage yourself at times, especially when the boat is upside-down and the water is fast and icy and stark terror seems the normal response rather than thinking about the mechanics of the Eskimo roll).

Nobody likes rules in their recreation, but unfortunately there are a few in just about every sport—and boating is no exception. The captain's job is to make them clear to the passengers and crew. That way everybody remains comfortable, happy, and safe while aboard.

Taking Care of Business: The Captain Is the Boss

A boat can't be run by committee. Although you can decide where you're going to cruise or what you're going to fish for by democratic vote, actual operation of the boat has to be under the control of one individual. The boss is the man or woman at the wheel—that's the individual who has to know what he or she is doing and be able to make decisions quickly. (On larger sailboats, the captain may not actually do the steering—she or he will leave that to a competent helmsperson while concentrating on navigation and crew management.)

You don't want to come across as Captain Bligh, of course, or you'll soon have all your crew jumping ship. But you can gently assert this authority, and also give new crewmembers a sense of security, if you give a brief explanation of procedures afloat before you leave the dock.

This talk should cover the following:

◆ Tell everyone where the life jackets are stowed and how they should be put on. Don't imply that their emergency use is imminent or you might have some folks stepping back ashore right there. But responsible skippering requires that everyone knows where the personal flotation devices (PFDs) are located and how to use them. Nonswimmers and kids should put them on before the boat leaves the dock, and in small, low-freeboard boats, in high-performance rigs, or in dicey conditions, all aboard should wear their PFDs. If there are small children onboard, it is critical that not only the children, but also the parents of the children wear life-jackets. This not only makes it easier to convince the children to wear them without complaining, but it also anticipates that if a child goes in, the parent is likely to follow only a fraction of a second later. The extra buoyancy will be very helpful for the rescue.

Look Out!

On large cruisers, the broad bow looks inviting, but it's a dangerous spot when the boat is underway. Children in particular should be told that they should *never* ride on the bow rail with their feet draped over the bow. A fall from this spot ensures a tragedy, and yet you see people riding this way every day.

- If the boat is less than 20 feet long, remind everyone that they must be sitting down when the boat is underway. On larger sailboats, trawlers, cruisers, pontoons, and deck-type boats that run at moderate speeds, some moving around is okay by those agile enough to deal with the ups and downs of life afloat.

- Explain the basic operation of VHF radio or your cell phone, particularly if you're the only "salt" aboard. If something happens to you, somebody else will need to know how to call for help. (For details on marine communications gear, see Chapter 14.)

- Explain your route of travel for the same reason. If you're in an area where there's a lot of shallow water, or if you'll be out during low tide, explain where the safe routes are.

- Select a second-in-command and explain basic boat operation to him or her. Again, if you're disabled, this person will have to keep the boat under control until the boat docks or help arrives.

- Tell everyone where the head or marine toilet is and explain how to use it.

- Remind all that there will be no smoking during refueling. None, period.

Make this all light and informational—the object is to make your crew aware without making them nervous.

A Few Words About Alcohol Afloat

Although waiting for the sun to drop below the yardarm and then enjoying a cup of "grog" is a longtime seagoing tradition, alcohol use afloat brings with it all the cautions of use ashore, and some additional concerns as well.

As with driving a vehicle, the skipper or anyone else who will be charged with a critical job should not drink any alcoholic beverages at all until the boat is securely tied up for the night. The standards for driving under the influence are the same on a boat as they are ashore in most states, and so are the penalties. In fact, in some states, a DWI on the water gets added to your driver's license ashore! As few as two beers can put a small person over the legal limit. Don't risk legal problems—and more importantly the safety of your crew and your boat—by drinking while you're at the helm.

Be aware that drinking afloat can have a more immediate and obvious affect than drinking ashore, too. Dehydration and overheating from long hours in the sun can cause alcohol to pack a lot more wallop than it does when you're sitting in an air-conditioned lounge. And those who have too much to drink can be at least as obnoxious afloat as they are back on land; keep an eye on drinkers and don't be afraid to limit their intake if you feel it's necessary for their own safety or that of others.

Protection from the Sun

I don't like to read health warnings any more than anyone else, but for those new to life afloat, the relationship with the sun is a whole new ball game. That friendly Mr. Sun that gives your cheeks a rosy glow when exposed during a walk in a park will fry your skin into purple blisters if it's not protected during several hours of open-water boating.

The fact that there's no shade and no greenery to soak up the rays at sea and that the water is reflective doubles or triples the impact of sun on human skin, and failure to protect yourself and your crew guarantees discomfort—and maybe lasting damage that can lead to the first stages of skin cancer. It's not an option to protect yourself; it's *mandatory*. Ask any dermatologist who deals with melanoma and you'll get the same firm advice: Avoid getting a sunburn.

Sunscreen: Don't Leave Home Without It

Sunscreen with UVA and UVB protectors is the ticket. Buy the generic drugstore versions, which are half as costly but just as effective as the name brands, and buy them by the gallon. SPF-15 is reportedly the most cost-effective buy. Higher SPF numbers cost more, but doctors say they offer no added skin protection.

Boat Bytes

White is the best color for any clothing worn in hot weather—it can make a huge difference in how much heat you feel. Dark, dull-finished material soaks up heat and sends it through to your skin. Keep cool with white.

Don't even consider leaving the docks without everyone aboard swabbing down thoroughly. Insist on it—many people think they'll go back to shore with a great tan if they don't use sunscreen, when in fact they'll go back with second-degree burns.

Wear a Hat

If your hair is at all thin, a hat is a must—skin cancers on top of the head are very common, as are those on the tops of the ears.

Even if your hair isn't thin, a hat can greatly reduce the heat you'll feel, and a broad brim reduces glare, protecting your nose and face and also enabling you to see better.

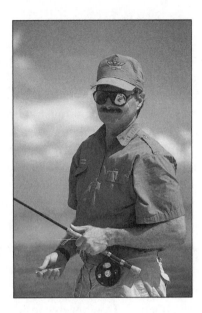

Sun protection includes a shirt with a collar and sleeves, a long-billed hat, and polarized sunglasses. And don't forget to cover all exposed skin with an SPF-15 sunscreen!

(Darla Sargeant)

Baseball caps, a favorite of anglers, don't protect the ears at all. Hats that have a full brim do much better, although it's hard to keep them on. The goofy-looking Florida flats guide hats, with brims fore and aft, are very useful and stay on well. They also protect the back of the neck—great hats, even though they do make you look a bit like Sherlock Holmes.

Note, however, that large-brimmed hats and sailboats don't always mix—they can obstruct the view of the sails or masthead wind indicator. That is why most traditional sailing hats have small brims, or brims that can be turned up.

Boat Bytes

A "cap-keeper" is a big help in keeping your cap on aboard boats that run more than 20 mph. It can be as simple as a cord around your chin. One useful model has alligator clips at each end of a cord; clip one to your cap and the other to the back of your shirt collar. Otherwise, be prepared to donate a hat to the "sea-gods" every once in a while.

Your Feet Need Protection, Too

Don't forget to protect the tops of your feet if you don't wear socks—the area between your ankle and your toenails is exposed to the direct rays at a near-vertical angle and will burn much quicker than your legs. Boaters often go barefoot or sockless in hot weather, so this area is highly vulnerable.

Wear Sunglasses

You and your crew *must* have sunglasses to go boating, and they should be polarized. Polarized glasses have a film built into them that acts like Venetian blinds, letting in light horizontally but not vertically. This gets rid of much of the blinding glare that's common when sun strikes water, making it much more comfortable afloat. Just as important, the polarizing effect allows the skipper to see through the surface of the water to any hazards that might be below. Anglers love polarized sunglasses because they allow easy sighting of fish and bait several feet below the surface. But check your navigational instruments or engine gauges that have LCD displays. Some displays become invisible through polarized glasses, especially if you turn your head sideways to read them.

The best boating glasses have side panels to keep out glare. They should have ear-pieces that fit snugly and stay put even when you tip your head forward.

However, even with good earpieces, sunglasses can be blown off your face by the wind blasts of high-speed boating. Don't even consider taking your $100 shades aboard until you equip them with a strap of some sort.

Coping with Seasickness

Seasickness is no joke if you're the one who's suffering from it. Although some old salts don't like to admit it, even the most seasoned captain can be touched by Big Ralph at times.

Fortunately, there are ways to ease the discomfort. Here's some advice you can give new crew members:

◆ Eat and drink moderately the night before a voyage and try to get your usual amount of sleep. Don't start at a disadvantage. If you wake up with a cold-sweats hangover, you don't have a chance.

◆ Eat a light breakfast—cereal and fruit, nothing greasy.

◆ Make use of preventatives early. Pills, acupressure wrist bands, or ear stick-on patches work for some people, but it takes several hours for these things to take full effect. If you wait until you start to feel queasy to use them, it's too late. It's not a bad idea to start the medications the night before, other remedies a couple of hours before you leave the dock. If at all possible, avoid experimenting with a new drug when you are already out on the water. It is much safer to do a trial run with the medication on land, well before the boat trip.

Scopolamine is among the more effective medications at present; it's applied via a skin patch that sticks behind the ear, and the medication lasts up to 72 hours. Many familiar with the product suggest putting on the patch the night before to get the best results. Like Bonine and most other pills, Scop—also sold by the brand-name Transderm—can make you drowsy, so keep that in mind if you're going to be driving. It's a prescription medication with some other possible side effects and should not be worn by pregnant or nursing women or young children. But it works well for thousands of users. Other prescription drugs that can help include Marzine, Meclizine, and Cyclizine, all used in antihistamines and with the some similar side effects; you might have to try several types before you find one that works best for you.

Homeopathic remedies can also work for some, though it's arguable whether the result is mostly psychological or physical. Ginger, either in tablets or chewable form, sometimes with additions of cayenne pepper, peppermint, and other herbs, seems to help many people. Some even report that ginger beer soda helps—it doesn't hurt to try all these remedies if your seasickness problems are persistent.

◆ A new electronic device called the ReliefBand has been highly successful for many people. The watch-like unit applies a gentle electric shock to the wrist at repeated intervals, and somehow or other seems to stop cold the cycle of seasickness for most.

This device, known as a ReliefBand, looks like a watch, but administers a tiny electrical current that pulses to nerves in the wrist. Many users report reduction or elimination of seasickness as a result.

(Martin Flory Group)

◆ Stay out of the cabin. Don't go below—stay on deck. There's something about the effect of swinging curtains and sliding cups (and sometimes the smell of diesel fuel) that makes the stomach unhappy. (Actually, it makes the inner ear unhappy, but you feel it in your stomach.)

- Stay well aft and on the lowest deck, off the bridge. Boats pitch worst at the bow, and wave action is accentuated when you get above the main deck.

- Avoid sitting next to the transom if there's a blow-back of diesel fumes. However, sitting near the stern is usually best because the boat rocks least there.

- Keep your eyes on the horizon. It looks still compared to those waves that keep rolling ... rolling ... rolling ....

- Take the helm, if at all possible. The person steering always seems to be the least likely to get seasick.

- Avoid sitting, especially in the cabin. Horizontal position with eyes closed is somewhat protective against motion sickness—although usually not as effective as taking the helm.

- Try drinking carbonated soda and eating dry crackers. Avoid smelly, oily foods.

- Keep in mind that no matter how bad it might be, it will end the instant you set foot on solid land again. (Shooting a skipper who refuses to take you in is not justifiable homicide, however.)

- Remember, caution is the better part of valor. When conditions are just too rough, those prone to seasickness should consider staying home.

The Right Footwear

Nobody requires regulation Topsiders aboard anymore, but it is definitely foolish to go boating in your Florsheim Oxfords. Advise anyone who will be joining you, in advance, that footwear is important. Anything without a rubberized sole is a definite liability aboard because it will sooner or later cause the wearer to fall on his keister. And yes, some nonboating shoes with dark soles do leave little black marks on white decks. Another problem with some nonboating athletic shoe designs is that the tread can pick up clumps of dirt or small bits of gravel and do a lot of damage to a boat's deck. Good boat shoes are designed to minimize this possibility.

Boat shoes should have soft vinyl or rubber soles so that they'll grip the deck. The most common "boat shoes" seen these days are jogging shoes, although the old salts for the most part wear the standard slit-soled slip-ons made by Topsider, Bass, Dexter, and

Nautical Notes
The herringbone pattern in the cut sole of the original Topsider design was copied from a dog's paw.

others. Some boat shoes now look like jogging shoes on the uppers and are just as comfortable, but have the unique "sticky" soles that keep you safe aboard. Prices range from $55 to $130.

These shoes have exceptionally soft rubber in the soles, and that, along with the razor-cut slits in the flat bottoms, make them sticky as flies' feet. (Personally, I think it's possible flies actually wear tiny little Topsiders so they can walk up walls.)

The leather laces that come on most boat shoes are constantly coming untied, and the knots in them look like the knots you tied in your laces when you were in second grade. Here's a tip: After your shoes are broken in so that they slip on easily with the tie secured, get rid of the shoestring tie and replace it with a neat, tight square knot. Then cut off the ends about one-half inch from the knot. This makes the shoe look a lot better, and they'll never again come untied.

It's a good idea to avoid rubber thongs or "flip-flops." On a rolling deck—they can slip off and cause you to lose your footing. And if you have to wade ashore in sticky bottom, the thongs will disappear into the muck instantly.

Boat Bytes

There's a reason traditional boating shoes are slip-ons: because they slip off just as easily when you fall overboard. Ever try to swim with a pair of Nikes on your feet?

Dressing for Cold-Weather Boating

The best way to experience cold-weather boating is via video as you sit in front of your fireplace sipping hot Earl Grey tea. A 20-knot north wind with temperatures in the 30s takes most of the pleasure out of pleasure boating.

However, for those who like to extend the season a bit, dressing appropriately can make it downright comfortable, even on those chilly November dawns. Warn your crew before they leave home if you suspect it might be a bit nippy on the water. If it's chilly ashore, it will be twice as chilly when you get on the water and are exposed to wind and humidity. And, even though that brisk air might feel fine in shorts and a sweatshirt when you go for your morning jog, it won't feel so good as you sit still in the boat for a few hours.

Boat Bytes

Just as wearing light colors is best when it's hot, wearing dark colors is best when it's cold. If there's any sun, dull, dark gray, dark green, or black material will soak up lots more heat. You'll be amazed at the difference it can make on a chilly but bright day.

As with so much in life, underwear is the answer. (The secret of happiness, my father used to say, is to buy your BVDs two sizes too large.) Long underwear, in this case. Polypropylene will wick away the moisture while keeping you warm. Add a pair of warm pants and a sweater; polyester fleece like that made by Polartec and other companies is the modern replacement for wool, much lighter, less bulky, quick to dry, and very warm. If it's really cold, add several layers of garments; the air space between them adds greatly to their insulation, and you can take them off a layer at a time as the day warms up.

Over the top of your soft inner clothes you need a windbreaker of some sort. A good rain suit (see the following section, "Singing in the Rain with Good Rain Gear") is the most common choice.

Gore-Tex gloves are also a must—waterproof, but they let sweat escape so your hands don't get clammy. The type with Thermax or other insulation is best for powerboat operation.

If you're fishing or running a sailboat, where you have to use your fingers frequently, lighter gloves are essential. Neoprene diving gloves are waterproof and give you a good grip, plus fairly good warmth. Standard sailing gloves, which expose your fingertips but protect your fingerpads and palms with canvas and leather, are good in moderate weather but not warm enough when it's frosty. Wool gloves don't hold out water, but they do remain warm when wet—they make a good extra pair to have in your pocket.

Singing in the Rain with Good Rain Gear

Rain might not make you sing, but it won't make you or your crew that unhappy if you have enough good rain gear aboard. Rain gear varies hugely in quality and price, from the $4.99 drugstore poncho that's about as durable as a garbage bag to some serious stuff suited for ocean crossings that costs over $400 for coat, pants, and hood.

Boat Bytes _____

Opt for a bright-colored rain suit: In the unlikely event that you or any crewperson ever falls overboard, yellow or bright orange is a lot easier to see in the water than green or blue.

The cheap stuff is worth what you pay for it, which is nothing.

The best rain gear is nylon, coated with neoprene rubber or PVC waterproofer. These suits might last for a decade or more if cared for properly, and they absolutely don't leak. Gore-Tex is good stuff, although quite expensive. It offers the no-sweat advantage—it lets your sweat evaporate through the fabric but keeps out rain.

I personally like bib-style pants because they prevent water from getting under the coat and down your waistband. Whatever style of rain gear you buy, be sure to get it large enough to accommodate the coats you will most often wear under it. Good gear also has heavy-duty, corrosion-proof zippers covered by wide "storm flaps" that keep wind-driven spray from penetrating.

You'll also want a hood, probably with a visor to keep rain from running down into your eyes. The best hoods have a broad, stiff brim that will act like a miniature umbrella to keep rain off your face—a big plus when it's really coming down. The brim can be rolled up for better visibility when you want it more for wind protection than to stop rain. (The hood is a major factor in keeping you warm, because a lot of lost body heat exits through the head.)

Ocean-going rain gear is not available at your local discount store—check with marine specialists like West Marine or BOAT U.S. for good prices on quality stuff.

Keep your rain gear washed clean, particularly if you boat on saltwater; it will feel a lot better next time you put it on if it's not clammy with salt-drawn dampness or crusts of dried salt. Stow it out of direct sun and excessive heat; don't leave it in the back of your SUV between trips or it won't last long.

Don't forget rain gear for your feet, particularly if you do your boating on cold water. Sperry and others make waterproof boots with cushioned insoles and razor-cut soles that are both dry and sticky when it comes to walking on a wet deck. And they kick off easily should you ever take an unscheduled trip overboard. Prices range from $35 to $60.

What's Bugging You?

Insects love the water as much as boaters do, and there are some unpleasant specimens out there in considerable numbers. If you run into lots of bugs and your crew is unprepared, they'll want to go home, pronto.

Mosquitoes are the most common problem and the easiest to deal with. They hate DEET, the basic ingredient of most commercial insect repellants, and if you use a spray containing plenty of it, they will leave you alone. Other problem bugs are no-see-ums and black flies. Avon's Skin So Soft Bug

 Look Out!

The so-called electronic insect repellers that fit in your pocket do not work, period. This is not just my opinion—the Entomology Department at the University of Florida has conducted tests proving that mosquitoes pay no attention to the noise these things generate. Save your money for DEET.

Guard or Johnson's Skintastic do a good job of keeping no-see-ums at bay. Heavy doses of DEET repellent and covering all exposed areas are the cure for black flies.

In general, if you can stay away from shorelines, you'll attract fewer bugs. Seek areas where the wind blows regularly—a narrow creek where the breeze can't stir will be alive with insects on any summer evening, while an airy beach just a mile away might be completely bug-free on the same evening.

There's also something to the idea of keeping the bugs upwind when you can—they find you by scent, sort of like little winged bloodhounds. So, if you have a choice, anchor on the downwind side of a heavily vegetated island. You'll get less wave action, and hopefully fewer bugs.

Of course, if breezes are light, you might need to go well offshore on the upwind side to stop and watch the sunset without lots of insect company.

The Least You Need to Know

- ◆ Let your crew know the basics of seamanship before you leave the dock.
- ◆ Sunburn and seasickness can ruin any day afloat—take proper precautions.
- ◆ Equip yourself and your crew for inclement weather.
- ◆ Insect protection is a must in warm weather.

8

Anchors Aweigh! Making Your Boat Stay Put

In This Chapter

- ◆ Types of anchors and what they do
- ◆ Offshore anchoring
- ◆ Anchoring at the beach
- ◆ How to avoid losing your anchor
- ◆ How to get your anchor back after you've lost it

Knowing how to handle your boat when underway is only part of successful skippering. You'll also want to know how to make the boat stay in one spot while you enjoy a sunset, try to winch up a snapper dinner, or maybe leave the boat on its own while you take the dinghy to a secluded beach.

The anchor is the key to making your boat stay put without being fastened to anything—except to Mother Earth. In this chapter, we'll look at what makes a good anchor, the gear or "tackle" that attaches the anchor to the boat, and the secrets of making the anchor securely grab the bottom in all sorts of depths and wave conditions.

Anchors by Design

Dead weight is one way of securing a boat—a rock on a vine was probably the first anchor. But dead weight has a major drawback: It's very hard to handle.

Heavy anchors go down easy but come up hard. Gross weight is not what makes an anchor function. The engine block from a '57 Buick would definitely hold your boat in place, but it would be hell to raise back up to the deck.

The trick in anchor design is to get the anchor to grab hold of the bottom and use earth itself as your security. Thus, "patent" anchors were devised to burrow their way into the bottom and use the weight of wet mud and sand to do the job in place of lots of specific gravity.

Anchoring in Style

Many styles or designs of anchors work well without excessive weight. The most common include the following:

- Danforth or fluke-style anchor
- Plow or CQR anchor
- Navy anchor
- Mushroom anchor
- Grapnel or grappling anchor

We'll take a closer look at each of these in the following sections.

Fluke (Danforth) Anchors

The fluke anchor (or Danforth anchor, as it's more commonly known) is the most widely used recreational boating anchor in the world. It's made of two flat steel or aluminum flukes on a pivoting shaft. The pointed flukes dig into the bottom when pressure is put on the shaft at an angle lower than about 60 degrees. When the angle of pull approaches 90 degrees vertically, the anchor turns over and comes out of the bottom, making it easy to raise.

Fluke anchors also stow flat, making it easy to fit them into a compartment until needed.

There are a wide variety of strength levels in fluke anchors, though, and the strongest cost a whole lot more than the weakest. For example, a standard galvanized-steel Danforth-design fluke anchor in the five-pound class lists for about $25. A high-tensile version of the same anchor from the same company lists for about $65, almost three times more!

The difference? It's not the label. The high-tensile model is rated for 500 pounds of holding power, the standard model just 300 pounds. The high-tensile version is a specially-treated steel that won't bend under pressure. If your boat is a 15-foot aluminum skiff, the less expensive version is fine, but if it's a 17-foot fiberglass inboard, the stronger anchor is the better choice.

Other versions of the fluke-style anchor are available in high-strength aluminum—which has the advantage of light weight but very good holding power—and stainless steel, which is a good-looking material, for those who stow their anchors in chocks on deck.

A recent variation of the fluke-style anchor is the C-Claw, which combines bulky bronze flukes with the typical Danforth type shank. The unique design of this anchor causes it to dig in fast, even without a chain, which has made it a favorite for anglers fishing shallow flats where the noise of lowering a chain can spook fish. It's about $90.

The fluke or Danforth anchor is relatively light in weight, has excellent holding power, and takes up little storage space.

Plow Anchors

Plow anchors, also called CQR anchors, look exactly like a plow. For those of you who haven't been on a John Deere lately, that means they have a sharp, curved spade fluke or blade attached to a long shaft that runs forward rather than up. When pressure is put on the shaft, the plow burrows its way down through weeds, mud, or whatever until it finds solid holding.

Plow anchors have excellent holding power, plowing deeper under heavy strain. They're a favorite yacht anchor.

Plow anchors are very strong and hold in extreme weather, but unless your boat has a bow pulpit where the anchor can hang when not in use, they are bulky and hard to store. They're also fairly heavy—most models start at 15 pounds. They're best for boats 25 feet and up. Prices range from $150 for a 14-pounder to over $700 for a 60-pounder.

Navy Anchors

Navy-style anchors look like anchors have traditionally looked (picture the one tattooed on Popeye's arm). They're the anchors that hang on the bow of older sea-going ships, and also, much smaller and in gold, on the necks of tanned, middle-aged guys throughout south Florida.

The navy anchor is strong and dependable, although it's heavier at a given holding power than a Danforth.

Navy anchors rely on both their weight and their hooked flukes to hold the bottom, and tend to start at about the weight of a Jeep and go up a whole lot from there. They're not often used on recreational boats because they're so heavy, but some small ones are used as storm anchors on larger yachts. In modern usage, the navy anchor is stockless, or without a shank, as seen on large ships. One of the most successful versions of the traditional style anchor is based on a design by Herreshoff, so traditional anchors are often called Herreshoff anchors in order to avoid confusion with the modern navy type.

Mushroom Anchors

A mushroom anchor looks like an upside-down mushroom, hence the name. It depends mostly on weight for holding power, although the cup does dig into the bottom to help a bit. These anchors are suitable only for boats under 15 feet long in protected water. They're also good for inflatable boats because they have no sharp edges like fluke anchors.

The mushroom is low in price and adequate for small boats anchored out of strong winds and waves.

Mushrooms are inexpensive, under $20 for an 8-pounder. PVC-coated models are available, with the coating protecting against rust.

Grapnel Anchors

Grapnels are useful when the bottom is too rocky for conventional anchors to grab. The prongs or hooks sink into a crevasse and hold on. They don't work at all in mud or sand, but for hard bottom they're great.

The grapnel is a handy extra anchor to put on shore during a lunch stop. It can also help you retrieve the fishing rod Junior dropped overboard, because it's light enough for throwing. Grapnel anchors cost $25 and up.

Look Out!

With grapnels or any other anchor, always avoid anchoring in areas with live coral bottom. Anchoring in these areas can cause damage that will take Mother Nature hundreds of years to repair; instead, drop the hook on sand to the side of the living bottom, then snorkel in for a look.

The grapnel or grappling anchor is capable of holding on to rocks where standard anchors drag. It's also useful for retrieving objects lost overboard.

Stronger Is Better

Why is it better to have a stronger anchor when your boat isn't going to pull all that hard on the line? There are two reasons:

- ◆ If you ever get caught in a really severe storm, the surges of your boat might well exceed the rated holding power of the weaker anchor as the boat rises and falls on tall waves. The forces can actually bend the flukes, leaving your rig at the mercy of the weather.

- ◆ If the anchor gets stuck on a rock and you try to use the motor to pull it free, the cheaper model will quickly turn into a twisted piece of junk that can never again be used as an anchor, while the high-tensile model will bring whatever it's latched onto up to the surface with it.

The following table is an approximate guide to the holding power needed for the working anchor, the standard everyday anchor suggested for various boats, according to the American Boat and Yacht Council. (The holding power of an anchor is a measure, in pounds, of the amount of pull it can sustain without breaking free in good bottom.) I've added the approximate weight of a standard fluke anchor providing the suggested holding power.

Boat Length	Working Load	Approximate Weight (in Pounds)
15 feet	250	5
20 feet	360	5
25 feet	490	9
30 feet	700	14
35 feet	900	14
40 feet	1,300	16
50 feet	1,600	23

A few high-tech anchors on the market advertise lower weights with higher holding power, such as the high-tensile aluminum alloy Fortress anchors. In tests conducted by BOAT U.S., these anchors proved their claims—a 6-pounder, although rated for 900 pounds, survived a 2,000-pound test load. Note the weight is less than half that of a conventional fluke anchor of similar holding power—nice when you're the designated anchor-puller. These are expensive anchors, as you might expect, with the 6-pounder going for around $90, but they're lifetime products.

Anchors That Float: Sea Anchors

Sea anchors, also called drogues, aren't really anchors in the conventional sense, in that they don't actually sink to the bottom to hold the boat in one spot. Instead, they're designed to slow the drift of a boat and maintain a heading without power.

Sea anchors are made of heavy nylon and fold up to the size of a loaf of bread when not in use. When put in the water, they open like a watery parachute, creating a huge amount of drag. The cost is $30 to $60 for lightweight models, $200 or more for "storm" models.

Why would you want one of these? They're handy for anglers who want to slow down their boat for live-bait trolling. The sea anchor can cut the drifting speed of a boat in half. And, should you ever be caught offshore in bad weather with a sick motor, the sea anchor trailed from your bow can keep the boat pointed into the oncoming seas. It can be a lifesaver.

Sea anchors are nylon or canvas bags that create drag when trailed from bow or stern. They're used to slow a drift rather than to hold the boat in one place.

In extreme conditions, the sea anchor is sometimes trailed from a bridle on the stern as a low-powered boat runs through an inlet. A bridle is a harness made from heavy rope, draped from each side of the transom lifting eyes (stout rings through-bolted to the transom) to form a secure, centered attachment for a sea anchor or for a line used to tow other boats. The idea is to keep the stern straight, preventing waves from pushing it into the trough and rolling the boat.

Anchor Tackle

Ground tackle is your anchoring stuff, the rope (called "rode" or "line" by old salts) and all the other gear that help you hold bottom. Anchors work a lot better if equipped with 3 to 6 feet of heavy galvanized chain between shank and rope. The chain lies along bottom, keeping the angle of pull on the shank low and helping the anchor to dig in.

A *shackle* is a C-shaped fastener with a clevis bolt used to secure the eye of the anchor to the anchor rode, usually through a *thimble*—a rounded, hard plastic or galvanized steel insert spliced into an anchor rode to prevent abrasion against the shackle.

The chain, because it produces a large amount of sag in the anchor line, also acts as a shock absorber as the boat rocks in the waves, keeping pressure off the anchor itself. And if there are sharp rocks or junk on the bottom, the chain helps prevent your anchor line from being cut.

BOAT U.S. suggests the guidelines shown in the following table for chain used on anchors.

A thimble is used to prevent chafing where the anchor chain attaches to the anchor rode or rope.

Boat Length	Chain Size	Chain Length
10–15 feet	$3/16$ inch	3 feet
16–32 feet	$1/4$ inch	6 feet
33–44 feet	$5/16$ inch	6 feet
45–60 feet	$3/8$ inch	6 feet

Galvanized chain does not rust—much. It does rust a little, leaving unsightly stains wherever it lies. If you're fastidious about this, choose vinyl-coated anchor chain.

You can also buy stainless-steel chain, which shows almost no rust. It's not quite as strong as galvanized at a given size, so you might want to consider going up a bit on the weight, and it's very expensive; but this is an item you'll never have to replace, so it's well worth the investment.

If you buy your chain at a marine store (and pay two to three times the price at the home store) you will get much better chain—it's likely to be two to three times stronger. (A table of working and proof loads is available at http://1st-chainsupply.com/technical/NACM%20Specs.pdf.)

Galvanized shackles hook the chain to the anchor at one end and the chain to the anchor line at the other. A thimble spliced into the rope prevents abrasion from the shackle. The shackle is secured with a little toggle bolt.

Shackles are used to attach anchor to chain and chain to anchor line. They allow you to remove the line for storage.

Put some waterproof grease on the toggle bolt before you tighten it, or you won't ever be removing it again. And use a keeper wire on the bolt, in case it comes loose on its own—a piece of stainless-steel wire is the Bristol fashion, but a couple of plastic tie-wraps work fine, too. (Bristol fashion means neat, orderly, and shipshape. The name comes from an English seafaring town.)

Deep Stuff: Anchoring Offshore

The deeper the water, the more difficult it is to make an anchor stay put, and anchoring offshore in deep, rough water to fish or dive can be a test of seaperson-ship. But it's usually not that difficult if you have the right ground tackle and some know-how.

Proceed uptide or upwind from the spot where you want the boat to hang, a distance at least 3 times the water depth in calm, nontidal water, 6 times if wind or tide is strong, and 8 to 12 times if staying overnight or in stormy weather.

This will give your anchor line adequate scope or length in comparison to the water depth to form a moderate angle of pull and keep the anchor buried in the bottom. A minimum scope of 3:1 (with "3" being anchor line length and "1" being water depth) is required to hold in anything other than dead calm.

For example, if you're anchoring in 10 feet, you go uptide of where you want the boat to be at least 30 feet, and then you're going to let out enough line to make that 3:1 ratio.

How do you know when you've let out 20 feet of line, or 50, or 100? The best way is to mark your anchor line. Some put little tags in the weave of the rope, but the easiest way is to mark your line with a waterproof marker. I start at 20 feet with one mark and add more marks for every added 20 feet—thus there are 2 marks at 40 feet, 3 at 60, and so on. You'll have to re-mark your lines about once a year—sun and salt cause the marks to fade, but it's worth doing, particularly as you're learning to estimate scope.

Nautical Notes

The moment when you lower the anchor is prime time for falling overboard. It's happened to me twice, and I'm supposed to know better. The problem is that you're up front on a sometimes slippery and rocking deck, you're leaning over, and you've got the weight of the anchor tipping you toward the water. One misstep or the rocking of a wave and you take a swim.

It's funny if it ends well (funnier for those watching than for those falling over, I'd say, based on my experience), but there's a grave danger here—if your hands or feet get tangled in the anchor line, you will follow the anchor to the bottom.

Never stand on an anchor coil for this reason, and if you feel yourself falling, the first thing to do is get rid of the anchor. (Then hold your nose and try to look as graceful as possible as you make a complete fool of yourself.)

Lower the hook—*never throw it*—from the bow and then back away, with the crew paying out line as you go. (Why shouldn't you throw it? Because if your foot or your favorite fishing rod happens to be wrapped in the line when the anchor is tossed, you or the rod will follow. Plus, throwing the anchor scares fish, if you happen to be fishing or diving. It also marks you as a boating dork.)

When you're over your spot, cleat the line, put a little tension on it by remaining in reverse for a moment to dig the anchor in, and you're set.

Anchoring in a Harbor

When anchoring in a harbor, it's important to allow enough "swing" space so that if the wind or tide changes at 2 A.M. you won't be slamming into neighboring boats. The boat may travel in a circle, the radius of which is about the length of your anchor line, as winds and tides change, so allow plenty of space.

What to Do When the Anchor Doesn't Hold

When winds or currents increase, or when tides rise significantly, you may find your anchor is not keeping you where you thought it would. This can be problematic if there are shoals or other boats downwind. The best cure for a dragging anchor is to let out more line, or scope, which will hopefully cause the anchor to dig in. (Or, truly the best cure is prevention—let out more scope anytime conditions become iffy.)

If your anchor does drag and won't take hold even when you let out more line, you'll need to start the engine, take in the anchor, and reset it, this time with more scope.

Anytime you drop anchor, firm sand is the preferred holding ground, and soft mud is the least preferred; it's worthwhile to search around to find good bottom, particularly if you plan to stay in a spot overnight.

When Two Anchors Are Better Than One

When anchoring larger boats overnight, particularly in a crowded harbor, you may want to use two anchors at a 45-degree angle from the bow. The extra anchor keeps your boat from swinging widely and banging into other boats, and also gives you added security in a storm.

If space is really tight, you might go to a pair of anchors set at close to 180 degrees, with the boat suspended in the center. This keeps the boat from doing anything but swinging in a tight circle by the bow as the winds and tide change.

Putting out a second anchor from a larger boat is easiest to do with a small dinghy to run out the second anchor after the first is set. But if you don't have a dink, two crewpeople handling lines from aboard the big boat can manage it.

You drop the first anchor, back away, and then motor at an angle to the second anchor-drop and have crewperson number 2 lower that one as crewperson number 1 pays out line. When both anchors are down, you back away, paying out line to give adequate scope and set them as described earlier.

> **Boat Bytes** _____
>
> Sea Tow and TOWBOAT U.S. are two of several franchised nationwide commercial towing companies. The companies have branches nationwide and can be reached via cellular phone as well as marine operators. Check your local phone directory for the number of a towing company and keep it in your wallet—you may need it in a hurry someday. Some companies sell towing insurance—you pay a modest amount each year and save a bunch if you ever need a long tow.

Beaching It

The first thing many families want to do with their boats is to go "beaching"—visiting those enchanting, private beaches far from the crowds. But you can't simply slide a powerboat up on the sand like a canoe.

> **Look Out!** _____
>
> Never approach a beach with a boat when the waves are much over a foot. The swell may seem gentle until you're almost on the sand, and then may rear up and deposit you and the boat high and dry. You never see people beaching on the open Atlantic or Pacific shores because waves are too tall. Beaching is doable many days in lakes, bays, and the calmer Gulf of Mexico in summer.

Well, you *can*, and many do through accident or ignorance, but then they have some unique problems in getting back afloat once again.

The best way of anchoring at a beach is bow to the seas. This presents the tallest part of the boat to the rolling seas, and also puts the swim platform, usually found at the transom, nearest to the beach.

Before you drop the bow anchor, touch the bow in on the sand (wave action permitting) and let everybody hop out so they don't have to jump out into waist-deep water to get ashore.

Drop the bow anchor well offshore and back down until the stern is within a few yards of the beach. In calm weather it can be within 10 feet. Remember to allow at least a 3:1 scope on your anchor line.

Also make sure that the beach is steep enough for the propeller to operate clear of the bottom when you come in close. And remember that a beach with a steep drop-off at high tide might be a very shallow slope at low tide.

When the Anchor Goes Ashore

A second anchor from the stern keeps the boat from washing sideways when you anchor near a beach. It also prevents you from having to make a long swim if the wind changes and starts to blow offshore.

Don't put the stern anchor in the water—the wash of even a gentle surf will prevent it from holding. Walk it up on the shore about 30 feet and bury it in the sand. You can sometimes tie the rode to a tree or rock on shore.

This approach not only keeps waves and boat wakes out of the boat, but in tidal areas it ensures that you don't come back to a grounded boat as the water flows out from under it.

> **CAUTION**
>
> **Look Out!** _____
>
> Never ground the boat on a full or falling tide, because the water will soon fall out from under it. This leaves the hull lying on its side like a beached whale—and about as easy to lift.

Grounding—On Purpose

On flat-calm rivers and lake beaches, when you're not going out of sight of the boat, you can simply ground the boat bow on, which keeps your prop well out in the water and hopefully not grounded. Put an anchor out from the stern so that the boat doesn't wash sideways and ground the prop, and tie a bow line to a tree ashore. On outboards and stern drives, you may want to tilt up the lower unit.

On a calm shore, it's possible to anchor bow to the beach temporarily. In rougher water or for a long stay, anchor bow to the water, and add a second anchor ashore from the stern.

(Grady White Boats)

If You Lose Your Anchor

It happens. Somebody forgets to secure the *bitter end* of the anchor rode to a cleat and the first thing you know, anchor and line are deep-sixed, or even worse, deep-sixtied. Sometimes an anchor can't be broken loose from bottom. Sometimes the anchor line is cut by coral or wreckage.

You can't just swim down to bottom, grab the anchor, and swim back up with it. If you lost the whole shebang including the anchor line, one approach is to swim down, grab the loose end of the line—not the one with the anchor—and swim it back to the surface. A safer alternative is to take a light line down with you, tie that to the anchor line, and then hoist line and hook once you get back aboard.

Salt Talk

The **bitter end** is the end you hold when making a knot, or the tag end of any piece of line.

Avoid losing your anchor by putting a foam crab-trap float on the bitter end of your anchor line. Secure it with a stopper knot like the figure eight shown in the following figure (for more on knots, see Chapter 9). Then, when Cousin Ermal lets the whole thing go over the side, the float will save the day. (It's also handy when you have to cast off in a hurry to chase a tuna!)

The figure-eight knot is a quick and easy "stopper" knot, used to prevent a line from slipping out of a block or float.

Snagged Anchors

A snagged anchor may have to be retrieved by diving, too. But don't push your abilities. If the water is cold or deeper than 10 feet, it's usually better to leave it there and buy another anchor. (A large, expensive yacht anchor can be marked by tying a large buoy to the anchor line, so that scuba divers can come back and retrieve it later.)

Breaking Free

Breaking free from mud is usually a simple matter of motoring uptide or upwind to a point well beyond the anchor, cleating off on an aft cleat, and then applying a little power. This "turns over" the flukes, pulling on them from the wrong direction, and the anchor pops free.

Anchors sometimes stick to whatever it is that made them grab bottom in the first place. This is particularly common over a rock bottom, and it also happens in harbors and commercial areas where cables and other snags cause problems.

The best way to avoid problems is to put a trip line on the base of the anchor, the crown. This is a lighter cord secured with light nylon tie-wraps that will break under stress and cause the trip line to pull from the crown instead of the top (see the following figure). This usually slides the hook free. The trip line is somewhat of a bother to handle, though, and isn't used except on a very snaggy bottom.

Look Out!

Be sure to keep the props well clear of the anchor line as you attempt to turn over the anchor.

Main anchor rode, 1/2" nylon

Nylon tie-wraps

Trip line, 1/4" nylon

Putting a trip line on the base of the anchor will help free the anchor from a snaggy bottom.

You may need to secure the anchor line to a transom lifting eye (not a cleat, because the cleat may pull out of the deck under heavy load), get well uptide of the spot where you dropped the anchor, and then apply increasing engine power until the hook pops free. The more line you let out, the better your chances of getting the anchor back.

The Least You Need to Know

- ◆ Anchors should be matched to the boat and the mission.
- ◆ The gear that attaches the anchor to the boat is as important as the anchor itself.
- ◆ Scope is as important as anchor design. The minimum scope is 3:1.
- ◆ Anchoring along a beach requires special precautions.
- ◆ The best way to avoid losing an anchor is to rig it correctly in advance; but even if you do lose an anchor, it can be retrieved.

Chapter 9

Nautical Knots

In This Chapter

- ◆ Getting a grip on cordage terminology
- ◆ Learning the ropes—types of line
- ◆ Caring for your line
- ◆ The most useful knots you'll need to know

Remember when you were in Boy (or Girl) Scouts and didn't pay attention while the scoutmaster was showing you how to tie the sheepshank? I didn't either. And you know what? I'm glad. I have never missed the ability to tie a sheepshank thus far in my life. I've never met anyone who said they have, either.

However, there are a lot of other knots that boaters use with some regularity. (Okay, there are some situations where you will find the sheepshank very useful, too.) In this chapter, you'll learn what ropes are, what sizes and types work best around a boat, and how to tie the most useful knots.

When a Rope Is Not a Rope: Nautical Cordage

First, let's take a look at what we tie. It's not rope—at least, not in the terminology of the sea. What we call "rope" ashore may be called *cordage*, *line*, *rode*, or *sheet* by salts, depending on how it's used.

Cordage is the term used to cover pretty much all the various ropes used on a boat, whether they're attached to the docks, the anchor, or used to hang out the laundry. In general, line is what you use to tie up the boat—dock lines, for example. Although we often think of line as string-sized ashore, it might be $5/8$-inch braid afloat. (This is not to be confused with fishing line, which is in fact called line, too.)

Salt Talk _____

Cordage is the general term used to refer to all the ropes, lines, anchor rodes, etc. used aboard a boat.

Line is what's normally called "rope" ashore—it can be of any size and either twisted or braided. It's usually classified according to diameter.

A **rode** is a line attached to an anchor.

Sheets are lines used to tension sails.

Running rigging is the term on sailboats for the lines used to control the sails, including the sheets, for tensioning sails and the halyards, and for pulling sails up and down the masts.

As noted in Chapter 8, the rope used on the anchor is most often referred to as the "rode," although it's also called the anchor line in practical use. And "sheets" are not what go on your bed afloat, but the ropes used to control tension in the sails of a sailboat. In general, though, anything that would be called a rope ashore is referred to as a "line" onboard. One common usage is to call it "rope" when it's still on the spool, but it becomes a line as soon as it's cut to length and given a specific function.

The strength of a rope or line is most affected by the diameter of the finished product, and lines used in boating are designated by their diameter. For example, a $1/4$-inch line is about $1/4$-inch thick. The strength of a line increases by a factor of about 3.5 to 4 for every doubling of diameter. The breaking strength of a typical $1/4$-inch braided nylon line is around 1,500 pounds, while the breaking strength of most $1/2$-inch braided nylon is around 6,000 pounds. (Different rope materials also have different strengths at a given size.)

What Is Rope Made Of?

To a landlubber, rope is rope—you go down to the discount store and buy whatever is handy and cheap. To a boater, the material and the way the line is built is important, even critical in some applications. Let's look at some of the most common rope materials.

Nylon: The Universal Soldier

Nylon is the preferred material for most boating uses, including for dock lines and anchor lines. The cost is reasonable—about 25¢ a foot for a ³/₈-inch line, up to 70¢ a foot for a ⁵/₈-inch line. Nylon is very durable, strong at a given diameter, and can withstand years in the sun.

Nylon also has a certain amount of stretch that acts as a shock absorber, making it more forgiving as an anchor line or for use in towing another boat.

Polypropylene: Low in Price, but Also Low in Strength

Polypropylene's only place aboard is to act as a clothesline for drying your swimsuit. It's not strong for its size, it frays easily, and it breaks down rapidly in direct sunlight. It's also a "hard" line, rough on the hands when used as anchor line.

However, it is in fact sometimes sold as very inexpensive anchor line. It's okay for little boats used in a pond, but just doesn't have the qualities to be suitable for anchoring or tying up large boats.

One legitimate use of poly is as a ski-tow rope. Because it floats, it's much easier to pick up than nylon, which sinks and might foul your prop. It stretches more than nylon, too, so it's easier on the hands and shoulders. The price is the lowest of any man-made fiber, around 15¢ a foot for ³/₈-inch diameter.

Polyester and Dacron: The Higher-Priced Spreads

Polyester lines, not to be confused with polypropylene, are excellent for many boating uses. They're very strong, flexible, and resist abrasion well. They are expensive, however, with good ³/₈-inch going for over 50¢ a foot.

Dacron lines stretch very little and are very strong, durable, and easy to handle, but also very expensive—up to 75¢ a foot for ³/₈-inch line. It's often used in sailboat rigging due to low stretch, but sees limited use aboard powerboats.

Sailors also use many more exotic materials, including Spectra-cored ropes encased in polyester weave that go for over $3 a foot in the larger diameters. These lines have only slightly more give than a steel cable and can wear practically forever (or not, depending on stress and sun exposure), but their high cost limits their use for the most part to rigging aboard the larger offshore sailboats.

Hemp: The Natural Ropes

Smoke 'em if you must, but don't ever use 'em aboard your boat. Hemp ropes and other natural fibers are not strong to begin with compared to the synthetics, and the fact that they rot easily if they're not kept dry makes them obsolete for boaters, even though they're very inexpensive.

Twisted, Stirred, or Shaken? How Ropes Are Made

Laid ropes are manufactured by twisting small strands together. There are usually three cord-sized strands in a typical marine line. Laid ropes are inexpensive, durable, and widely available.

Braided rope is woven from hundreds of small strands into a smooth, even finish that's easy on the hands and that runs through fittings without excess friction. Braids are also more flexible than laid ropes and less subject to kinking or fraying. Braided rope also comes in decorative colors, making it nice for dock lines. However, you can't splice braid as easily as you can laid rope, and it's about twice as costly as laid rope in the usual form.

Twisted or laid rope (left) is made up of three strands of smaller material. It's inexpensive, strong, and easy to splice. Braided rope (right) has a smoother surface than twisted rope, making it easier on the hands, and it is available in a variety of colors.

Size Counts

Line sizes should match the weight of the load they'll be expected to bear. Thus, you need bigger lines to tie up bigger boats. BOAT U.S., the nation's largest boating organization, suggests the following:

Boat Size	Line Size
20–30 feet	$^3/_8$-inch
30–40 feet	$^5/_8$-inch
Over 40 feet	$^3/_4$-inch

Note that a premium laid rope in the $^3/_8$-inch diameter has a breaking strength of 12,800 pounds, many times the strength it takes to hold even a 40-footer at the dock under normal conditions.

But you don't buy for the norm—you buy for the hurricane or for the day when a barge wake sends a 3-foot swell into the harbor. The larger lines also maintain their strength many more years than smaller lines, so it pays to buy large—but not so large that it won't fit the cleats on your particular boat.

For anchor lines, most experienced boaters use $^3/_8$-inch for boats up to about 25 feet, $^1/_2$-inch for boats 25 to 35 feet, $^5/_8$-inch for boats 35 to 50 feet, and $^3/_4$-inch for larger yachts.

However, many charterboat skippers rely on $^5/_8$-inch even for 20-foot boats. It's easier to handle, lasts forever, and doesn't tangle as readily as thinner diameters. On the downside, $^5/_8$-inch is more than twice as expensive as $^3/_8$-inch for a given length, heavier, and takes more storage space. It also won't fit around the undersized cleats on smaller boats, although it works fine with larger (at least 8-inch) cleats.

Boat Bytes

Lines used in sailing can sometimes be subjected to surprising stresses due to wind force on the sails, so you might need to check recommendations from the boat builder or from others sailing the same class of boat regarding diameter, material, length, and load-bearing properties.

Line Care

Nylon requires almost no care, which is what boaters love about it. Even with nylon, though, you'll improve its longevity if you wash off salt and sand with freshwater after each trip. Otherwise, the grit gets inside the weave, causing abrasion and eventually weakening the line.

Dry the line in the sun (this avoids mildew) and then store it in the shade inside your anchor box. Long-term exposure to sun gradually burns out even the best lines.

Look Out!

Avoid splashing the lines with bleach when you're washing down your boat—it will weaken the fibers. If the lines are soiled with fish offal or oil, put them in a 5-gallon bucket, add some dish detergent and warm water (not hot!), and let them soak overnight, agitating now and then. Rinse thoroughly, and then let them dry in the sun before storage. Lines stowed wet often grow slippery green mildew.

The Bitter End

When lines are cut, they leave unsightly ends that are subject to fraying. The standard method for treating this problem used to be "whipping"—wrapping the end of the rope with small cord.

Look Out!

Be very careful when melting nylon. It is extremely hot, and if it drips on your skin, it will burn you badly! Also, remember that nylon ignites easily—the drips can start a fire. It's a job best done out-of-doors, and not aboard your boat.

Boat Bytes

When you have to cut a line and don't have other means of securing the ends, plain old duct tape will do the job temporarily. Just make three tight wraps around the line and presto, it's whipped.

These days, there are better ways. If you buy nylon in a marine store, they'll probably cut it with an electric hot knife. The heat melts the nylon and instantly secures all strands. If not, you can do it yourself. A soldering iron will do the job neatly.

This step is particularly important with lines that have a separate core and cover; with these, you might need to whip the ends with smaller line, and then cut them with the hot knife to seal everything together and prevent the core from creeping into or out of the cover.

No soldering iron? If you're careful, you can use a cigarette lighter or a candle to burn the ends slightly until the nylon becomes liquid. As it cools, roll it between two pieces of 2 × 4 to make a rounded end. This gives a solid end on the line that will never unravel.

There are also commercial whipping compounds or rope dips that act as a glue. You dip the ends of the rope in them, let it dry, and it secures the strands.

There's also a heat-sealing tape with which you wrap the end, and then apply a flame; the tape shrinks and seals to form a permanent whipping. This is quick, relatively safe, and forms a dependable bond—carry some aboard.

Coiling Lines

Take care of your lines every trip, and they'll take care of you when you need them.

The first rule is to never put a line away without coiling it. There's a little trick to this with laid line.

You can't simply pick up some line and make a bunch of loops over your hand. It won't lie "fair" or flush, one coil exactly like the next, and this will lead to tangles when you use it.

The trick to getting it flat is to give the line a little half-twist, to the right or clockwise, each time you go over the hand holding the coil. Make the coils about 18 inches in diameter, a comfortable handling size in most lines. To prevent kinks, make the coils in a clockwise direction.

This technique has one disadvantage: It results in a steady twist being put into the coil from the little half-twists per loop. Another way to do it is to *not* twist the line, and let the coil assume a gentle half-twist as it hangs down. That way, when the line uncoils, it comes out with no new twisting. It looks a little less neat hanging up, though.

After you've got it all laid in, secure the coils by taking a turn counterclockwise around them with the bitter end (the end you hold while making a knot, or the tag or cut end of any piece of line). Then pass a short bight or bend through the loop, passing above the turn at the back side of the coils. Bring the bitter end up through this loop, draw it tight, and you've got the coil complete and ready to hang or stow. (Just be sure that anyone who wants to uncoil this line understands that first you pull the loop back over the top and unwrap the turns, or you'll have a mess!)

Braided line has less of a tendency to kink than laid line, and there's no need to impart the twist as you coil it. It will lay in a fairly regular loop or sometimes in a figure eight, but these run out without tangles.

Proper coiling keeps a line tangle-free and ready for immediate use.

Handling the Anchor Line

Many boats have an anchor hanger in the box, and this should give you a tip about how the tackle goes in—first you put in all the line or rode, then the chain, and then the anchor—not vice versa. This is so that everything comes out in the order you want it when you need it.

Salt Talk

A **hawse pipe** is a tube above the anchor locker that lets you feed the line in without opening the hatch—handy and salty-looking. Many well-designed boats have a pipe or at least a groove in the anchor hatch where line can feed out without the hatch being ajar.

There's no need to coil the anchor line—just feed it in hand-over-hand and take it out the same way. Don't store other equipment on top of it because this leads to tangles.

On some boats, line is fed through a *hawse pipe* or fitting through the front deck into a rope compartment or locker.

Cleating Off

Cleats are two-horned monsters that will murder a bare toe, but they are a boater's best friend when the boat must be secured. Instead of tying a knot around the steering wheel or your mother-in-law, you simply make a few turns and a half-hitch over the horns of the cleat and the boat stays put. (A half-hitch is the most basic of knots—see the "Getting Hitched" section later in this chapter for details on how to tie it.) And, when you want to leave, the turns come off easily, unlike most types of knots.

First, you need line that fits the cleats. A ⅝-inch line won't work on a 4-inch cleat because it won't fit under the horns for more than a single turn. Quarter-inch line is adequate for tying up small boats under 16 feet long, and ⅜-inch line is a good choice for securing boats from 16 to 30 feet long.

Horn

Cleats make for quick tie-ups. They're usually located at the bow and stern, with spring cleats sometimes added amidships. They're also found on most docks.

To cleat off, take a turn under the away side of the horn, completely around the base, make a figure eight by going over the top center and under each horn, and then finish off with a half-hitch around one horn. The following figure shows you how to do it.

You haven't really made a secure knot with this arrangement, but the friction of the line against the horn does the job so that there's no pressure against the half-hitch. It won't slip.

It doesn't take 10 half-hitches to hold your boat. You can add a couple more turns around the base and a final half-hitch if you're leaving it for a long period—it will make you feel better, even if it doesn't hold the boat any better.

Coil any excess rope neatly on the dock as near the edge as possible, so it won't tangle with people's feet.

Boat Bytes

Always store the same lines in the same boxes. Be compulsive about this—put all the gear you use into the same boxes all the time. That way, in an emergency or hurry-up situation, you can quickly find what you need and it'll be ready to go.

Note that no knots other than a half-hitch to finish off are required to secure to a cleat.

To boat

Bitter end

Bitter end

To boat

Bitter end →

To boat

A neat coil of line next to the cleat is a mark of good seamanship. The easy way to make this coil is to start with the bitter end laid flat on the dock. Turn it clockwise to form a circular loop on the dock. Continue to turn it to pull in all the remaining line, right up to the cleat, forming a series of neat, concentric coils that won't tangle with the feet of passersby.

Knots You'll Use Most Often

There are dozens of knots that the salts and scoutmasters of the world would have you learn, but between surfing the Internet and figuring out how to program your VCR, you probably don't have time for all that stuff. It's better to learn only a couple knots really well so that you can tie them fast and flawlessly, even under the most challenging of conditions.

Here are four knots that you'll use most often while boating, plus a bonus knot for you anglers:

- Bowline
- Half-hitch
- Two half-hitches
- Clove hitch
- Uni-knot

I'll discuss each of these knots in the following sections.

The Ubiquitous Bowline

If you were to learn only one knot that could get you through many different situations, it might be the bowline. It's simple and fast to tie and can do a lot of things well. It's pronounced *bo-lin*, by the way, as in "Bo knows sports," not *bow-line*, even though that would seem to make more sense, nautically speaking.

The bowline is used to create a secure loop that can be dropped over a piling, its most common use. It can also be tied through a mooring ring, and two bowlines can be used to join a pair of lines. A running noose (which functions like a hangman's noose or choker) can be made by passing the free end of the line through the loop.

Basically, the classic method for tying the bowline is this, as taught by Scoutmaster Rex Morgan back in Jeromesville, Ohio: Rabbit comes out of the hole, rabbit goes around the tree, rabbit goes back in the hole. The "rabbit" is the bitter end, the "hole" is a closed bight or loop, and the "tree" is the standing part of the line—the working part of the rope that runs from your knot to a cleat, piling, etc.

The only trick is to get the small loop with the free end on top of the standing part of the line. (If you put it beneath the standing part, the tree collapses and kills the rabbit; the knot simply refuses to tie.) Then, rabbit out of hole, around tree, and back into hole. Draw up both ends at once and you've got it.

Confused by the rabbit method? Here's a step-by-step guide for tying a bowline:

1. Make an overhand loop in the line about 2 feet from the bitter end. Make sure the loop lies on top of the standing part of the line.

2. Run the bitter end through the loop and around the standing part of the line, making a "working bight"—the larger main loop you'll drop over a piling.

3. Bring the bitter end back through the overhand loop.

4. Adjust the size of the working bight so it fits the piling.

5. Draw the knot tight by pulling on the standing part of the line and the bitter end.

There you have it—a perfect bowline.

Getting Hitched

The half-hitch is made by passing a loop around the standing line, the working part of the rope that runs from your knot to a cleat, piling, etc., usually after passing through a fitting or over a post. The finishing steps of the common shoelace tie is a half-hitch, but with the ends "slipped" or looped so that they can be drawn loose with a tug on the bitter ends.

A single half-hitch won't do much more than support the weight of the line itself, but it's the starting point of several other knots. Add a second half-hitch, making a knot not-so-cleverly called "two half-hitches," and you've got a secure and very quick knot.

Two half-hitches tend to jam under strain, so you don't want to use the knot where you might have to untie it quickly, but it's a good knot for lines that are left in place, such as line that remains attached to the bow eye of a dinghy.

You can keep a half-hitch, or any other knot, from jamming by making several round turns around the piling or eye you're tying to before starting the knot. Friction will keep pressure off the knot and prevent it from jamming.

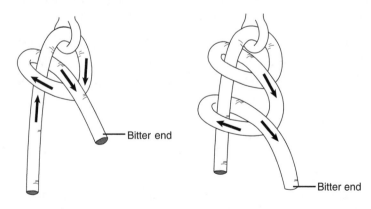

The half-hitch is the simplest of all knots and is the beginning of many other knots.

Two half-hitches make a stout knot that won't slip and that can be tied by anyone quickly.

Clove Hitch

The clove hitch is used to tie up to dock pilings when you're not staying long, as for a waterside dinner. It's basically a couple of loops tossed together and is very easy to tie and untie.

Start by making the first loop over the piling so that the standing line passes over the top of the running line. Then, make a second loop around the piling so that the bitter end passes under the running line. Pull on both ends and the hitch snugs down.

You can convert this into a permanent knot for dock lines left in place at your slip by adding two half-hitches over the standing line. Because the clove hitch bears all the strain, the half-hitches won't jam, but they secure everything.

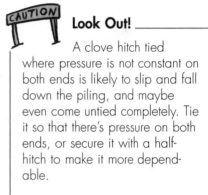

Look Out!

A clove hitch tied where pressure is not constant on both ends is likely to slip and fall down the piling, and maybe even come untied completely. Tie it so that there's pressure on both ends, or secure it with a half-hitch to make it more dependable.

The clove hitch is a good temporary tie-up to a piling but might slip down the pole if there's no strain on the lines.

One Knot That Fits All: The Uni-Knot

This is a knot originally invented for the slick monofilament used in fishing line, and it won't work with large, rough ropes. It's sometimes useful in light rope, especially if started with a *round turn* so that it doesn't take extreme loads and thus doesn't jam. Its most important use, though, is for anglers. It's quick and retains almost 100 percent of the line strength.

The nice thing about the uni is that it's an all-purpose knot, good for tying on a lure, tying a leader to running line, or tying two equal-size lines together. Learn this one and you won't have to worry about most of the other fishing knots.

Salt Talk

A **round turn** is made by passing a line through a fitting or around a piling twice, thus forming a complete loop around the object.

Basically, you make a loop so that the end overlaps the running part of the line about 6 inches, make five turns through the loop, and then pull the tag end tight to jam the wraps. Pull on the standing line and the loop closes to form the knot.

To use the uni to tie on a leader, make a loop in the running line overlapping the leader, and a second in the leader overlapping the running line, and then tie the knots. Draw them down, clip off the tag ends close, and you're done.

Microfiber lines, which have become very popular with anglers in recent years, are so thin that they tend to cut through monofilament leaders. You can avoid this by doubling the microfiber before tying the double uni-knot to make the attachment.

The Least You Need to Know

- Nylon is the most commonly used material for anchor and dock lines.

- Line diameters must be matched to load, determined mostly by boat length.

- Don't ignore basic line care to keep your lines in good condition and ready when needed.

- Learn a few knots well, so that you can tie them in a hurry under stress.

As Personal as It Gets: Personal Water Craft

In This Chapter

- ◆ Deciding which PWC is for you
- ◆ Operating basics
- ◆ Riding safely
- ◆ Being a good citizen
- ◆ Taking care of your PWC

Personal Water Craft or "PWCs" are motorcycles on the water. For powerboaters who crave a wet and wild ride, the feel of instant response, and amazing handling, they offer an exciting alternative to powerboats and sailboats. And these days, they're becoming the second boat of many families who already own a larger cruiser, deck-type boat, or pontoon rig.

PWCs are typically 7 to 12 feet long, and nearly all of them are designed so that you sit "on" them rather than in them; you straddle a saddle, similar to riding a motorcycle. That similarity extends to the handlebar steering and throttle—and to the cycle-like performance that makes them such a blast to ride.

Most modern PWCs are powered by four-stroke engines from 50 to 165 horsepower. Because they typically weigh less than 800 pounds, performance can be spectacular! And the jet-type lower unit allows for incredible turns and cuts, and also means there's no spinning propeller to add danger should you take a spill. Prices are moderate compared to many boats, ranging from as little as $5,000 to a max around $10,500.

PWCs combine amazing acceleration with incredible handling. Most are designed for one or two riders, but some versions can carry three in comfortable, molded, saddle-type seats.

(Bombardier Sea Doo)

Which PWC Is for You?

Though all PWCs look fairly similar, there's a great deal of difference in what the various models can do, based on seating capacity, beam width, and power. Look at the following parameters before you make your choice.

Size Counts

If you're new to personal watercraft riding, bigger is better. The three-person models, though more expensive than the single-rider models, offer stability and a forgiveness in handling that make them very easy to ride. And if you have youngsters in the family who are too young to ride on their own (under 16 in many states, 14 or even 12 in some), then the aft seats enable them to get the feel of the PWC with you at the helm.

In general, "standup" PWCs are smaller and tougher to ride than "sit-down" models; you can expect to spend a couple days on the water before you feel confident with the ski-type machines, while with the sit-down jobs, basic operation is a matter of turning the key and taking off. The secret to riding the standups is getting your weight in the right location on the foot pads and learning to shift, while keeping your balance in the corners—it takes a few trips, but like riding a bicycle, it's something that anybody can master.

Standup PWCs like the original Jet-Ski™ from Kawasaki are a bit more challenging to learn than the sit-down models, but provide for breathtaking thrills after they're mastered. Among the secrets are getting your weight in the right fore-and-aft location on the foot pads and learning to shift your center of gravity in turns.

(Kawasaki Motors U.S.A.)

Power Up

When it comes to power choices, consider how you'll be using the PWC. If you buy a three-person model and you expect to have all three seats occupied most of the time, you're going to want plenty of power to get the rig on plane. The same is true if you're a hair-on-fire sort of rider who wants to enjoy mile-a-minute speeds out there in open water; because jet-drives are not as efficient as prop power, you need plenty of horsepower, even though the boat is relatively small and lightweight.

On the other hand, if your main concern is price, less power means a lower initial cost. And you'll burn less fuel. If inexpert teens will be riding the water-bike, you might want to choose a moderate horsepower model as a way of governing their speed. (Yep, it won't be long

> **Boat Bytes**
>
> All PWCs are propelled by impellers, which is a sort of enclosed propeller inside a metal housing. The impeller sucks in water through a grid on the bottom of the PWC and shoots it out in a jetlike stream from a nozzle at the back, pushing the boat forward. The boat is turned by directing the nozzle, via a connection to the handlebars.

before they'll be crying for a more powerful model, but at least they'll be safer while they're learning.)

Cost Control

Other factors in cost are selecting two-stroke or four-stroke models; two-strokes are cheaper, but burn more fuel, make more noise, create exhaust smoke because they burn oil, and are being phased out by the industry due to pollution regulations. So even though you might save money initially, you won't get as much back in resale if you opt for a two-stroke PWC.

Because PWCs are much more seasonal-use craft than most boats, you can often save considerably by buying at the end of summer; dealers will want to get rid of their inventory rather than store it over winter, and you can sometimes save 20 percent or more.

Riding Basics

Riding a PWC is a lot like driving a boat in terms of basic handling. However, the controls vary considerably, and so does the steering. You can get a lot of good basic information by taking an on-line PWC course; one of the best can be found at www.boatus.com. PWC rental agencies will also provide basic instruction to get you started.

At the Controls

On most PWCs the ignition system is on the left handlebar—a green button to start, a red button to shut down. A "kill switch" or ignition safety lanyard must be in place for the motor to start. No matter what you do, it won't run without that lanyard in its clip. Put the clip in place and attach the lanyard to your wrist or to your personal flotation device; that way, if you fall off, the engine shuts down immediately.

On the right handlebar is the throttle, typically a spring-loaded lever that can be held down with one or two fingers as you grip the handlebar. Let go of the lever and the speed drops to idle immediately, another safety factor.

Some high-end PWCs also offer trim control on or near the left grip; the trim functions somewhat like that on an outboard or sterndrive boat, enabling you to vary the angle of thrust. You trim the lower unit up to raise the bow, reduce wetted surface, and increase speed; and down to put the bow lower, make the hole-shot or takeoff faster, soften oncoming waves, and improve cornering.

Some models also have reverse, which is achieved by a "reverse gate," basically a bucket that can be dropped over the jet output to redirect it forward. It's not much of a reverse, but it's enough to get you on and off a dock—a big help in many situations. This is typically controlled by a shift lever on the right side of the frame.

PWCs do not come equipped with the running lights required for after-dark operation, and it is illegal in all states to operate any boat without running lights illuminated between sunset and sunrise. So plan your outings with plenty of time to get back to the dock before the sun disappears below the waves.

Boat Bytes

Most PWCs are equipped with a fuel reserve rather than a gas gauge. When you run out of fuel on the main tank, you flip a switch, restart, and the reserve gets you back to the gas dock. (Just make sure you head directly there—there's no "reserve" reserve!)

Make a Clean Start

Attach the emergency stop key, hook up the lanyard, and you're ready to power up. Hit the starter button, usually a green button on the handlebars, and the motor fires up. If there's no neutral gear, the boat might start to ease forward immediately.

However, unlike prop-drive boats, jet-drive boats require some rpms to provide steering; you can't really idle away from the dock because the boat will pretty much wander wherever it wants to. So you turn the handle bars the direction you want to go and briefly goose the throttle to kick the back end of the boat around so that you're headed in the right direction. Just a brief shot of power will do it; no need to leave the marina at full tilt—and if you do you're sure to draw plenty of heat from surrounding boaters, and maybe a ticket if the marine patrol happens to see you. (Some recent models do offer much-improved "trolling speed" steering, a major assist around the docks.)

Look Out!

If you've got ideas of speeding along with your head low to cut wind resistance, as you've seen PWC racers do on TV, it's best to forget them for the moment; one of the most common injuries among beginning riders comes from banging their chin into the handlebars when they hit a wake!

After you're clear of the docks and other boats, you can put the PWC on plane. As with other boats, it's best to do this by going to near full-throttle until the boat jumps up on plane, then ease back to a cruising speed around 3,000 rpms or so.

Larger PWCs can carry two or even three adults with ease. These larger craft are easier to learn to ride because they are more stable than small models, but they're more expensive to purchase.

(American Honda Motors)

Testing Your Wings

As soon as you're on plane, buzzing along at 25 mph or so, start keeping a sharp eye out for boat wakes from distant boats—at this speed, they might give you a pretty good jolt if you hit them head on.

After you've got the feel of the PWC, make a few gentle turns. You'll notice that the boat leans into the curve, just like a bicycle or a motorcycle. The faster you go and the shorter you turn, the greater the lean—and as you gain skill, you'll learn to shift your weight to the inside to help the boat stick in the corner.

> ### Nautical Notes
>
> Make it a habit, before making a turn, to look over both shoulders and check for traffic coming up behind you. Particularly where lots of PWCs are ridden in close proximity, such as around rental docks, turning into the path of an overtaking craft is a common cause of accidents. By the same token, avoid riding too close behind another PWC— if it stops abruptly or turns in front of you, a collision might be unavoidable.

As with all boats, there are no brakes; to stop, let go of the throttle. You won't stop immediately—manufacturers caution that many models traveling at top speed will travel over 100 yards after you cut the power. And in jet-drive boats, as soon as you get off the throttle, there's very little steering response. If you need to turn and stop, as you might to avoid another boat that suddenly crosses your path, you'll have to keep some power on to maintain steering as you slow down.

Easy Does It

PWCs ridden carefully by mature riders are no more dangerous than any other performance boat. But in the hands of untrained riders with no knowledge of boating laws and very little sense of self-preservation, they can be deadly both to the riders and to anyone they run into. PWCs are involved in a disproportionate number of accidents and injuries.

Particularly when you're learning, riding with a buddy on another PWC is a great idea. That way, if one of you gets in trouble, the other can step in to help. In fact, riding with a buddy is a good idea even for the most experienced riders, and it makes riding more fun, too.

But when you do ride in close proximity to another PWC, remember to signal when you intend to slow down or turn—otherwise, the safety measure can become another cause of accidents.

Taking a Spill

For those who like to experience high-speed turns, extreme wave-jumping, and other dramatic maneuvers, falling off is fairly common. Taking a spill should be no major problem for skilled swimmers wearing the required PFD; all PWCs are equipped with emergency shutdown devices that shut off the motor or put the machine into low-speed idle, in a circle, if the rider falls off.

On a Roll

PWCs are one of the few powerboats where a rollover is not a disaster. The motor compartments are sealed except for a convoluted air inlet that traps and dispels any water, even if the boat turns completely upside down, so the usual mechanical problems are not a concern.

However, in many PWCs, the water trap system works only if you roll the machine upright in the proper direction; if you roll a boat to the left and it's designed to be rolled right, it might scoop water into the air intake and then into the engine, causing all sorts of costly problems. PWCs that can be rolled only one way typically have a large arrow on the bottom or lower sides to indicate the direction they should be turned to get them upright safely.

Look Out! _____

Age and experience count in safe PWC riding. The minimum age varies by state from 12 to 16—know the laws for your area and follow them to the letter. Wear a PFD at all times, secure the safety lanyard, and never ride after sundown or before sunup.

Getting Back Aboard

After the boat is upright, you should remount from the rear. Place both hands on the back end, push it down slightly, and hoist yourself aboard. Get back in the saddle, reattach the safety lanyard, and you're ready to crank up and take off again. Note that there might be water inside the bilge from the rollover, which can make the boat hard to get up on plane. Trim down all the way if your rig has a trim control, get it out of the hole and up on top, and in most models an automatic bilge pump will take care of most of the water.

Beaching

Be careful when beaching your PWC. Don't power all the way up on the sand or you're sure to suck sand or weeds into the intake. It's best to stop a few feet out, step off the machine, and push the hull until the nose is up on the sand. When you leave, follow the same route, pushing the boat out until the water pickup is in a couple feet of water before you climb on and start the engine.

Be a Good Citizen

"Social awareness" is an important term in PWC riding, at least among manufacturers concerned about the many lakes, rivers, waterfront communities, and nature preserves that have already banned water-bikes. The combination of engine noise and rough wakes can make PWCs unwelcome in some areas.

Boat Bytes _____

Most manufacturers recommend that you don't run in water shallower than 2 feet, not only for safety's sake, but also to prevent your jet pump from sucking up sand and gravel, which can damage the cooling system or the pump.

If you travel through residential waterfront, keep on going and find a remote area for doing the circles, turns, and tricks that will keep you in one location for extended periods.

Stay well clear of other boats. They might be seeking a little solitude, and your sending up wakes time after time won't help that. Stay well away from large boats if you want to try a bit of wake-jumping—a minimum of 200 feet is a good safe rule that also will keep you far enough away not to aggrieve the skipper.

Fishermen are particularly sensitive to fast boats passing close—they believe this spooks the fish. So again, as much as possible, stay well clear.

And remember that just because your PWC will run in foot-deep water doesn't mean it's a good thing to do, especially over delicate grass flats in a mangrove creek where your passage might disturb rare wading birds from their nests.

Look Out!

The water jetting out of the back of a jet drive can be dangerous to nearby swimmers. Always be careful on takeoff that you don't hose anyone with your jet blast—it can contain bits of shell or other debris that can cause injury.

Gearing Up

If you ride in cool weather, you'll want a wet suit to keep you warm. Even in fairly warm weather, it's easy for wet skin to chill rapidly in the wind, so it's always a good idea to have the top of a wet suit handy. And you also must wear a pair of neoprene shorts or pants to protect your "lower unit" from getting a high-speed enema should you fall and skid fanny first. It sounds funny, but it can cause serious injuries. Standard swim trunks provide no protection on this count.

Basic PWC riding gear includes sunglasses or goggles, a vest-type PFD, and protective neoprene swim trunks or wet-suit bottoms. Many riders also wear neoprene gloves and booties.

(Kawasaki Motors U.S.A.)

You'll also appreciate a pair of neoprene diver's gloves and lightweight neoprene dive booties on cooler days, allowing you to stretch your season at both ends of summer.

If you're one of those northern riders who can't wait to get on the water after the ice goes off the lake, you will probably want to opt for a "dry suit," which is a tight-fitting, gasketed, and waterproof version of the wet suit. It prevents water from entering around the neck, wrists, and ankles, and also acts as a windbreak, so you can stay dry even if you take a spill. Of course, you lose most of your body heat through your head, so a matching water- and windproof hood is also part of the gear for riding in extreme weather. Some addicts wear snowmobile helmets, complete with visors, to deal with temperatures approaching freezing.

Whenever you ride, you'll also want to wear eye protection. Curved sunglasses that fit the contours of your face are a good start—and be sure to wear a "keeper" of some sort to prevent them from blowing off and sinking. As in operating a conventional boat, polarized lenses are the best choice because they enable you to see through surface glare and note areas that are too shallow for safe operation. If you ride faster than 50 mph, you'll probably want to opt for full goggles to protect against spray and insects.

Other Stuff

PWCs are required by law to carry the same safety gear required of other power-boats, including a fire extinguisher and a signaling device; check your state's laws. You'll also want a small anchor and line for your PWC. Some companies make anchors that you can fill with sand when you need them, then empty out for compact storage.

You might also want to carry a tow strap or a length of stout rope for that inevitable day when the motor won't restart after a spill, or when you simply run out of gas.

If you carry a rider behind you regularly, it's not a bad idea to invest in a life-jacket "harness," which slips over your PFD to provide heavy-duty handholds for your rider. This is more comfortable for you, safer for them, and less likely to result in your life-jacket getting damaged in tight maneuvering.

A siphon can be a big help for that day when you just can't bring yourself to go home after you switch to the reserve tank. A model sold as the "Super Siphon" has a self-primer in the tip, so that you don't have to suck in gas fumes to get it started flowing—it's well worth the $10 price.

You'll also want to carry chilled beverages—most PWCs have a built-in drink box, or at least a small storage space where a compact cooler can be fitted. That's also a good spot to stow, inside several layers of sealing waterproof bags, a rescue flair, horn, and your boat registration.

Because everything you carry on a PWC is likely to get wet, special care is required when stowing things like your wallet, car keys, and cell phone. It's a good idea to get several heavy-duty watertight locking bags of the sort whitewater kayakers use to keep your stuff dry—and off the bottom of the lake.

Trailering Your PWC

PWCs are easy to trailer because of their light weight. You can tow a single personal watercraft behind even the smallest compact car, and larger vehicles can tow specialized trailers that load up to four PWCs at once.

However, the light weight can create special problems. For one thing, it's very easy to bounce a PWC off a trailer if it's not secured both front and rear. And don't depend on the winch hook alone to hold the bow in place; add a heavy nylon strap with a tensioner to pull straight down from the bow eye to secure the front end. And put another strap over the seats. (Place a towel or a strap guard under this strap to prevent it from cutting into the seats.)

Launching a PWC from a trailer is pretty straightforward, again due to the light weight. Remove the tiedowns, attach a bow line, make sure the drain plug is in place, and back the trailer in until the stern of the boat starts to float, then push it free. If your boat is a little "sticky" on the trailer, you can make it let go more easily by spraying the bunks with silicone spray. Applying silicone makes it easier to winch the hull back on the trailer at the end of the day, too.

> **Look Out!**
>
> PWC trailers have little 8- or 10-inch wheels that rotate much faster than those on your car. As a result, the tires wear out rapidly—in as little as 10,000 miles. Keep an eye on them, keep them inflated to the maximum recommended pressure, and change them promptly when they show signs of wear or cracking.

When you tow your rig to a distant lake, one of the most disappointing discoveries you can make at the ramp is that you left the emergency stop clip at home. Avoid this by attaching the clip to the ignition key of your car the night before a trip—or get a spare and hide it somewhere inside the PWC.

Care and Feeding

Because PWCs operate in heavy spray and most experience occasional roll-overs, they require a bit more maintenance than conventional powerboats. And the jet system also takes some special attention at times.

Cleaning the Impeller

You'll occasionally get debris in the jet intake, no matter how careful you are. The tipoff is when the motor revs high but the boat slows down; it means the impeller is sucking in air rather than a solid stream of water. The cure is to shut down, take the emergency-stop lanyard off its connection to make sure the motor is not started accidentally while you have your hands around the intake or impeller, and then get off and clear away the debris.

The intake is located on the bottom of the watercraft, just ahead of the jet outlet; it's covered by a metal grate. The obstruction might be weeds, a plastic bag, fishing line, or whatever. In some cases, you might have to turn the rig over on its side to get at all the junk (keeping in mind that most PWCs should be turned over in only one direction) but be persistent, because running the motor with debris inside the impeller housing is a very bad idea—plus, it cuts way down on your speed.

At the End of the Day

Because PWCs get more water inside than other boats, maintenance has to be a bit more intense than usual. If you ride in salt, you must hose down the whole rig with freshwater after each trip. Remove the drain plug so that any water inside the bilge can drain.

PWCs operate in an environment of heavy spray and occasional turn-overs, so a freshwater washdown is a must after use in saltwater. Drying the interior and oiling all metal parts is also essential after every trip.

(American Honda Motors)

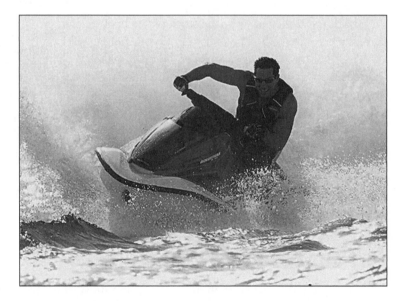

And it's wise to remove the seat or motor cover, and use a dry towel to wipe down the entire motor (after it has cooled) and sop up any water left in the bilge. Then fog the motor lightly with a corrosion preventative like Corrosion-X. Make sure to hit steering and throttle cables and any other metal parts, too. When you're done, leave the cover off and let the rig dry in the sun for a few hours before closing it up.

If you can't store your rig in a garage, it's a good idea to invest in a fabric cover. This will prevent humidity problems to some degree, and also keeps the sun from fading the finish and cracking the seats.

Get Ready for Winter

If you'll be storing your PWC for the winter, you'll want to winterize it at the end of the riding season. The first step is to run the motor briefly, out of the water, to blow out water left in the cooling passages. It's basically just an on-and-off run, no more than 30 seconds, so the motor won't overheat. This is an essential step—otherwise, the water could freeze and crack the cooling passages, resulting in engine failure.

Remove the drain plug and store it where you can find it; this prevents humidity from building up in the bilge and freezing. And again, fog the exterior of the engine and all metal parts with a protective oil designed for the purpose. Remove the spark plugs and put a light spray of oil into each cylinder, then replace the plugs. Add a fuel preservative to the tank, then top it off; a full tank is less likely to have water condensation problems.

 Boat Bytes

Unhappy with your PWC's performance? It could be your impeller; a pitch that's too high for the load can cause holeshot problems, and one that's too low can cause the engine to over-rev frequently, and also reduces top-end speed. A PWC shop can change the pitch or install a new impeller for you.

The end of the season is also not a bad time to have a shop that specializes in PWCs take a look at your impeller. If it's badly worn or out of pitch, they can replace it for around $200, or rework it for around $125.

The Least You Need to Know

- ◆ PWCs come in a wide variety of styles and performance levels—choose one that fits your needs.

- ◆ Riding a PWC is simple, but start slow and learn skills gradually before you push the envelope.

- PWCs are involved in numerous accidents; follow the rules of safe riding to make sure you don't become a statistic.

- Be a good on-the-water citizen to ensure the future of PWC riding.

- PWCs take extra care to keep them functioning—clean, dry, and lube your machine after every trip.

Part 3

Getting from Point A to Point B: Marine Navigation

You don't know the players without a program, and you don't know the waters without a chart! In this part, we'll take a look at where to find charts—including the new generation of digital versions—and how to get the most out of them.

You'll also learn how to apply what you see on the chart to the markers and buoys you see out there on the water ahead, and we'll explore the basics of using compasses and electronics to "find yourself." Thanks to GPS and chart plotters, it's far easier than ever before.

And when you feel you're ready for that first long cruise, turn to this section for a chapter on how to go about it.

THE CANS AND NUNS MAKE IT JUST LIKE A ROAD, DAD.

YES- EXCEPT THE ASPHALT MOVES AND ROCKS ATTACK FROM UNDERNEATH.

11

Nautical Road Maps: Marine Charts

In This Chapter

♦ Using nautical charts to find your way around

♦ Decoding the colors on charts

♦ Learning about latitude and longitude

♦ Making sense of scales for determining distances

In boating there are no corner filling stations where you can stop and ask for directions (or refuse to, if you're like some people). Either you know where you are or you have problems. Maintaining a good sense of where you are on the water is called *navigating*.

There are several ways to avoid getting lost afloat. The first is simply never to go out of sight of the boat ramp, although this considerably limits your boating opportunities. But if you hope for broader horizons, a bit of navigating might be called for. Navigating starts with a nautical road map called a *chart*—a map of the water that shows depth and navigational details. These days, the map might be a digital image on a screen, but whether it's hard copy or electronic, it shows you a lot of information that you'll need to know.

In this chapter, you'll learn where to buy nautical charts and how to use them, as well as the basics of latitude and longitude, the imaginary lines that help boaters navigate.

The Art of the Chart

Charts show the shape of the waterway, and just as importantly, the depth. Boaters view depth as aviators view altitude—if you have plenty of either, your craft will not have problems from colliding with the earth. (These collisions tend to be less serious in boating than in flying, fortunately, but they're still to be avoided.)

A navigational chart can cover any area ranging from a single harbor to an entire ocean, but all show the same basic information:

- Water depth
- Shape of any land masses
- Location and description of navigational markers
- Latitude and longitude lines

Some privately produced charts, both digital and paper, offer additional information, including location of launching ramps, good fishing spots, artificial reefs, and so on, but these, too, include the basic data on depth and geographic locations. Some of the better digitals these days even include tide information projected many years into the future; click on designated marks on the electronic screen and you can see exact tide heights in real time.

Thus, no wise boater will ever take on anything more than a pond he or she can see across without looking over a chart first. On the chart, the hazards are all marked, the safe passages all clear, the navigation markers and shoreline landmarks all obvious. All you have to do is figure out how to translate what's on the chart to what you see from the wheel and follow the safe water. It sounds easy, and it should be.

So why do highly paid professional skippers still run ships aground on occasion? Hard to say, but if *they* do it, you might do it. Learn the art of the chart and keep it in mind any time you're underway and you'll have few problems.

Charts Are Where You Find 'Em

Charts are produced by the U.S. National Oceanic and Atmospheric Administration, or simply NOAA, which everybody pronounces "Noah." The government produces the charts because nobody else can afford the time, money, or manpower to survey the world's oceans. But they are plagiarized, legally, by everybody who can think of a profitable use for them, including me—I've written two books of fishing maps.

You can get the official charts from NOAA at Distribution Division, N/ACC3, Riverdale, MD 20743-1199, 301-436-6990. Local stores listed under "maps" in your telephone directory also carry charts in coastal areas, as do marinas and outdoor stores.

Charts used to be dirt cheap, but when the government figured out that they were selling them at a loss, they started charging more. They're about $18 to $20.75 each at present. Visit http://chartmaker.ncd.noaa.gov/ for details or go to a local map shop. You don't have to know exactly which chart you want to shop for a chart—chart catalogs, available at map dealers, will guide you.

The Profit Motive: Commercial Charts

When NOAA raised prices, they opened the door for privately-produced commercial charts, allowing competitive pricing. Now there are private charts based on the NOAA charts that are actually better than the originals because they include two charts on one piece of paper—one on the front, one on the back.

Some add lots of specialized information especially for recreational boaters and anglers. And some of the private versions are printed on waterproof paper and include neat stuff such as the location of good fishing reefs, which the government charts don't.

Whatever form of chart you select, remember that it will eventually go out of date as sandbars migrate and markers are repositioned. It's a good idea to update your charts regularly, and particularly anytime you head into waters you're not familiar with. Some electronic charts can be updated via the Internet, a major advantage over paper charts.

Electronic chart plotter-GPS units use postage-stamp–size chips to create coverage of vast areas of coastline. The units enable you to see your boat moving across the screen, and to plot your course through use of a cursor, just like on your desktop computer.

(Lowrance Electronics)

International Sailing Supply (320 Cross Street, Punta Gorda, FL 33950, 941-639-7626; www.waterproofcharts.com) is a great source, and their charts are printed on a paper so tough that you can hardly tear it if you try. (Do not say this to a six-year-old stoned on Slurpees, or he will prove you wrong.) The charts are $21.95 for two-siders, which is to say you get two charts for just a bit more than the price of one official government chart. The company also offers collections of charts—you can get 26 charts covering the whole west coast of Florida, for example, for about $50.

You can also get entire regions on CD for viewing in your computer. A typical package covering 300 to 500 miles of coastline goes for around $200, and includes many detailed harbor maps as well as aerial photos of inlets, photos of lights or markers, tide information, marina lists, pre-plotted courses, and lots more. (This same electronic information is available in chips for chart-plotters—we'll take a closer look at them in Chapter 13.)

By the Book

If you go boating in a lot of different areas, you might invest in a book of charts, available from several suppliers. These books offer up to 80 pages of large-scale charts and are super-useful for planning cruises and fishing trips outside your home waters.

They also indicate local boat ramps, compass courses between popular destinations, and mileages. You'll pay $70 to $110 for one of these books, but they're a real bargain if you use a lot of different charts, and the chart books are a more convenient size to use and stow than the loose government charts.

One good source of chart books is MapTech. Their "Embassy Guide" series includes not only marked charts, but also aerial color photos of harbor entries and passes and step-by-step navigation information on entering any waters new to you. They're a great investment at about $60 per cruising area. Learn more at www.maptech.com. The same company offers large CD packages covering, for example, all of Lake Michigan in minute detail, including large-scale charts and photos of all harbors. Prices are around $250 for these interactive charting systems—hook up a miniature GPS receiver via USB and you've turned your laptop computer into a chart plotter.

Whether you buy government or private charts, paper or digital, it's wise to invest in the official "Chart #1" from NOAA, because it's the key to all the markings and symbols on all other charts. It's an education in itself, opening the wealth of information the chart series provides—get it and use it.

It Was Deep Enough Yesterday

The charts show the depth at "mean low water" (MLW), which is the average low tide at the indicated spot.

Note that the average low tide is not necessarily as shallow as it gets in that particular spot. Maximum "spring" tides might subtract several feet of water from the depth, as can strong winds blowing seaward. And areas that might be too shallow for your draft on low water might be fine on high tide. Use the chart in conjunction with the tide tables to be safe. (Many marinas and bait shops offer free weekly tide cards for their local waters, and you can also get them online at many sources, including www. capmel.com.)

By the way, depth-indication or "hydrography," as the chart-makers call it, is not necessarily updated regularly in areas where commercial ocean traffic never travels. Thus, some of the shallow areas that are very attractive to boaters and anglers might display depths that were last ground-truthed—by sending in a boat with a depth finder or sounding lead—50 years ago.

So always take chart depths with a grain of salt, so to speak. This is particularly true around all inlets, where depths can change due to storm waves and currents from day to day, let alone year to year.

> **Look Out!**
>
> Inshore charts usually show depths in feet. Offshore charts often show depths in fathoms. One fathom equals 6 feet. Make sure you know which form is being used in the chart you're depending on to keep you from going aground.

The Color of Water

Charts are printed in color, not to make them pretty as wall-hangings in your beach house (although many wind up that way) but to convey navigational information. Here's what the colors usually mean, both on paper and in pixels—but note that there is some variation on some charts:

- **White:** Water deeper than 3 fathoms (18 feet), safe for navigating most any recreational boat.

- **Light blue:** Water deeper than 1 fathom but not more than 3 fathoms. Still safe for anything but large yachts or keeled sailboats.

- **Medium blue:** Water 1 fathom or less, potentially dangerous for larger recreational boats.

- **Light greenish-tan:** Shoals that sometimes uncover at low tide—good for fishing, bad for boating.

- **Light tan:** Sandbars and oyster bars that go dry at low tide—very dangerous spots if you're not an oyster or a crab. (Also used in Florida for low-lying coastal land currently inhabited by lots of people, but that will be inhabited by fish after the next major hurricane.)

- **Medium tan:** High, dry land, terra firma, where your boat will be if you don't keep a sharp watch on the chart and the horizon.

- **Magenta:** Navigational information—danger zones and markers. Red navigational markers are designated in magenta on the chart.

- **Dark green:** Green navigational markers.

Buoy, Oh Buoy

Navigational aids and buoys are numbered on the charts, just as they are out there in reality. The channel marker numbering system begins at 1 on the most seaward marker of each channel and goes up as you head toward the harbor. In long channels, the numbers might run into three figures by the time you get to port. As you head inland, odd numbers always go on the port side, even numbers on the starboard side.

By comparing the buoy numbers with those on the chart, you can tell exactly where you are in the channel without the help of any electronic navigation device. They're like the street names on a landside map.

Navigation by Degree

Marked along the edges of the chart are the *latitude* lines (on the left and right) and *longitude* lines (on the top and bottom). The intersections of these lines make it possible to give a number coordinate for every point on the earth on both land and sea, and thus anyone in any nation can understand the system.

There's also a scale of miles along the top and/or bottom of the chart, but the scale is in nautical miles (6,080 feet), which are slightly different from the statute miles (5,280 feet) measured by your car's odometer.

Nautical Notes

Why can't a nautical mile be the same thing as a good old U.S. land mile? Because the world's oceans touch nations around the globe, and many of them have different measures for their land miles. The nautical mile is an agreed-upon international distance recognized by everyone for marine navigation worldwide. Here are some numbers you might want to know:

- The earth is divided into 360 degrees of longitude, with the lines running north to south.
- The earth is divided into two halves, east longitude and west longitude.
- The earth is divided into degrees of latitude, with the lines running around the globe east and west.
- Each degree is subdivided into 60 minutes.
- Each minute is subdivided into 60 seconds.
- A nautical mile is 1 minute of latitude.
- A nautical mile is 6,080 feet.
- A nautical mile is 1.15 U.S. statute miles. (And a "knot" is one nautical mile per hour.)
- A statute mile is about 0.87 nautical mile.

So when an old salt tells you his boat will go 40 knots, he will take affront if you tell him your boat is faster because it runs 45 mph. Forty knots × 1.15 is 46 statute mph; therefore, his boat is faster.

Longitude Lines Are Long-Ways

Didn't pay attention when your teacher went over latitude and longitude in ninth-grade science, did you? Okay, me neither—I was checking out Andrea Horowitz's mini-skirt, which is why I had to learn navigation later. Here are the basics, one more time.

Longitude lines (meridians of longitude, the experts say) are imaginary lines running from the north pole to the south pole. The zero longitude line (the Prime Meridian) arbitrarily runs through Greenwich, England. (Guess who made up the system?) From there, meridians or imaginary lines from pole to pole mark off the degrees east or west of the line.

This large-scale harbor chart shows details that would be omitted on a small-scale coastal chart. Note the mileage scale at the bottom and the latitude/longitude indications along the edges.

The International Date Line

Yes, it's true that the International Date Line is a great name for a pickup bar in Switzerland. However, that's not what we're talking about here.

The numbers on longitude lines go up to 180 degrees in each direction. They meet at the International Date Line, which runs through the mid-Pacific.

Traveling west, every 15 degrees of longitude lengthens the day by one hour, while traveling east the same amount shortens the day by one hour, which is why there are different time zones worldwide. Where the zones meet, east of the line is designated as one day earlier than west of the zone. The name for this line is—yep—the International Date Line.

Avoiding Platitudes About Latitudes

Latitude lines begin with zero at the equator and rise as they proceed toward the poles. Those north of the equator are designated north latitude, those south as south latitude.

Latitude lines are spaced 60 nautical miles apart. And one nautical mile is $\frac{1}{60}$ of the distance between latitude lines, designated as a "minute" of latitude.

"X" Marks the Spot

The crossing of latitude and longitude lines provides a precise means of navigation. Particularly now that satellites linked to electronic reading devices can instantly measure the location of any spot on the globe, the latitude/longitude system makes for very precise navigation even in open ocean.

The latitude/longitude numbers correspond to the numbers you see on an electronic machine called a Global Positioning System (GPS), so they show your exact position on the chart.

A Fading Acronym: LORAN

LORAN is the acronym for the Long Range Navigation system in U.S. waters, based on a network of radio towers that send out directional signals over coastal areas.

LORAN lines, which are slightly curved, are shown on many older charts, although LORAN has now virtually been replaced by inexpensive and highly accurate GPS. By reading coordinates from two towers, the LORAN machines provided fairly accurate navigation, usually to within 100 yards.

GPSs, Global Positioning Systems, enable you to pinpoint your location via latitude/longitude information received from satellites. The system works almost worldwide. We'll learn more about its use in Chapter 13.

The Compass Rose

The compass rose is a direction-indicator printed at several locations on most charts. It's used in laying out compass courses. The "rose" is a circle about the diameter of a grapefruit printed on the chart, aligned with true north toward the top. It's printed in a reddish maroon ink, thus the "rose" designation.

The circle is divided into 360 degrees. There's a second circle within the outer circle, also divided into degrees. This inner circle is an indication of magnetic north, which moves around as much as a sitting president's politics, left one day, right the next.

By use of *parallel rules*, you can measure the direction of a course you want to follow from this rose. Line up the course, and then walk the rulers to the nearest rose and run one through its center to get the course.

(Yes, this is a bit like geometry class, which is why electronic chart plotters are becoming so popular. With them, you simply move the cursor to where you want to go, hit enter, and the computer tells you the course. However, you never know when the infernal machine might decide to blow a fuse, so it's best to learn the old skills, too, particularly if you anticipate taking long ocean voyages.)

If you're not going far—say you're in a shallow-draft boat and you're heading toward a large, visible landfall such as a lighthouse—the common method is to look at the compass rose, estimate the direction as, say, north-northeast, and head in that direction. That way, if rain or fog moves in before you get there, you can still hold course via the compass.

For longer voyages in deep-draft vessels or when you need to find a small object such as a navigational buoy, it's standard operating procedure to use the parallel rules and the compass rose to compute an exact course. (This is assuming you do not have a chart-plotter type GPS, which we'll learn lots more about shortly.)

Salt Talk

Parallel rules are two pieces of clear plastic connected by swiveling arms that allow them to be "walked" across a chart while maintaining a measured angle. See Chapter 14 for details.

Variables of Variation

Look closely and you'll note that the inner circle doesn't show exactly the same "North" as the outer circle. Does this mean mapmakers are afraid to make a decision? No. But it does indicate something even more unsettling, which is that the magnetic poles of the earth are in motion! Don't call FEMA on this one. It's been going on for a very long time and nobody is concerned.

The outer circle of numbers on the compass rose indicates true north, the inner circle magnetic north—the north your compass points to. They're not exactly the same in many parts of the globe, because the magnetic centers of the earth are not exactly the geographic centers. The difference between magnetic and geographic north is called *variation*, which we'll look more closely at in Chapter 13.

The difference can be significant in some areas, and particularly for longer voyages it must be included in calculations or you could wind up many miles from your intended destination.

As another example of nature's sense of humor, the variation does not remain constant. It changes a few minutes (sixtieths of a degree) or so each year. It takes a long time for this minor change to be significant, but you don't want to try an open ocean crossing with hundred-year-old charts.

The concern with variation is gradually disappearing due to GPS navigation. But if you're in the middle of that 2,000-mile run to Tahiti and your electronics go out, you'd better know something about variation.

What You Don't Know Can Hurt You: Bottom Conditions

One of the objects of safe skippering is to stay out of areas where the bottom is too close to the top, and charts tell you how to do that with their depth indication.

But there are times when you must enter shallow areas, as when you want to have lunch on the beach, and knowing whether the bottom along the beach is soft sand or hard rock can be critical to the safety of the lower units of both your boat and your passengers.

You also need to know the bottom conditions when you look for a spot to anchor. Soft mud and grass make for tough anchoring, as does smooth rock. Hard sand is the preferred anchorage—it's soft enough for the anchor to dig in, yet firm enough to hold against heavy strain when it does.

How do you find out what's down there, short of donning a mask and fins? Again, you look on the chart:

- "Grs" indicates a grassy area where fishing might be good.
- "Hrd" indicates a sand bottom that's good for anchoring.
- "Rky" is rocky, maybe good for bottom fishing, not good for anchoring.
- "Oys" is a good place to find hors d'oeuvres, but a bad place to run your boat—it marks an oyster bar.

- ◆ "Sft Md" means soft mud—no place to go wading, and not a good place to try anchoring either, because the anchor won't hold.

- ◆ "Obstr" means obstruction—a broken-off channel marker, rock, or other danger—steer clear!

- ◆ "Shoaling" means that currents and waves create unpredictable movement of the bar, and passage is not recommended.

Scale Models

There are scales on fish, scales in bathrooms, and scales of justice, but the scales that concern boaters most are the scales on charts—the ratio of size on the chart to size in reality.

Some small-scale charts show hundreds of miles of coastline and are only suitable for offshore voyagers. The scale on these charts is commonly 1 inch = 550,000 inches. That is to say, 1 inch on the chart equals about 8.7 statute miles.

Inshore charts offer a larger scale, with 1 inch = 94,000 inches common; an inch on the chart is equal to a bit over 1.5 miles. These charts are much more useful for weekend boaters, showing greatly expanded views of the coastline and offering the details needed for navigation.

This inshore chart shows a navigable river running many miles inland from Tampa Bay on Florida's west coast. Note the marker numbers and shapes along the channel.

Harbor charts sometimes go as large as 1 inch = 35,000 inches; an inch on the chart equals only about a half-mile on the water. This will show every little creek and sandbar, so it's the one most useful for inshore boaters and anglers.

If you're looking at a digital chart, you can simply hit the zoom-in or zoom-out button and get any scale you like—another reason electronic navigation is rapidly converting those picturesque old roll-up charts to wall decor.

Measuring Chart Distances

Mileage scales are printed along the bottom of most charts, making it possible to easily measure distance with a set of dividers. A divider is a two-legged device with sharp points on the legs that is designed to let you transfer a measurement from the chart to the mileage scale along the edges or at the bottom of the chart.

Digital Navigation

With a computer and electronic charting software, you can plan your voyages in advance. Numerous companies offer CDs with not only nautical charts but also thousands of coordinates for prime fishing, diving, and gunk-holing. With the computerized systems, you can lay out your course for a day or a week, determine the cruising times required, estimate how much fuel you'll need to make the trip, and even add typed notes on things to watch for, and then print out hard copies to take with you on the boat.

On larger boats with enclosed cabins, you might want to simply take along a portable computer and run the chart software as you need it. Just remember, computers are not happy long if you keep them around salt air and away from air conditioning.

The ultimate chart is one that's coupled with a GPS system and shows you where your boat is in relation to the chart on a real-time basis. These are available as add-ons for portable computers and also built into charting GPS systems, which we'll cover in Chapter 13.

The Least You Need to Know

- Charts are water-going road maps.
- Charts contain depth information based on color and numbers as well as shape of landmasses and shoals.
- Markers shown on charts help to locate your position afloat.
- Choosing the right scale for your type of boating makes a chart much more useful.

Chapter 12

Buoys and Rules of the Marine Road

In This Chapter

- ◆ Reading buoys
- ◆ Using your horn as a signal
- ◆ Passing etiquette
- ◆ Boating after dark

Part of the appeal of boating is that there's a certain freedom you don't feel ashore—fewer people, less traffic, fewer rules. But there are some basic regulations known as the "rules of the road" designed to keep everyone safe, and these are "musts" in your boating education.

You have to learn exactly what these rules mean and react to them properly *every time*, just as you have to react to a stop sign ashore every time, or you can get into serious trouble.

In this chapter, you'll learn what the buoys and markers you see on the water mean, the driving rules that apply when you meet or pass other boats, a bit about sound signals afloat, and some tips for operating safely after sundown.

Where the Buoys Are: Aids to Navigation

Nautical *markers* or *buoys* are the street signs of the sea. They tell you where the safe course lies, directing you around the rocks, shoals, wrecks, and snags that can otherwise spoil your boating life.

In U.S. waters, markers are usually big, stout, permanent fixtures placed by the Coast Guard, although some can be as simple as a stick with a can on top, put there by your Uncle Bill who hit a rock on that spot a few years back. Only the Coast Guard and state marine agencies are authorized to put up markers, but many private citizens do it anyway.

Salt Talk

Markers are generally fixed pilings or tripod towers set into the bottom, and are most commonly used inshore in waters less than 4 fathoms (24 feet) deep. They're also called "day markers," although many are equipped with lights for night navigation. **Buoys** are floating navigational aids and can be used in waters of any depth.

The government markers are dependable, the private ones are suspect. Do you go to the right of the stick, or the left? Only a busted prop will tell.

When I was a guide in a little Gulf Coast town called Homosassa, some of the locals who didn't like the weekend yuppie invasions put out markers directing boaters onto oyster reefs and rock piles! (I always suspected the guy who owned the prop shop had something to do with it, too.)

The government markers have a system or language that offers lots of information to those who understand it. Unfortunately, it's quite a bit different from the rules for driving ashore. Red and green do not mean stop and go at sea. Remember these two basic rules:

- As you return from the sea, red markers go on your right and green markers go on your left.

- As you proceed inland, the red markers on your right will have even numbers and the green markers on your left will have odd numbers.

This is called the *lateral buoyage system* because the marks lie along the side of the safe channel, and it's easiest to remember when you start out by memorizing Red/Right/Returning/Even (RRRE, for you retired military folks), and Green/Port/Odd/Entering (GPOE). Or you can remember it like this: RRR2, GP1E. That is, the red ones start with the numeral 2, the green ones with the numeral 1. After dark, some of the red markers display red lights, and some of the green ones display green lights. But not all day markers have lights, and there's no particular rhyme or reason to which do and which don't. Usually, markers in heavily traveled routes such as the

Intracoastal Waterway (ICW) will all be lighted, but those to local harbors might have only the outside marker lighted, and maybe one or two others at danger points along the route. Always proceed slowly and have the next marker in view via moonglow or spotlight before passing into a channel without lighted marks.

Nautical Notes

The Intracoastal Waterway (ICW) runs from Boston, Massachusetts, to Brownsville, Texas, along the length of the Atlantic and Gulf coasts of the United States. It provides a clearly marked channel with adequate depth to float most private boats, except for deep-keeled sailboats. The waterway often runs inside the barrier islands that are found along most coastlines, providing an all-weather passage as well as thousands of inviting places to visit.

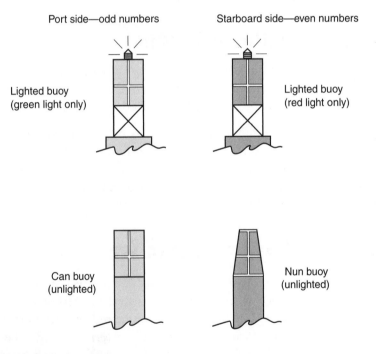

The lateral buoyage system places red, even-numbered, nun-shaped buoys to the right or starboard side of a ship entering a channel and green, odd-numbered, can-shaped buoys to the left or port of an entering vessel.

Shaping a Course

The shape of the markers is also informative. The red buoys are frequently conical on their upper sections, while the green buoys are cylindrical. And on marker posts, the GPOE symbols are square, the RRRE symbols triangular (see the following figure). On a foggy day or after sundown, you can often pick out the shape before the color, so this is a useful thing to know.

Some boaters call buoys with conical tops *nun buoys*, because the outline does look a bit like a nun's hat from a distance. The cylindrical buoys are sometimes called *can buoys*, again for their shape. It's expected that you will know if someone tells you to watch for the can buoy that you are looking for a green or black buoy with an odd number.

Day markers, displayed on pilings, feature green, square-shaped, odd-numbered markers to port; and red, triangular, even-numbered markers to starboard of a boat heading landward.

Port side—odd numbers   Starboard side—even numbers

Look Out!

Slow down when you're operating at night, or in fog or rain. At these times, the markers themselves can become hazards to navigation, and you might collide with them if you don't slow down and keep a sharp eye out. Slowing down also cuts engine noise, allowing you to hear the warning sounds from the bell, whistle, and gong buoys.

Salt Talk

Port is the left side of the boat, as you face forward (it helps to remember that "port" and "left" have the same number of letters), while **starboard** is the right side. These are two basic terms used daily in boating; they help avoid confusion, so learn them.

Sound Decisions

Offshore buoys with lights, bells, gongs, or whistles are usually taller than the nun and can buoys. Their shape is not significant, although their color is.

Why should buoys come with bells and whistles, so to speak? Because when visibility goes to zero, as it sometimes does in fog, rain, or snow, the strange moaning "OOOOAAA" of a whistle buoy can save your boat by telling you where you are.

Heading Out to Sea

The color/number/shape system is seen in reverse order when you head downstream, or from land toward the open sea. Now, the red, even-numbered markers are kept on the left or *port* side, while the green or black, odd-numbered markers are kept on the right or *starboard* side.

With this lesson firmly grasped, you can confidently enter any harbor anywhere in the United States and in most other nations throughout the Western Hemisphere. (Unfortunately, there's a different system in the Eastern Hemisphere, where the colors and routes are almost exactly opposite!)

The same system applies in the Great Lakes and in any rivers that lead to the sea, as nearly all large ones do.

Special Situations

Okay, but what about a channel that heads north and south, when you know that the ocean is to the east? There, a designated landward is used; that is, the government agency placing the markers decides which ways will be considered landward and seaward.

For the Intracoastal Waterway, one of the most-used recreational boat routes in the world, the designated landward course is south along the Atlantic shore, north and then west along the Gulf of Mexico. ICW markers usually have a yellow horizontal band added to the conventional color to indicate that they are not part of the main harbor-marking system.

On the Pacific coast, traveling northward is considered heading toward land. The steep and often rocky shore here offers no protected waterway or inside passage until you get to Puget Sound, however.

Note that the coastal marker system, proceeding clockwise around the U.S. coast, keeps the red markers always on the landward side, making it easier to remember.

Inland Buoyage

The states have agreed among themselves on a system called the Uniform State Waterway Marking System (USWMS). It follows the lateral system discussed earlier, except that it substitutes black for green in the GPOE system, and there is no meaning in the buoy shape—all are cans.

Also in the USWMS system, informational markers indicating rocks, idle zones, swimming areas, or directions to distant lakes or rivers are displayed on white cans or signs with orange borders and symbols and black lettering.

> **CAUTION**
> **Look Out!**
> Range markers are effective only when you're in a specific portion of a channel. Many are built in shallow water, so if you get too close, you could leave the channel and run aground.

Other Navigational Aids

Lighthouses are not likely to be overlooked by anybody—the blinding sweep of their lights can be seen for many miles and can act as an auxiliary compass point anywhere you are within range. You can see the tower by day for miles, too.

Range markers are two markers set one behind the other so that when they are viewed from the safe channel, they appear in perfect alignment, one directly above the other. The rear marker is taller than the front one. If one marker is off to one side, you're not in the center of the channel the towers are indicating (see the following figure). They're sometimes lighted, and for night operation you try to put one light atop the other with your course.

Radio towers and smokestacks also work well as long-distance markers. A tall stack can be seen from 20 miles away by day, and the red- or white-strobe aircraft warning lights on tall structures are visible at long distances after sundown.

Range markers line up perfectly when your boat is in the safe channel but appear to be out of alignment when you are off course.

Range markers as seen when boat is off-course to starboard

Range markers as seen when boat is in channel

By knowing where these fixed structures are in relation to your intended course, you can roughly fix your position even if you have no compass or electronics. The positions of many towers are shown on navigational charts. (A group of tall buildings can also work this way—many a Bahamas crossing has come to a happy end when anglers sight the towers of Miami Beach or Palm Beach beckoning them home!)

Pleased to Meet You: Meeting Situations

When two boats under power meet head to head, the preferred method to avoid collision is to pass port to port (left side to left side) by both boats altering course to starboard, or to the right of the driver.

There are obvious situations in which you can't do this; if there's a marker or rock pile in the way of a starboard turn, for example. In that case, usually the best thing to do is to pull back to dead slow and let the other boat pass through the obstructed area first. If a collision looks like a possibility, sound your horn with five short blasts, signaling danger.

There are two things to remember in this situation:

1. You are supposed to use horn signals to tell the other boat what you are going to do.

2. Very few people do!

The vast majority of recreational boaters simply don't use their horns as signals, except in the same way they use them as signals ashore—to indicate displeasure. However, to be legally correct, you should know the sound signals and use them any time there's danger that an approaching boater might not understand your intentions.

Many skippers use VHF radio (which I'll cover in Chapter 14) to inform other boats of their intentions. This is really a better approach than sound signals because you can convey more information. However, some small boats don't have VHF, and the situation might not allow you enough time to make a connection by radio, so it's important to know and use sound signals.

The correct ways to signal with your horn on inland and coastal waters are as follows:

- **One short blast**   I am turning to starboard and will leave you to my port side.

- **Two short blasts**   I am turning to port and will leave you to my starboard side.

- **Three short blasts**   I am reversing engines.

- **One long blast**   I am getting underway (used when leaving a dock).

- **One long blast followed by one short blast**   Please open the drawbridge.

- **Five short blasts**   Danger—get out of the way, or don't do what your signal says you intend to do.

The other vessel (or the bridge tender) should repeat with his horn what he heard from your horn to confirm. If the other vessel does not repeat your signal, he either didn't hear it or doesn't understand horn signaling. If he does not repeat your signal but issues five short blasts, he is telling you that your intended action is dangerous. In either case, it's prudent to slow to idle and review the situation before proceeding.

Just remember, if you do use horn signals when approaching a small boat, there's a chance the other skipper won't have any idea what these signals mean, so keep a very close eye on the situation and maneuver to avoid the other boat. Or better yet, make contact on your VHF radio and find out his or her intentions.

Making a Pass

You can pass a slower boat moving in the same direction as you are on either side. The horn signals are the same as listed earlier, and they can be just as important in the passing situation as in a head-on meeting because the skipper being passed is unlikely to know you're there until you're right beside him. He or she might make a sharp turn right into your path if you don't signal or make VHF contact.

By marine law, you are not supposed to pass another vessel until he acknowledges your horn signal or responds via VHF. However, in actual practice among small out-board boats in inland waters, this rule is universally ignored. But be aware of it and do your part correctly—if the overtaken skipper doesn't know the rules and doesn't respond to your signals, you'll have to pass with extra caution, being aware that you are responsible for keeping clear should he make an unexpected maneuver.

After you signal and the skipper turns to look at you, go ahead and make the pass smartly, before other traffic comes along or you enter a narrow area where passing will be difficult.

So what if you're the vessel being passed? If you agree passing is safe, return the passing vessel's signal or VHF message and maintain your course and speed. (Accelerating like some drivers do when somebody tries to pass them on the interstate is a no-no!)

Who Has the Right-of-Way?

The "right-of-way" applies in a crossing situation on the water even more emphatically than it does on shore. A boat approaching from your right is supposed to hold its course and speed and pass in front of you; it has the right-of-way (unless you are in a sailboat under sail; see the following section). Your job is to slow down or alter your course so as not to get in the way. A boat approaching from your left is supposed to slow down and/or alter course to let you pass in front of it.

But you might ask "Yes, but how far to the right does this right extend?"

The rule reads that a boat "112.5 degrees or less off the starboard bow" has the right-of-way. So if a boat approaches from 112.6 degrees, you're within the law to assert your rights—but put on your crash helmet first! (Of course, if there's any question as to who has the right-of-way, it's always wiser to defer to the other boat and allow it to pass in front of you.)

Other Situations: Sailboats and Ships

Sailboats under sail and boats powered by oars or paddles usually have the right-of-way over powerboats. Even though they're coming from the left or port, don't cut close in front of them—they have a hard time changing course abruptly, and it's easy for powerboats to do so. It's also common courtesy to slow down when passing small sailboats and rowboats to avoid rocking them with your wake.

And the rules for two sailboats approaching each other under sail vary considerably from those for boats under power.

Boats on the port tack, that is those with the wind coming over the port side, must give way to those on the starboard tack. When two boats under sail have the wind on the same side of the vessel, the boat to windward must give way to the one to leeward. This is because the leeward boat could have its wind blocked, thus reducing its ability to maneuver.

 Look Out! _____

Ship crews do not always maintain a lookout. They often run on autopilot when they're offshore, and if you get in the way, they might run you down without ever knowing you're there. Give them a wide berth. A large ship might take up to 3 miles to come to a complete stop, so even in bays and rivers don't tempt fate by cutting close in front of them—it's like crossing a railroad track on a dare. Even if your motor has never stopped before, it might choose to stop then.

Note that these rules apply only to sailboats under sail; if a sailboat is operating under auxiliary engine power, it must follow the same rules used by powerboats, and a sailboat under power must give way to a sailboat under sail.

The same is true for ships: Never argue with a 1,000-foot oil tanker. (Remember, the ship can't stay afloat outside of marked channels inside shallow bays, and actually have the right-of-way there no matter what the meeting situation. Also, a big ship at speed can't stop for several miles. Stay well clear.)

One signal ship crews do use is the five short blasts that signify danger. Remember that one—it usually means, "Get the heck out of the way if you want to keep breathing."

Other Ship Cautions

Ships are fascinating to watch, but they can be extremely dangerous to recreational boaters who get too close. Here are some basic rules to keep you safe if you boat where the big boys pass nearby:

- Never pull a water-skier across the path of a ship—if he falls, you might not be able to get him out of the way in time.

- Never tow a broken-down boat across the path of a ship—if the line breaks, the towed rig will be in deep doodoo.

- Keep your eyes open for passing ships, even if they're a long way off. Remember that ships put out tremendous waves from both bow and stern. If you're close as they pass at speed, these waves might roll right over your gunnels. Even if you're several miles away, the huge swells a ship produces can send a fast boat airborne. If your passengers don't expect it, they might go up when the boat goes down, and vice versa, with painful results. And when the swells roll onto a shoal or bar, they become breakers that can turn over a canoe or jon boat.

When passing a ship, recreational boaters must stay well clear (at least 100 yards) and observe sound warnings. Since 9/11, strict laws have been passed regarding approaching a military vessel, some bridges, and many government ports.

(Frank Sargeant)

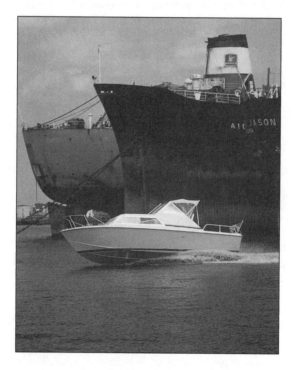

Night Moves: Signals After Sundown

Most recreational boaters don't intend to operate after dark, but sooner or later wind up staying out late and having to do so. Boating at night is pleasant and safe, cooler than in daylight hours, and also less crowded. Provided you keep your eyes open and understand the rules, it can add a whole new dimension to your time on the water.

We've already touched on the use of red and green lights on navigation markers. Some marker lights blink out a little code so that they can be positively identified at a distance. Their code is indicated on the navigation charts for the area. For example, if you are entering a harbor and see a green light give three short flashes, you can be sure that's the outside marker or marker number 1, and not marker number 3, which is identified by three long flashes, and which might be separated from open water by a dangerous sandbar.

Boats also have lights for night operation so that they can be seen by the skippers of approaching boats. In small boats it's common for the forward running light to be a single light on the bow, with a red lens on the port or left side and a green lens on the starboard or right side. On larger boats, there are usually two separate lights: red on the port bow quarter, green on the starboard bow quarter. These lights can only be seen by boats from dead ahead to 112.5 degrees on either side.

The aft light on most open powerboats less than 12 meters (about 40 feet) long is a white light visible from 360 degrees. The most common aft light on cabin vessels and larger recreational boats is a white light visible from 135 degrees astern only.

Boat Bytes _____

If you see a red light and a white light on an approaching boat, it's going to pass port side to. Green plus white, it's going to starboard. Red and green at once, it's headed right at you—change course! (On boats without a masthead light or a 360-degree stern light you will see only the red on boats passing to port, only green on boats passing to starboard, and only red and green as it approaches head-on.)

Boats longer than 12 meters must also carry a masthead light forward of the stern light, and it must be at least 2.5 meters (8.2 feet) above the gunnels. The masthead light is visible only in an arc of 225 degrees ahead of the boat.

Sailboats also display the bow and stern lights described above when underway, and alternatively might display masthead lights that include both the red and green lights visible only from ahead and the white light visible only from astern. Sailboats can also put a red light above a green light on their mast.

All small boats at anchor are supposed to display a single 360-degree white light. This may be the stern light in outboard boats or a masthead light in cabin boats and sailboats. (The "mast" on a powerboat with a cabin is a short staff, usually no more than a yard long, that supports the light.)

A few words to the wise when boating after dark: Red light doesn't wipe out night vision like white light, so it's wise to have instruments lighted dimly in red. And if you must use a white spotlight to find an unlighted marker, avoid looking at the beam—have the light-handler stand well ahead of the skipper if possible.

Be sure you never shine a spotlight directly at the skipper of another vessel underway. You'll temporarily blind him, and there's actually a rule against doing so, making you liable should he run aground or into another boat shortly after.

The Least You Need to Know

- Navigational markers convey information by their color, shape, number, sounds, and lights.

- Horn signals are useful in keeping clear of other boats.

- The "right-of-way" gives boats approaching from starboard the right to pass ahead of you.

- Sailboats, boats powered by oars or paddles, and ships always have the right-of-way over recreational powerboats.

- Boating at night can be safe and pleasant, provided you take the proper precautions.

Tools and Tricks of Navigation

In This Chapter

- ◆ Making sense of the marine compass
- ◆ Calculating variation and deviation
- ◆ Navigating electronically
- ◆ Using GPS, chart plotters, depth finders, and other amazing gadgets

Before you graduate to traveling far enough in your boat that you can no longer see the dock or the launching ramp, you might want to start learning the art of long-range navigation afloat.

Although there's a certain mystery to plotting a course through untracked water far from land, there's also a delight to it, and knowing where you are at all times will quickly build your confidence as a competent boater.

Modern electronic navigation systems are absolutely wonderful, the ultimate navigation tools that can convert anyone into an open-sea navigator in short order. But there will be times with these systems when the batteries go dead, a wire comes loose, or a fuse blows. Whatever can go wrong will go wrong sooner or later on a boat.

In this chapter, you'll learn how to navigate by compass and how to make the adjustments necessary to make this time-tested navigational tool accurate anywhere you boat. We'll also take a look at modern electronics and touch on their basic use, and I'll offer some suggestions on which might be the best value for the type of boating you do.

The Unfailing Compass

Basically, a *compass* is a magnet suspended on a nearly frictionless pivot point. The compass always finds magnetic north, and with that single bit of information you can usually get home, or at least find land, even at night or in a heavy fog.

The compass is always there, right in front of you, always "on," and never breaks. So compass basics are an essential part of the navigator's educational kit.

Note that the *compass card* or magnet itself doesn't move—the compass, attached to the boat, pivots around it. In fact, the boat itself pivots, while that nearly weightless card steadfastly maintains position—it's magic when you visualize what's truly happening.

Salt Talk _____

A **compass** is a magnetic navigational instrument that orients to the magnetic north pole of the earth. A **compass card** is the free-pivoting, circular card that is mounted inside a compass, marked with the points of geographic directions.

The compass card is a disk marked every five degrees into a 360-degree circle, and compass courses are designated by degrees on that circle. If you run due east, you are on a course of 090 degrees; due south, 180; west, 270; and north, 000.

Compass courses are designated by three digits when written on charts, to help emphasize that they are courses and not angles. A course of 1 degree east of north is written "001."

Salt Talk _____

A **lubber line** is a sighting line on the forward part of the compass dome or housing that's aligned with the keel. Thus, when you turn the boat so that the lubber line aligns with the 090 marking on the compass card, you are headed due east.

The compass is usually secured on the console as nearly dead center with the steering wheel as possible and aligned parallel with the boat's keel. A *lubber line*—a dark line that's aligned with the centerline or keel of the boat to make steering easier—is marked on the compass dome.

In compasses, bigger is better. The larger the compass card, the easier it is to read and the more accurately you can follow a course. Larger compasses cost more but are worth the investment in boats that run regularly out of sight of land.

Compasses vary in price from as little as $30 to over $1,000. Larger compasses make it easier to read precise courses than smaller models.

Variable Variation

Compasses point to magnetic north, but meridian lines on a chart are laid out relative to geographic north. The difference between the two is known as *variation*. Variation is a compass error resulting from the fact that magnetic north and geographic north are not identical directions on most parts of the earth.

For short voyages and in some locations, variation is insignificant. For longer journeys and in other spots, particularly in more northern latitudes, it can be very significant.

Variation approaches 20 degrees along the coasts of Maine and Washington, and 10 degrees along the California shore. On a long coastal voyage, that much alteration in the course could put you hundreds of miles off course, run you aground, or get you lost for days.

The error introduced by variation is westerly on the East Coast and easterly on the West Coast. Thus, easterly errors are added to the true course you wish to follow as laid out on a chart, and westerly errors are subtracted.

For example, if you want to follow a course of 45 degrees true—that is, relative to the geographic north pole—along the coast of Maine, you would have to add about 16 degrees, the variation in that area, to the magnetic course shown. It looks like an Algebra II equation, but it's simple addition or subtraction:

$$45T + 16W = 61M$$

In this simple equation, *T* stands for the true course (one accurately measured in relation to the geographic north pole, with corrections

Boat Bytes

Hand-held "fluxgate" or digital compasses operate on built-in batteries and can be moved from boat to boat. They also act as a hand-bearing compass, allowing you to check your navigation by getting the bearing of landmarks ashore and markers at sea. They cost about $150.

made for variation and deviation of the compass), *W* stands for the variation or compass deflection to the west from true north caused by the location of magnetic north, and *M* stands for the magnetic course, or the compass course you would steer to adjust for or "compensate" for the variation.

So to travel 45 degrees true in that area, you'd steer 61 degrees on the compass.

Devious Deviation

As if this were not enough to remember, there's also a second possible compass error called *deviation*. Deviation is compass deflection from magnetic north caused by ferrous (iron or steel) materials or electrical currents aboard your boat.

It doesn't change with location, but it does change with the heading of your boat. Ideally, you want to make deviation as small as possible by keeping all materials that can affect magnets well away from the compass. Wiring should also be kept clear, because it can create a magnetic field in some cases.

Deviation is determined by "swinging ship," taking bearings on a known course line to a distant marker as the boat is rotated in place, and writing down any deflection at a number of headings.

It's not something normally done by weekend boaters, but you should at least be aware that this is where deviation tables come from. If your compass deviates more than a few degrees, it's best to have it compensated or adjusted by a pro at a good marina.

However, most marine compasses can be compensated for moderate deviation errors by adjustment screws that move tiny internal magnets nearer or farther from the card.

Putting It All Together: Can Dead Men Vote Twice?

The entire equation for canceling out compass errors for variation and deviation can be remembered via the nautical question "Can Dead Men Vote Twice?": *CDMVT*.

- ◆ *C* stands for the compass course.
- ◆ *D* stands for the deviation.
- ◆ *M* stands for the magnetic course.
- ◆ *V* stands for the variation.
- ◆ *T* stands for the true course.

So if you have a true course written on a chart and want to know what compass course to steer, you add or subtract the variation, which gives you the magnetic course, and then add or subtract the deviation, which gives you the compass course:

$$C + D = M + V = T$$

In this case, the rule is to add easterly errors and subtract westerly errors. If you know the compass course to a landmark ahead and want to know the true bearing, you work the equation the other way: Add or subtract the deviation to get magnetic course, and then add or subtract the variation to get true course (which is useful in plotting your exact position on a chart):

$$T + V = M + D = C$$

In this equation, you subtract easterly errors and add westerly errors.

Electronic Navigation

Now that you've seen this much about compass navigation, you probably want to forget all about it.

Fortunately you can, most of the time. Modern electronic navigation gear takes care of all the calculations for you and puts you exactly where you want to be every time—as long as it doesn't break.

Although electronic navigation is as good as it gets, it's always wise to have a backup if your primary set goes down and a compass in case all else fails.

LORAN Waves Good-Bye

Long Range Navigation Systems (LORAN) are on their way out, but you'll still see a few used by older offshore anglers.

The reason is that all these folks have their bottom-fishing spots located with LORAN numbers, and LORAN has proven itself strong in the "repeatability" department—that is, it returns your boat to almost the same exact position time after time for a given set of numbers.

However, these days, GPS or Global Positioning Systems are the universal choice because they're more accurate than LORAN. And GPS units have become incredibly cheap, with some handheld units selling for barely $100.

GPS: The Ultimate Navigator

GPS units can locate any point on the globe to within a few meters. The systems pick up satellite signals to work their magic, and unlike LORAN, they do not have to be in range of a shore-based transmitter to work.

Global Positioning Systems with chart plotters can be dash-mounted units, like this one, or portable units. The dash-mounted models rely on a separate antenna about the size of a hockey puck, which can be mounted anywhere with a clear view of the sky.

(Lowrance Electronics)

Global Positioning Systems also work on the tiniest lakes hundreds of miles from the nearest coastal navigation systems. In fact, they work on land, as well, and are now a much-envied option in luxury cars—the landside models include street names and even voiced instructions to your next turn.

GPS receivers rely on a fleet of U.S. military satellites circling the globe to provide precise navigation anywhere on earth. Modern units are typically accurate to within 10 feet, sometimes as close as 3 feet. And the units also provide speed readings to a tenth of a mile-per-hour, which can be a benefit to those trying to troll at an exact speed for gamefish, as well as for sailors trying to squeeze the last bit of speed out of their boat. They can also automatically calculate your arrival time at a distant marina or buoy.

Boat Bytes _____

Do you really need electronic navigation gear? If you do your boating on small inland lakes and rivers, you'll probably never miss it, although it could be a help in finding your favorite offshore fishing spots at times. On the other hand, if you operate on the Great Lakes or the coasts, out of sight of land, electronic positioning equipment is a must. It's by far the most reliable and easiest way of keeping track of where you are.

Basic Global Positioning Systems are becoming more affordable each year, and some are now available in console versions for around $200. Unlike radios, portable or handheld GPS units are just as useful as fixed units and just as accurate. They burn batteries rapidly, but converters allow you to hook them to the boat batteries. Some cost as little as $100, or less than a tenth of what the first units to hit the civilian market went for!

Do-It-All Chart Plotters

The ultimate inshore navigational tool is a chart plotter with a built-in GPS. On the screen, you zoom in on a navigational chart of the area you're cruising, usually via postage-stamp–sized chart cards that insert into the machine.

The GPS then positions your boat on the chart, and you can see your progress as it tracks your course. Even the buoys and other navigational aids are shown, and you can track your boat on-screen as it zooms past Marker 1 and heads for home.

Recent models enable you to simply place a cursor on a distant location, click a couple of buttons, and the machine plots a course to that location.

You can insert as many *waypoints*, locations along the way where you might want to check your navigation or simply stop for a picnic, as you like. You can even get a graphic tide chart of the area as part of the display.

The machines can also lay down electronic tracks, sort of like a trail of breadcrumbs, that enable you to travel through tricky shallows by day, and then follow your reverse course after dark or in bad weather with complete confidence.

Some GPS units now provide interfaces for your computer, allowing you to plot out a longer voyage on your desktop or laptop, then transfer that routing into your GPS for use aboard. And you can electronically save any routes you run while out on the water back into the computer when you return home. It's handy for saving those secret fishing spots, too.

Simpler, handheld chart plotter/GPS units have fewer bells and whistles, but many of them also offer charts on-screen. Battery life can be a problem for some, but all offer 12-volt battery hook-ups.

Boat Bytes

On a "cold start" of a new GPS or one that has been moved to a new location many miles from its home port, it can take up to 5 minutes for the machine to lock on to the satellites passing overhead and locate itself again. The display will blink to warn you not to try navigating until the system locks in.

GPS units look a bit intimidating because of all the buttons, on-screen menus, and numbers, particularly if you're not into computers. But, in fact, anyone can learn to operate most within about 30 minutes. (Most companies offer videos for those who need a bit of extra help.)

Handheld GPS units are compact, lightweight, and accurate, and they can be carried from boat to boat. Charting models like this one can even be used on shore to navigate your car.

(Lowrance Electronics)

Basically you just turn them on, let them lock on to the nearest satellites, and then punch in latitude/longitude numbers to tell the machine where you want to go.

If you already have waypoints saved in the machine, you can simply hit the "Go To" button and punch the number of the waypoint you want to seek.

Or you can move the electronic cursor to the spot you want to visit and tell the machine to take you there. (It will go straight to the mark, though, with no concern that there might be a rock or an island between you and your target, so you might want to plot this sort of trip in a series of steps.

However you select your destination, the unit guides you there, suggesting you steer right or left if you wander off course due to inattention or the effect of the wind or currents. When you approach your destination, it sounds an alarm so you don't over-shoot. And throughout the run, it gives constant updates on your exact speed, course made good, distance to go, time to go, and course to the destination.

Given the remarkably low price of the handheld models these days, there's no reason for any recreational boat not to have one tucked in the glove box.

Navigating in Depth: Depth Finders

Depth finders, basically recreational sonar units, are commonly called "fish finders" by anglers, and they do work well for locating fish and bait. But they're also very important navigational tools for all boaters. The readout can be an LCD screen, a rotating dial, or simply digital numerals; each type of unit basically measures depth.

Depth finders give you underwater "eyes" to evade shallows and avoid running aground by following deeper, safer channels. In low visibility, it's possible to find your way home following the depth contours as listed on a large-scale nautical chart; you compare the depth contours on the chart to the depths shown by your machine, and this can give you a pretty good idea of where you are, even if you have no GPS and there are no markers in sight.

Sonar systems send out a pulse of sound, measure the time it takes the echo to return and the intensity of the echo, and convert these signals to visual data.

Most inexpensive depth finders have liquid crystal display (LCD) screens, which draw a mono-color chart of the bottom on what looks like the screen of a portable computer.

You can also view the depths in color. Cathode Ray Tubes (CRTs) are not space guns but color depth finders. They function much like a small television set and are about as big—the box on these machines is three to six times larger than a typical LCD. In the past, that size factor kept them out of most small recreational boats as did the price, from $1,000 and up.

Fortunately, recent tech advances now provide LCD color depth finders/GPS units that are much smaller than CRTs. In fact, they're about the size of black-and-white LCD machines but with far more features. They're still fairly costly; prices start at around $800, but if you're serious about bottom fishing, you'll want one. Or opt for a combination depth finder/GPS/chart plotter, all in one box. Prices begin at around $1,200 for black-and-white units, and around $1,900 for color.

> ### Nautical Notes
>
> Digital depth finders show the depth in numbers only via an in-dash display smaller than a hockey puck. They're moderately priced, starting at under $100, and take up no space on the dash. If you're not a serious angler, a digital might be all the depth finder you need.

> ### Boat Bytes
>
> Most depth finders have a depth alarm function that allows you to preset a "safe depth," typically a foot or more deeper than the draft of your boat. That way, if you ever wander into water that's dangerously shallow, the alarm warns you, hopefully before you run aground.

Radar Shows It All

Radar is rarely seen on smaller recreational boats because of its high cost ($1,500–$3,000), but on larger boats used regularly offshore and in inclement weather, it's a basic part of the navigational tool kit. Radar is similar to sonar, but it operates above the surface and sends out radio waves rather than sound pulses to measure distance.

Radar can draw the shape of a coastline, show the presence of other boats ahead, and measure both distance and bearing to anything appearing on the screen. It's a great asset, particularly at night or in low visibility.

The Least You Need to Know

- The compass is the most basic but most dependable of navigational tools.

- Compass courses should be corrected for variation and deviation in many areas for longer voyages.

- Electronic navigation systems offer a wide variety of features and prices. Review the way you'll actually use your system aboard and select those that provide the most bang for your buck.

Chapter

14

Nautical Radio Gear and Procedures and Your First Longer Cruise

In This Chapter

- ◆ Using marine communications and other electronic gear
- ◆ Planning a voyage
- ◆ Creating the skipper's checklist
- ◆ Figuring your position without the use of electronics

If you've read the rest of Part 3 you're almost ready to try a limited off-shore cruise, a longer cruise on inland waters, or maybe a trip from one river port to another.

In this chapter, you'll learn about the marine communications systems important on offshore trips, how to plan the longer voyage, how to take care of the important details on the morning of your trip, and a bit about the art and science of dead reckoning or figuring your position without the use of electronics.

Marine Communications

There are a few more items you'll want in your cockpit before you watch that thin blue horizon that marks land disappear behind you for the first time—or even before you cruise down your local river.

The most important electronic doodad to carry aboard is some sort of communications device. It's a handy way to find where the fish are biting or which beach the sundown rendezvous is planned for. It's also useful when you want to talk with the harbormaster in a new port to learn which slip he wants you in, and even to call the waterfront restaurant and reserve a corner table.

And if things ever go really bad—sinking boat, life-threatening injury, heart attack—you need dependable contact with the world ashore, pronto.

Reach Out and Touch Somebody: Cell Phones

For lakes and inshore areas, you can't beat a cellular phone. It's immediate, easy to use, dependable, and something that most families already own. Just be sure to put the phone in a waterproof container, and keep the battery charged—a connector to the 12-volt system is a great plus. However, most cell phones won't work when they get too far from the nearest tower—many won't function more than 5 miles offshore.

Anglers like the cell phone because it doesn't broadcast information on where the fish are biting—they can share secret spots with their pals and not find a fleet bearing down on them. On the other hand, in an emergency the "party line" aspect of an open radio channel can sometimes bring help from another nearby boater.

Nautical Notes

You can sometimes increase cell phone range by taking the phone up on the bridge of a flybridge boat. The higher position gives a better chance for the antenna to pick up signals from towers ashore. Touching the antenna of a cell phone to a steel outrigger can also increase range at times. There are also aftermarket "cell phone range boosters" available, although quality (and possibly legality) might vary.

Satellite Phones: World Rangers

Satellite phones like Iridium have the same sort of world-wide coverage as GPS, and for those who regularly travel far offshore, they're a huge safety net. Prices are high, at $1,300 to $1,500, plus about $2 a minute talk time, but when you really, really need help, they're worth whatever they cost. Many can be set up to receive e-mails, too, making them doubly useful.

VHF: Everyman's Radio

VHF stands for Very High Frequency, the most useful of marine radio communications gear.

VHF works where cell phones won't, many miles at sea, enabling you to reach out and touch nearby boats or passing ships even if you don't have their telephone numbers. And you can call as often as you like, at no charge whatsoever!

Most people monitor a single channel, channel 16, so any time you need to make contact, you can simply broadcast a hailing call and all nearby boats will hear it. The Coast Guard and many marinas also monitor channel 16, so that's where you go if you ever need to broadcast the dreaded MAYDAY call. (Channel 9 is also used as a hailing channel, but it's not monitored by the Coast Guard.)

Channel 16 was the hailing channel for many years, and most boaters still use it that way, but it is now supposed to be used only for emergency hailing. Channel 9 is now the hailing channel for recreational boating. Use it for initial contact, and then jump to a "working" channel, typically 68, 69, 71, 72, and 78. For details, visit http://wireless.fcc.gov/marine/vhfchanl.html.

Boat Bytes

On small fishing boats, the tall antenna of a VHF gets in the way of the backcast. On these rigs, it's better to opt for a low-profile "whip" style antenna that's only 3 feet long, yet rated for 6 dB. It won't match a full-size antenna over a long reach, but it's adequate most of the time and a lot less likely to snag your lures.

VHF radios cost $160 to $300. It's a good idea to buy waterproof models for small, open boats. The system requires an antenna about six to eight feet long for good performance, another $75 to $100 or more.

Even with a good antenna properly mounted, the range is limited to about 25 miles max. But along the coasts of the United States, it's rare to be more than 25 miles from another VHF-equipped boat, so you can usually reach someone when you need to.

VHF radios are small—about half the size of a fax machine—and fit easily inside even the smaller consoles on open boats. They're built to withstand the rigors of life afloat. Some are completely sealed and will operate totally submerged. (Unfortunately, *you* won't—so call for help early if you have problems.)

Boat Bytes

The factors that most affect VHF transmission are the "gain," or amplifying ability of the antenna, and its height. A 6-dB gain model or higher is needed for good range (provided the antenna remains approximately vertical). And an antenna atop a flying bridge or on a sailboat mast can reach out miles farther than one on a center console. However, for best performance from a sailboat frequently at a high angle of heel, a lower-gain antenna is preferable, because it doesn't concentrate the signal into such a narrow horizontal disc.

This well-equipped console includes two VHF radios (right), one flush-mounted into the dash. Particularly for offshore operation, a backup is wise.

(Frank Sargeant)

In the Palm of Your Hand: Handheld VHFs

Handheld VHFs are not a whole lot bigger than a cell phone. They have built-in batteries and can be carried with you from boat to boat. They're great in small boats that have no permanent radio system. They're not significantly cheaper than console units, with prices ranging from $100 to about $200.

However, they put out only 5 watts, versus the 25 watts of a fixed system, and the antennas are only about 6 inches long, so the range is limited to about 5 miles. Also, they can't be left on continuously because their batteries soon run down, so they're not the best "first" radio for your boat. However, most have rechargeable batteries—just plug them into a charger attached to an AC outlet, and they're back to full power overnight.

Rechargeable batteries in handheld VHF radios tend to lose a lot of reliability as they age, especially battery types that have a "memory" and must be fully depleted before being fully recharged. Rechargeables also have poor shelf life when away from the charger. For these reasons, many boaters who don't have an onboard charging system for their VHF have a strong preference for disposable batteries instead of rechargeable. That way, all you have to do is carry a spare set of alkalines, and you'll always have radio power in an emergency.

Also keep in mind that VHF radios use very little power on receive, so you can listen all day and hardly make a dent in the battery condition. But transmitting gobbles up the electrons very quickly.

> **Boat Bytes**
>
> Want to talk over your handheld all day long? Buy an optional 12-volt accessory hookup with a cigarette-lighter plug, so you can tap into your boat's power system. As long as the main battery is charged, your VHF will be ready to go.

The Lingo of VHF

There's a routine format for speaking on the VHF, primarily because you can't both talk at once as on a telephone. You can only transmit when you key your microphone (push the button on the side of the part you hold in your hand), and you can't hear any incoming message while your mike is keyed. So radio conversations are a sort of dance, a timed pattern of communications that keeps everybody from getting stepped on.

You no longer need to register or license a VHF radio used in U.S. waters. There are some requirements for radios used internationally; check with the FCC for details (1-888-225-5322; www.fcc.gov).

Standard operating procedure is to always begin your hail with the name of the vessel you're trying to contact. Identify your vessel secondly, so a typical conversation with your buddy aboard the nearby "Done Rovin'" might go like this:

> **Nautical Notes**
>
> You don't have to keep your radio turned on at all times, but if you do have it on, you're supposed to monitor channel 16. If you try repeatedly to call another boat and get no response, his or her radio is probably off.

> "Done Rovin', Done Rovin', Done Rovin', this is the Busted Flush, come back."

Or for a sailboat it might be:

> "Race Committee, Race Committee, Race Committee, this is Twilight Zone. Over."

You repeat the name of the boat or place (if you're calling the marina) you're trying to reach three times to make sure they hear you. The "come back" is the sign you're done speaking for the moment and will listen for the reply. (Some people say "over.")

If you get no response after 30 seconds or so, repeat the hailing call. If the other boat hears you, the reply is likely to be:

> "Busted Flush, this is the Done Rovin', come back."

Now you know you're connected, so it's time to get off the hailing channel to a working channel where you won't interfere with other people trying to reach each other:

> "Charlie, let's go to 72, come back."

> "Roger, going to 72, over."

You both now switch your channel selectors to 72 and get on with your conversation. At the end of the communication, it's normal to identify your boat name again and indicate you're finished by saying "out."

Weather Stations, Too

VHF has the added advantage of including several weather channels that give immediate and continuous access to National Weather Service radio forecasts (see Chapter 15). You simply press the "WX" button to get the continuous reports.

You can also use the VHF to make phone calls to people ashore by going to channels 24 through 28 or 84 through 87 and contacting a marine operator. This is fairly pricey, so don't chit-chat—reserve it for urgent information.

SSB for Maximum Range

Single sideband radio, or SSB, has far greater range than VHF, in part due to an output of up to 150 watts, six times the maximum VHF output. They're usually hooked to monster antennas more than 20 feet long. The long range of SSB is not because of the big antenna, but because the longer wavelengths are refracted around the curvature of the earth more easily. SSB is a kind of "shortwave" radio, but the wavelength is really much longer than VHF. The longer antenna is required to transmit the longer waves.

The range is awesome, but unfortunately so is the price—a set, with antenna, goes for $1,000 and up. The cost is prohibitive for weekenders, but those who move up to Caribbean crossings and the like might want to make the investment.

Doing Your Pre-Cruise Homework

After you understand the basics of charts, markers, navigational tools, and marine communications, you're ready for your first long cruise. Long is relative—we're not talking weeks or even days here. Navigating to anywhere you can't see from the boat ramp is a good first effort.

Step one is to get the appropriate chart before your trip and study your route, from the put-in point to the destination and back.

Look for areas that might cause problems— doglegs or S-curves in a channel, unmarked oyster bars close to your route, or inlets that might be rough if wind and tide oppose each other.

If you're in a coastal area, you should check the newspapers or a tide chart for the times of high and low tide or any special currents on the day of your cruise—you'll need to know them if you cross shallow areas. (Currents and tidal flows are particularly important to boats operating under sail; a strong opposing flow can bring your headway to a stop, despite a favorable wind. Currents tend to be strongest around passes, inlets, and narrow channels between bays.)

> **Boat Bytes**
>
> You don't have to go through the chart study after you've traveled an area a few times—you'll quickly become familiar with the local navigational aids and landmarks, know the compass routes by heart, and have the secret grouper holes and diving reefs programmed into your GPS. It's only on the first visits that the chart work is critical.

If you'll be making a run beyond the marked channels, you'll want to pencil in your courses, using the parallel rules to make them neat and to get the compass courses from the compass rose (see Chapter 11). Indicate the distance in miles by measuring with the two-legged dividers and transferring that measurement to the distance scale on the chart. Write both course and distance along each leg of the trip. Always use a soft pencil to mark your courses on a chart, so that you can erase the marks when they're no longer needed. Permanent markings may be used for fixed locations, such as the latitude/longitude numbers of a fishing reef, but if you mark your courses in ink, the chart will soon have so many tracks on it that it will become illegible.

You'll usually have several waypoints along the way, fixed objects such as offshore buoys where you can check your route. Or you might have to lay out your course in legs to avoid shallows or other obstructions. If you have a GPS, your waypoints will be electronic. And if you have a chart-plotting GPS, it will pretty well take care of the navigation for you—provided it does not have one of those "blue screen" moments we have all become familiar with in the computer age.

Straight-line courses between waypoints allow you to stay aware of exactly where you are, so an extended route along a coastline sometimes looks like a connect-the-dots puzzle when it's completed on a chart or electronic screen.

If you're more casual about your route, you might someday look around and discover you don't realize whether that distant marker is the one for your destination or for another harbor 10 miles up the coast—it's amazingly easy to lose track when you're out of sight of land, and sometimes even when you're near shore in unfamiliar waters.

If you get serious about navigation (and you'd better before you make any long voyages), you can preprogram these waypoints into your GPS during the week before the cruise, either by punching them in directly or perhaps downloading from a navigation program on your desktop or laptop PC. Then, when you're ready to leave the docks, you simply turn on the machine and go for it.

Cruising Day

On the day of the planned cruise, the skipper should get up early and check the weather. Sources include Internet weather stations, The Weather Channel on television, and the WX station on the boat's VHF. If the weather is iffy, it might be best to let everybody sleep in and wait until another day.

It's important to drop off a "float plan" (see Chapter 18) with someone ashore, so that people will come looking if you don't return as planned. Run a quick check of all gear. Make sure the boat is gassed up, the sandwiches made, the coolers full of ice and drinks, the PFDs aboard, and the charts and navigational tools handy. Only then should you head for the dock.

Finding a protected and private beach you can access safely might take a bit of chart study and a careful watch on the depth finder, but it's time well spent.

(Chris Craft Boats)

At the ramp or dock, check the chart or your chart plotter, note the shape and direction of the channel, and look out across the water to locate the markers that correspond to the route as shown on the chart.

Follow the markers to open water (red ones go on the left or port as you head out to sea, remember) and from marker 1 you punch in your first GPS waypoint toward your destination, or take a compass course in that direction. You're on your way!

Most cruises are straightforward and without problems if you've done your homework. You'll want to keep an eye out for landmarks as you travel—points of land, radio towers, and tall buildings—noting them on the chart as you pass so that you confirm what your GPS is telling you.

 Boat Bytes _____

To steer a compass course, don't look at the compass. At least, don't look at it continuously. Get the boat headed in the right direction and the compass stabilized, and then look into the distance ahead of the boat and pick out a landmark—or a cloud in open ocean—and steer for that. If you try to steer by watching the compass, you'll create a crazed "snake-wake" as you chase the oscillations of the compass card with the waves.

It's also prudent to turn on your depth finder the minute you leave the dock and leave it on until you return. Keep an eye on it—any time there's a steady shallowing trend, you might want to slow down and check what's ahead according to the chart and your position.

The Color of Water

In many areas, a seasoned skipper can measure water depth simply by looking at its color. To be sure, in the muddy waters of the Mississippi River, not even a catfish can navigate by eye, but in the clear waters of the upper Great Lakes and in most coastal areas, navigation by water color is a useful and accurate art, and one you'll no doubt want to employ on any cruise you take.

Water captures most colors of sunlight but reflects blue, so the deeper the water, the bluer it looks. Extremely clear water like that in Lake Superior offers only shades of blue, while water with a bit of sand in it, like that along much of the coast of Florida, might look pale green in depths to 40 feet.

In most areas, the lighter the shade of water, the shallower it is. Thus, pale blue, pale green, or whitish water might be anywhere from a couple feet to only inches deep.

Moderate blues and greens are probably anywhere from 4 to 40 feet deep, and deep blues and greens are usually deeper than 40 feet. The green water fades to blue as you move farther offshore and escape the stirred-up sand.

The deepest ocean waters are an indigo to violet shade that is spectacularly beautiful on a sunny, calm day. (The colors on the back of a marlin or a sailfish mimic this magical color.)

There is also a catalog of colors in inshore waters. Here are the most common:

- Dark-green spots surrounded by light-green spots: patches of grass or rock on sand bottom.

- Broad, dark-green to gray areas in water that you know is fairly shallow: sea grass, often prime fishing waters.

- Brownish spots: oyster bars or rocks dangerously near the surface.

- Dark blue or emerald through an otherwise pale-green flat: a deep channel, good for boating (also good for finding spiny lobster to grill for dinner).

In general, dark-green water is deeper than light-green water, and water shading toward white is water too shallow for your boat. A pair of polarized sunglasses is a great help in noting color changes.

(Frank Sargeant)

Understanding water colors will serve you well, even when you're just buzzing out to wet a line before sundown. And in many areas with extensive shallows, such as the Florida Keys and the Bahamas, it's essential for safe navigation.

In general, that's about all there is to it. Ninety-nine trips out of 100, you'll have a completely enjoyable trip without the slightest glitch, particularly after you get the first voyage or two behind you. However, there's always that hundredth trip—so it's best to do your homework before setting out.

Murphy's Boating Rules

It is true that, occasionally, whatever can go wrong will go wrong. In fact, on my boat, it's true that sometimes things that *can't* possibly go wrong go wrong. You have to expect a few problems now and then.

Suppose you're motoring happily along toward your third waypoint, a sea buoy over the horizon off the coast of Maine, when suddenly the GPS goes blank.

Now what?

If it's a long run and your target is small and in danger of being missed, stop the boat and break out the chart; otherwise, you might wind up out on St. Georges Bank eating raw cod. Without the sweet rice and seaweed, you won't like it.

You can figure about how far along the leg you were when the electronics went kaput using an ancient art known as "dead reckoning."

Dead Reckoning Is Alive and Well

Dead reckoning is the art of estimating position by calculating course, speed, and time, without the aid of electronics.

It's not as accurate or as simple as turning on the GPS chart plotter, to be sure, but it's a backup for when everything breaks, and it will usually get you within sight of the marker or the harbor you're looking for.

On a long cruise, particularly when you're traveling at night, it's standard procedure to track your course on the chart via dead reckoning to make sure your electronics have not gone bonkers. And if you don't have a GPS, you can use dead reckoning to calculate about how long it will take you to get from point A to point B.

The basics are the relationships of distance (D), time (T), and speed (S) you learned in elementary school:

Distance = Speed × Time

Speed = Distance ÷ Time

Time = Distance ÷ Speed

So, for example, if you are traveling 30 mph for two hours, you can easily calculate distance covered thus:

D = 2 × 30 = 60 miles

> **Nautical Notes**
>
> It's not called "dead" reckoning because you'll be dead if you don't do it right. The term comes from "deduced" reckoning, meaning that you must deduce your position from indirect information.

To calculate using minutes, the equations look like this:

$$D = S(T) \div 60$$

$$S = 60D \div T$$

$$T = 60D \div S$$

Maybe you're going from your marina to another at the other end of a big lake and you want to know if you'll arrive in time for lunch. The distance is 40 miles and your boat does 15 mph.

$$T = 60 (40) \div 15 = 160 \text{ minutes} = 2 \text{ hours, } 40 \text{ minutes}$$

It takes a bit of doodling to keep track of your location with a pencil rather than electronic memory bytes, but after a few trips it becomes second nature, and one more interesting skill you can use as skipper.

Vectoring In

If there were no winds or currents, boats could simply head straight for their destination, like a car traveling down a road, and wind up where the skipper wanted to go.

But boats are greatly affected by both winds and currents, and the slower the boat, the greater the effects.

Boat Bytes _____

In crossing the Florida Current between the Bahamas and Florida (commonly but inaccurately known as the Gulf Stream), it's common for slower boats to be offset by many miles due to the northward push of the ocean current measuring 2.5 to 4 knots. Sailboats and trawlers out of Miami's Government Cut must steer southeast to arrive at Bimini, which is almost due east. The difference for a 5-knot boat can be over 30 degrees!

If you never venture offshore, the offset of wind and current is less important, but not completely irrelevant. When you're heading for a distant shoreline in a low-speed boat such as a pontoon rig, and facing heavy side winds, you might have to steer far above or below your target to travel directly toward it.

The same is true with strong river currents—set the boat at an angle into the current, pointing upstream of your intended landing point, to get to the spot you want to reach. Those trying to get boats back on trailers at river ramps soon learn this tactic.

There's a bit of science to figuring the appropriate vectors for long ocean crossings. The process is more than the beginning boater might want to wade through, but for those who go on to the blue horizons, the current edition of *Chapman's Piloting* (Hearst Marine Books, 2002) has an excellent chapter on how it's done.

The Least You Need to Know

- Every prudent skipper carries some type of communications device, enabling access to emergency services ashore.

- It's wise to plan any extended voyage well in advance, and to study the route both before you leave and while you're underway.

- Keep track of your position when you cruise, both electronically and via the art of dead reckoning. Someday, you'll be glad you did.

Part 4

Nature's Triple Play: Wind, Weather, and Tides

Boaters soon learn that the weather is both their best friend and their worst enemy. This part tells you what to expect, based both on listening to the professionals and on listening to nature's clues (sometimes they're more reliable!).

And if you're a coastal boater, you'll definitely want to give some attention to Chapter 16 on tides. Their ups and downs and ins and outs are both fascinating and challenging, and affect everything from safe navigation to properly tying a boat to a dock.

Weather You Like It or Not

In This Chapter

- Becoming your own weatherperson
- Understanding how winds and waves affect you as a boater
- Interpreting clouds
- Handling squalls, lightning, and other dangerous conditions

You quickly learn to become adept at reading the weather when you spend much time afloat, particularly after the first few times you get caught out in a howling thunderstorm when the TV forecaster promised a calm, sunny day.

Conditions change rapidly on the water, and those white, puffy clouds that look so welcoming when you leave the dock can quickly build into towering black thunderstorms during the time you're taking a nap to the gentle slap of the waves against the hull.

This doesn't mean you have to learn millibars and isobars and the names of all the types of clouds (another item to which we all should have paid better attention in ninth-grade science), but there is a lot of practical weather lore that will help you avoid sticky situations wherever you boat.

In this chapter, you'll learn how to become your own weather forecaster. I'll also tell you how winds affect waves so that you'll know when your favorite waters are likely to be too rough for enjoyable boating. And we'll cover how to deal with dangerous elements such as lightning.

Forecasts: Don't Leave Home Without Them

The favorite source of weather information for most boaters at home has become television's The Weather Channel. It runs 24 hours a day and offers not only the national weather picture repeatedly, preparing you for major, wide-scale changes, but also the local weather, including radar, every 10 minutes.

The radar view is particularly useful—any bad weather likely to be in your area within a few hours will appear on the screen. If you've got cable or satellite TV, you won't want to miss checking the data. (Regular news programs' weather forecasts are just as useful, but often aren't on when you need them.)

Newspaper weather information gives a broad view of what might be headed your way, but the information is likely to be at least 24 hours old by the time it gets printed and delivered.

Boat Bytes

For those with Internet access, check out the weather information on your local newspaper and TV station sites. This information is updated regularly and often includes live-action radar. Also see www.weather.com, www.accuweather.com, and www.intellicast.com on the Internet.

The U.S. Weather Service also maintains offices in many coastal areas with telephone-available recorded weather information, updated regularly. Check your local directories for the number.

When you're at the boat, NOAA Radio offers continuous weather broadcasts that can be picked up on any VHF radio, and these are keyed to the mariner, which The Weather Channel forecast is not. You get data on sea conditions both inshore and off, currents, and so on—all for your localized area of the coast. Press WX-1, WX-2, or WX-3 on your VHF to hear the continuous broadcasts, which are updated several times a day.

The Highs and Lows of Air Pressure

Air pressure as measured by a barometer is a useful indicator of likely weather in your immediate area. A barometer going south in a big hurry indicates a major blow, maybe even a hurricane, as a major low-pressure system approaches. However, it's also true that a rising barometer can foretell strong winds, even though there's unlikely to be rain and lightning attached.

Here's how it works: Unequal heating of the earth between the poles and the equator causes north-south airflows, which are twisted into east-west flows by the rotation of the planet. As they're twisted, they form whirling masses of air that contain pressures that are either higher or lower than the average weight of calm air—weather highs and lows.

Some barometers have "rain" marked on the readings below 29.00 inches, "fair" marked on those above 30.50. But in fact, both rising and falling barometers can mean wind or bad weather. Rapid change is the determining factor, because an abrupt change from high pressure to low pressure or vice versa is sure to create a rapid air-flow and lots of wave action with it.

A Feel for Nasty Weather

Although there's a lot of weather lore that just ain't so, there's also a body of "weather sense" that you should not ignore among those who make their living on the water. When a grizzled fishing guide or commercial fisherman looks at the morning sky and advises you to stay at the docks despite a rosy forecast on the morning news, listen to the locals. You, your crew, and your boat will thank you.

The idea that lightning never strikes twice in one place, for example, has repeatedly been proven incorrect. And although the "fish may bite least when the wind's in the east," an east wind does not always foretell a coming storm. The winds blow toward lows approaching from the west, true enough, but whirling storms can also blow from the east after a low passes.

Some skippers can "feel" rain in the air. How? It's a combination of extreme humidity, low-hanging clouds, and usually a soft but persistent wind out of the southwest, the source of most rain in the United States.

Wind out of the east? In many areas, the skippers will avoid starting a long cruise because they know an east wind is often being sucked toward a low-pressure area to the west.

Some can even look at the way the leaves are blowing on a tree and tell when rain is coming.

> **Nautical Notes**
>
> Another sure rain forecaster is sound carrying farther and clearer than normal. When low clouds full of rain approach, they trap sound and bounce it back to earth, and the reverberations travel well. If you hear a train whistle blowing miles away, expect rain coming from that direction.

How do they do it? Prevailing or fair-weather winds cause leaves to blow in one direction. The reversal of winds that comes as a low approaches flips the leaves over and exposes their light-colored undersides, which the savvy mariner views as a warning sign.

Weather Proverbs

One of the first proverbs sailors learn is this one:

> Red sky at morning, sailors take warning;
> red sky at night, sailors delight.

Surprisingly, meteorologists agree with mariners on this one. A red sky at dawn results from the sun lighting up the edges of storm clouds moving in from the west, while a red sky at night means the sun has popped clear of the progressing clouds and fair weather is approaching (although it might be windy for a day or two after the front).

Look Out!

Although a red sky at night might be a sailor's delight, "orange or yellow can hurt a fellow." Clouds that turn these colors at sundown indicate that humidity is moving in, rain is likely, and storms are possible.

Here's another mariner's favorite:

Mackerel scales and mares' tails make tall ships carry low sails.

Mackerel scales are altocumulus clouds that form a scale-like pattern overhead, while mares' tails are cirrus clouds with the tails swept upward. Both are harbingers of wind and rain, although the weather usually takes 24 hours or more to arrive.

Mackerel-scale clouds often mean rain tomorrow, although they show only when the day is sunny.

(Frank Sargeant)

When the sun wears a halo, a luminescent ring that scientists say is ice crystals forming in the atmosphere, it's a good sign that there's a front coming in soon. "Sun dogs" or mock suns, bright spots in the sky displaying the spectrum of colors, show the same conditions, and also are most common when bad weather is on the way.

A rainbow is the mythic promise of an end to flooding, but in reality it depends on when and where you see the phenomenon. A rainbow in the west in the morning might mean rain on the way. In the east in the afternoon, it's usually a sign that the rain has passed.

Wind Speeds

In general, winds are an enemy to the powerboater and friend to the sailor—to a point. Most powerboat drivers would just as soon see the water dead calm every time they leave the dock, offering a smooth surface where they can let their horses run at full speed without pounding the crew to Jell-O.

However, for a powerboater, winds up to 10 knots are generally not a concern. Ten to fifteen knots makes things uncomfortable, and over fifteen knots, only the tough head out.

Sailors hate dead calm with a passion, love 10 to 15 knots, and the young and reckless might take on 20 knots or more in a catamaran. It's wet, wild, and risky, but you go fast.

Small Craft Advisories (SCAs) are posted on weather stations and at some large marinas when winds are predicted to exceed 18 knots. The signal is a triangular red flag, or at night a red light over a white light. They're an indication that anything less than a ship should stay in port.

Boat Bytes _____

Although the most common weather pattern in the United States is west to east, there are times when rain and storms come from the east. It's common in Florida in summer as storms drift off the Atlantic, and in New England in winter, as particularly vicious storms sweeping in from the southwest rotate as they hit the sea and strike back toward the mainland, producing the dreaded "nor'easter."

Fetching Considerations

The wind is only half of the equation in determining when it's going to be too rough for you and your boat. The other is the *fetch*, or the distance the wind will blow over unobstructed water. A long fetch can create big waves even on an inland lake with 15-knot winds; a short fetch will prevent much stronger winds from making the water too rough for comfort.

In the central west coast of Florida where I live, it's common for anglers to go king-mackerel fishing along the beaches in 25-knot winds, as long as the blow comes out of the east or off the land, which it often does after fall fronts pass through. They find flat water in close, and it stays fishable out to several miles. The same wind coming from the west in this area would produce very dangerous water along the beach, because it would have a fetch completely across the Gulf of Mexico.

The Beaufort Scale

The Beaufort Scale, devised in the 1800s by a British admiral of the same name, is best known as an indicator of gales and hurricanes. But everybody knows you don't want to leave the harbor—or even be around the docks—when winds reach these levels.

The lower levels of the Beaufort Scale are more generally useful to recreational boaters, not because they rate the winds on a 1 to 12 scale (with "Force 1" being the lowest wind speed and "Force 12" the highest), but because they give the usual sea conditions at a given wind speed. This enables a skipper of moderate experience to have some idea what he or she will face at various wind speeds. The Beaufort Scale is based on open sea conditions with a broad fetch. It's shown in the following table.

Beaufort Wind Scale

Beaufort Number	Wind Speed (in Knots)	Description	Effect on Water
0	Less than 1	Calm	Mirror-calm surface
1	1–3	Light air	Scale-like ripples
2	4–6	Light breeze	Wavelets, no breaking
3	7–10	Gentle breeze	Crests begin to break
4	11–16	Moderate breeze	Waves $1^{1}/_{2}$–4 feet, numerous whitecaps
5	17–21	Fresh breeze	Waves 4–8 feet, some spray
6	22–27	Strong wind	Waves 8–13 feet, whitecaps everywhere
7	28–33	Near gale	Waves 13–20 feet, white foam, wave streaks

Beaufort Number	Wind Speed (in Knots)	Description	Effect on Water
8	34–40	Gale	Waves increase in length, foam blown off sea, sea streaks white
9	41–47	Strong gale	Waves over 20 feet, limited visibility
10	48–55	Storm	Waves 20–30 feet, sea heavily streaked
11	56–63	Violent storm	Waves to 45 feet, sea nearly white
12	64–71	Hurricane or extremely violent storm	Waves over 45 feet, sea completely white, visibility near 0

By the time SCAs would be posted, you'd be looking at 4- to 8-foot waves in areas with a long fetch. That's a whole lot more wave action than most leisurely weekenders want to deal with, even though it's not necessarily dangerous in a larger yacht.

In reality, most boaters don't want anything to do with steady seas over 3 feet in boats that are 20 feet long or less, and as you note from the scale, winds of just over 10 knots might bring these in exposed areas.

Land and Sea Breezes

Land and water heat up at different rates. This causes a pressure differential between the two, and breezes result if no stronger weather system interferes.

During the daytime, the land heats up faster and the air rises and loses density. As a result, the denser, cooler air from the sea blows inland.

In various areas, the time when this breeze starts to blow is very predictable. In my area of the Gulf Coast throughout spring, summer, and early fall, it nearly always starts between noon and 1 P.M. in otherwise calm weather. For that

Boat Bytes _____

Sea breezes send moisture inland and this becomes clouds as it rises. It's common in summer for the sea to be clear and the land covered with clouds and even thunderheads. Provided there are no reverse currents in the upper air, the rain is likely to stay over land as long as the sea breeze blows.

reason, a lot of fishermen like to get out in the morning and come in at lunch when it starts to get bumpy, while sailors might have to wait until some time after noon to get reasonable winds.

At night, the land cools rapidly while the sea temperature remains nearly constant, so a breeze from land to sea might result. Again, this most often begins several hours after sundown, when the difference becomes most significant.

Thunderheads

In some 40 years of bouncing around the waterfronts, I've yet to hear a skipper take a look at the sky and say something like, "Looks like some nasty cumulonimbus clouds forming up this morning—we're going to get some weather." What he or she does say is, "Uh-oh, thunderheads."

The towering, anvil-shaped cloud is a thunderhead. If the anvil points in your direction, expect a lightning storm in short order.

(Frank Sargeant)

A thunderhead is an anvil-shaped cloud (technically, it's called a cumulonimbus) that foretells a serious thunderstorm. The direction the anvil points tells you where the storm is going—if it's headed for you, you should be headed for shelter. Seen at a distance, thunderheads appear to be white and fluffy and might appear in an otherwise blue sky. As they draw near, they tend to spread out and turn the sky gray, and then nearly black. They can develop quickly and move rapidly—a thunderhead on the horizon can reach you within an hour with the right winds.

Squall Lines

A low, black bank of clouds stretching from horizon to horizon is a squall line, one of the nastiest of the nasties that boaters have to deal with from time to time. Squall lines can travel a mile a minute and bring winds from near zero to gale force in nothing flat. They're frequently found on the edge of advancing weather fronts, but these are well forecast and easy to avoid.

Harder to foretell are the smaller but no less dangerous localized squall lines that form along the bottom of fast-moving thunderstorms. These storms run across the sea as fast as most powerboats, and passing through one can be a mind-altering experience, particularly if you're trying to get through a crowded and very angry inlet along with a bunch of other boaters who stayed out too long.

Look Out!

Any time you see a black line of clouds approaching on the horizon, it's time to head for home at flank speed. If you're far at sea in a slow boat, the only alternative is to batten down the hatches, put on the PFDs, rain gear, and life lines, and prepare for some excitement.

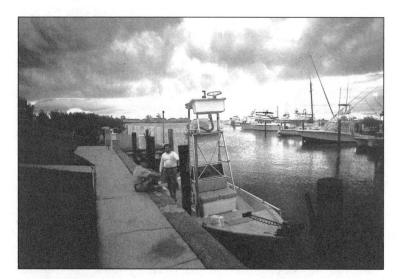

The best place to be as a squall line approaches is tied up to the dock. The bottom edge of a series of thunderstorms always brings violent weather.

(Frank Sargeant)

Lightning

Lightning is more dangerous than wind and waves for the inland and coastal boater, because the wind and waves can readily be avoided by timing your crossings of open water. Lightning, however, can arc across miles of open sky to deliver a knockout punch to you and your boat while the sun still shines brightly overhead—it can leap many miles from a distant thunderhead to strike.

The old rule about determining how far off lightning is striking by counting the seconds and then dividing by five does indeed give you the approximate mileage to the last strike, but unless it's more than 5 miles off, you are not necessarily safe. With 30 million volts to play with, nature can reach out and touch you at remarkable distances.

Look Out!

Anytime lightning gets remotely close to you—within even five miles—head for the marina!

There will be times when you get caught out in lightning, however. There's no point trying to run for cover after the bolts start to fly—chances are the storm will be over before you can get there. Here's what to do to ride out the storm:

◆ *If you're in a powerboat or sailboat that has a cabin*, go below and keep your hands off grounded metal objects, particularly the steering wheel.

◆ *If you're in an open powerboat or sailboat*, try to make the boat's profile as low as possible by dropping radio antennas, fishing rods, and anything else projecting above the gunnels. Stay as low as possible yourself, try to avoid touching anything that might conduct electricity, and say a prayer or two if you're so inclined.

Sailboats get struck by lightning with some frequency, but their masts are grounded and conduct the charge into the water instantly, usually without injuring passengers. (The fact that a mast is grounded doesn't mean it won't be damaged by a direct strike, however.)

Water Spouts

A water spout is a waterborne tornado that comes out of the bottom of a strong thunderstorm. Spouts don't possess the power or size of a tornado ashore, but they are still strong enough to damage a recreational boat in a direct hit. The spouts vary from 20 feet to several hundred feet wide, and they come spiraling down from the bottom of low-hanging cumulonimbus clouds.

Spouts are a scary sight, but they move slowly and can be outrun in a powerboat. (They're usually accompanied by wild thunderstorms and strong surface winds, though, and these can be more of a problem than the waterspouts.) It's not uncommon for offshore sailors to have several in sight at once on a stormy summer afternoon off Florida—most seasoned skippers in seaworthy boats keep their distance but don't necessarily run for cover.

The bottom line is that weather can present some dangers afloat, and that discretion is the better part of valor. Anytime conditions are iffy and you have any doubt about your abilities or those of your boat to handle the likely conditions, it's better to stay at the docks and play cards.

The Least You Need to Know

- Learn to use weather forecasts as they apply to your local area. Find an around-the-clock source you like and trust.

- Nature's clues on approaching weather are always on the mark—learn to read them.

- Don't try to out-tough dangerous weather—when the going gets tough, the tough get going … for the docks!

Chapter 16

Mastering the Tides

In This Chapter

- What causes tides and currents
- How tides affect boating
- Understanding tide tables
- The effect of wind on tides

Tides can make rivers run backward 100 miles from the sea. They can lift 500-ton ships off sandbars—and push them right up through reinforced concrete bridges!

Like time itself, they wait for no man … or woman.

Tides can also make you miserable. I don't think I'm that paranoid, but it seems like the tide-caused currents are always against me. Especially when I'm in a canoe or sailboat.

Traveling on the right tide can make you look like a hero, but leaving the docks on the wrong current—the flow caused by the tides—can make trouble for the most skilled skipper. So every boater who cruises coastal waters needs to know how tides work.

The daily coming and going of the ocean's visits to land is controlled by the gravitational pull of the sun and the moon, centrifugal force, and the rotation of the earth, as most of us learned in high school science. Okay, so maybe we didn't really learn *exactly* how it works, but you don't need to know all this scientific stuff to go boating. What you *do* need to know is how the tides create currents and raise and lower the depth of the water, and when they do so. That's what you'll learn in this chapter. (If you're an inland boater, you might want to skip this chapter; lakes and rivers have no tides large enough to affect boaters, though the Great Lakes do have a rise and fall of a few inches.)

How the Moon Influences the Tides

The moon is the strongest factor affecting *tides* via gravitational pull. Although the moon is tiny compared to the sun, it's a lot closer to Earth. As a result, tides are very obviously influenced by the moon phases.

Gravity causes the water of the oceans to bulge slightly toward the attracting bodies. The results we see are very long (thousands of miles between peak and trough), low ocean waves. They're not evident at sea, but when they hit land the motion of the waves causes the water to rise and fall, and also creates tidal currents as the water flows over shallows and through narrow passages. Anyone who spends any time around the coast knows this much. The flow varies dramatically based on the shape of the land it meets.

Salt Talk

Tides are the vertical rise and fall of the oceans created for the most part by the gravitational pull of the moon and the sun on the waters.

The strongest tides are on new and full moons when the sun and moon are aligned; the weakest tides are at the moon quarter-periods, when the moon is at a 90-degree angle to the line of pull of the sun. Because of the progression of the moon phases, today's high tide at noon will become a low tide at about noon 7 days from now, and a high tide very close to noon once again 14 days from now.

The moon rotates around the earth not every 24 hours, but every 24 hours and 50 minutes. Thus the tidal periods are 50 minutes later each of our Earth-days.

Tide Ranges

Tidal ranges can be as little as a foot from high to low water. On the other end of the scale, in some areas the range exceeds 50 feet—the Bay of Fundy on the coasts of Maine and New Brunswick is the most famous tidal spot in the world, with a maximum range of 53 feet, the result of tidal waves oscillating with each other inside the confines of the bay and one tide stacking atop another.

The result, when these monster tides go out, are big, sucking whirlpools, logs skimming along like racing canoes, and a flow that looks like a fast river—mariners beware!

In other areas, the tide movements are so gradual and so minimal that they go unnoticed by most boaters. But even minimal tides can have a big effect on boating. In shallow areas, a tidal drop of six inches can sometimes bare hundreds of acres of bottom, and a few inches of depth sometimes makes all the difference in whether or not the draft of a boat will be excessive for entering some waters.

Playing the Tides

Tides affect both the depth of the water and the current in coastal areas, and both factors are important in operating many types of boats.

Tide heights listed in tide tables are given as plus or minus heights from the *zero line*, which is the average, or mean, of the lower of the low tides at that spot year-round, over the previous 19 years. A tide indicated as −1.0 is expected to be one foot lower than the mean low, and one listed as +4.0 will be four feet higher than the mean low.

The greater the variations from zero—that is, the taller the wave—the stronger the tide flow. Because the earth has a slight wobble in its rotation around the sun that repeats on 19-year cycles, the tides today won't be exactly the same until 19 years from now. But for "government purposes," it can be said that tides repeat on yearly cycles in terms of height and current— that is, the December full moon high tide at the mouth of the Chesapeake Bay this year will have about the same height and volume on the December full moon next year, although the full moon will fall on a different date.

So what does this mean to you?

Let's look at an example. If you attempt to cross a bar with a *controlling depth* of 3.0 feet and there's a −0.5 tide and you have a 3-foot draft,

Boat Bytes

Note that mean low water is not mean sea level or just plain sea level that is often referred to when measuring altitudes ashore. Sea level is very near the average between mean low and mean high tide levels—it's not a number used regularly by boaters.

Salt Talk

Controlling depth is the maximum draft of a vessel that can pass over a given spot in a channel at low tide. For example, a vessel with a 4-foot draft will go aground in a channel with a controlling depth of 3'11" at low tide.

you are going to be doing the sandbar boogie for a while. On the other hand, if you try to cross the same bar on high water of a +5.0 tide—or even a +0.5—you will have no problem whatsoever. Knowing both the time and the magnitude of the tide can be critical to coastal boaters in many instances.

Large sailboats might require 5 feet or greater depth to keep their keel from touching bottom. Knowledge of tide heights is critical for inshore navigation in deep-draft boats.

(Beneteau Yachts)

For sailors, the tidal currents can be a major factor in both speed and course. Because sailboats travel at relatively slow speeds, proceeding with a strong current can as much as double their speed, and traveling against it can cut speed in half.

Salt Talk

Course made good is the actual course the boat takes, as it is affected by wind and currents, as opposed to the course steered via the compass or GPS.

Running at an angle across a tide can also greatly change the *course made good*—the tide becomes a vectoring force that can push you far off course over a period of hours. (For a closer look at how this works, see Chapter 14.)

So where do you get this information?

Tide Tables

The tide tables, plotted by the National Ocean Service, provide forecasts of tide height and current data for locations around the world.

All this information for any coastal area in the nation is now available free online. Go to http://co-ops.nos.noaa.gov/tide_pred.html and click on the area where you want to find predictions for a full year.

The tables also come in book form and are available at many boating-gear stores as well as chart and map stores. The book you want will probably be either *Tide Tables, East Coast of North & South America* or *Tide Tables, West Coast of North & South America*. They sell for about $15 each from BOAT U.S. and many other sources. Similar volumes, such as *Tide Current Tables*, are available for the Atlantic Coast of North America and the Pacific Coast of North America, for about $12 each.

The tide tables make it evident that tides arrive at different shore locations at dramatically different times. Note that all times are given in "standard time," as opposed to "daylight savings time," and that they are adjusted for time zone (Eastern, Central, Mountain, or Pacific).

The high tide at the Chesapeake Bay Bridge will be many hours before the high at Annapolis, 100 miles up the bay. In fact, a distance of just a few miles can make several hours' difference in when a tide arrives and leaves.

> **Nautical Notes**
>
> For boaters who always stay in their home bay, the full-size tide tables offer more information than you might want. Most bait shops and marinas offer handy tide charts for free that list local tides, and these are much easier to use than leafing through the tables and converting the data to your home port.

> **Boat Bytes**
>
> For those with computers, TideMaster tide charts are super for planning your trips on prime tides as far as a year into the future. For details, contact Zephyr Services, 1900 Murray Avenue, Pittsburgh, PA 15217; 412-422-6600; www.zephyrs.com.

In general, north/south differences are less than east/west differences along the Atlantic and Pacific coasts of the United States. For example, there's only about an hour's difference between arrival of high tide at Anna Maria, on Florida's west coast, and Anclote Key, 40 miles northward along the coast. But the time difference from Anna Maria to the Little Manatee River, just 20 miles east/northeast inside Tampa Bay, is over 90 minutes. Constrictions of the bay cause the flow to lag as it moves inside, while the tidal waves in the open Gulf move more rapidly. And if there are any constricting passages, narrow channels, or shallow flats, these slow the tidal wave and retard the times even more. That's why it's possible within a shallow estuary to have rising water at the mouth and falling water up inside the tidal creeks at the same time. The movements are not part of the same tidal period.

The tide tables don't give exact tides for every port on earth, but they do provide conversion tables for a huge number of locations, so you can make time adjustments for nearby ports.

Tides can be expressed in charts as well as in numeric tables. This chart, from the Tampa Tribune *in Tampa, Florida, uses a graph to show highs and lows for a week.*

Using the Tide Tables

The tables list tidal locations in geographical order from north to south and east to west; thus Miami, Florida, comes ahead of Brownsville, Texas. There's an index to look up the station nearest your location.

The table for a given spot lists dates; time of the tides in military time, with 0100 standing for 1 A.M., 1200 for noon, and 1800 for 6 P.M.; and the height of the maximum and minimum tides for the day. Be sure to check that the times have been adjusted for Daylight Savings Time when it applies—there should be a note in the book.

Tide Heights and Navigation

If your boat has a draft of 3 feet, the lowest part of it, probably the skeg, will touch bottom in water that's 2'11" deep. If the mean low tide at a given spot is 3.0 feet and you cross on an average low tide, you won't touch bottom. If you cross on a –0.2 low tide, things will scrape and bump and possibly bend.

But there's more. If there are waves rocking your boat up and down, the water on the shoal will go from deeper to shallower with every cycle of peak to trough. On the bottom of the trough, you might strike bottom, even though you could cross the bar in calm seas. You have to use your judgment and perhaps wait for the tide to flow back in before you cross that particular spot. Refer to the tide tables to see when the water will be rising, and "guesstimate" about when you can cross by looking at the time of high tide and the sea conditions.

By the same token, perhaps there's only a foot of water over a bar at a creek mouth at mean low tide, and that's 2 feet less than you need to get in. But wait until the peak of a +3.0 tide, and there's no problem. That is, there's no problem unless you want to leave that creek at low tide. You're locked in until the next high tide, so keep that in mind any time you go exploring in the shallows.

The tide tables also list nearby locations with time corrections for the nearest main reporting station. They list the latitude and longitude of the location so that you can confirm with your GPS, and the difference in time from the nearest station. The difference might be anywhere from a few minutes to several hours, and is not the same for high and low tides. You subtract minus differences and add positive differences.

For example, suppose you want to figure out the tide for a fishing spot that's 15 miles up your favorite bay from the mouth, and the tides are only reported in the tables for the mouth. Say the report indicates a noon high at the bay mouth, and a +2.0 hours time difference for your fishing location. You would figure it this way:

12:00 + 2 = 2:00 P.M., the time of high tide at your spot

There are very slight variations in tide height at various locations on a given tidal period. In most of the southeastern United States, this difference is insignificant, but in the northeast it can be considerable. The tide tables list this variation as well, and it should be considered if you're making an iffy passage across a bar.

> **Nautical Notes**
>
> It's always best to punch around in the backwaters on a rising tide, and to head back for deeper water shortly before the tide peaks and starts to run back out. That way, if you go aground inside, the rising water gives you a good chance to get off and escape; if you ground on falling water, you're stuck until the next incoming tide.

Bridge Clearance

Do you ever need to know the tide heights if you're not crossing a shallow bar? Maybe.

It could be that problems arise above the water. A low bridge can block passage for fly-bridge cruisers and sailboats on high tide, yet let them pass with space to spare on low. Sometimes even runabouts can be blocked by low-hanging roadways.

You obviously need to know your boat's *bridge clearance* if you navigate anywhere that passage beneath one of these structures is common. The bridge clearance (BC) refers to the height from the waterline (where the surface meets the hull) to the highest point of any structure on the boat, including the mast, tuna tower, or outriggers. (If your radio antennas and riggers fold down, you don't have to measure them in the equation.)

Salt Talk

Bridge clearance is the distance from a boat's waterline to the highest point on the topsides. It indicates the height of a bridge under which a boat can pass. It's indicated as (BC) on marine charts.

Bridge clearance is listed on marine charts, with the height above mean high water given. So, if you want to pass under a bridge that has 20-foot listed clearance with your sportfisherman boasting a BC of 19'6'', you aren't going to be able to get through at the peak of a spring tide that's a foot taller than normal high tide (more on spring tides later in this chapter). On the other hand, you can get through that bridge with a 19-foot listed clearance on the bottom of a –1.0 low.

Nautical Notes

In most areas there's a normal progression through four tides, but some days have only three tides. How can this be?

As the 50-minute-per-day regression takes place, the P.M. tide gradually advances past midnight, thus leaving one 24-hour period without four tides, even though the tidal movements maintain their steady procession.

Tides in the Estuaries

Tides follow wider, deeper channels first. That's why tide flows show up in major coastal passes long before they arrive at docks and boat ramps several miles inland.

In a bayou fed by several tidal creeks, you might see that the inflow begins on the main arm and is already flowing strong there while it's dead or even going out on the smaller feeders.

The tide comes into an estuary in a plume that you can see on the surface when the water is calm. It has a rounded leading edge, and it stays separate for a time from the residual water left in the backwaters on the previous low. Differences in salinity or temperature probably account for the edge.

The life in the estuaries responds to this pulse—you'll see fish start to jump and gulls start to whirl on tide movements. For anglers, it's often a good time to wet a line.

There are times, too, when the current tables can actually help you predict sea conditions to some extent—if a strong flow is coming out of a big pass and a wind is blowing in, you can be sure that there will be steep, nasty waves in the passage.

In a powerboat, you might want to stay at anchor until the flow reverses and begins to go with the wind, even though you'll then be working against the current, because the water will be much smoother. In a motorized sailboat or low-powered diesel trawler, you might have no choice but to take advantage of the push of the current to get you outside on the outflow.

Boat Bytes

Knowing when currents will be strongest in a pass or inlet can be critical for sailboats, which have less powerful engines than powerboats.

Spring Tides

Spring tides are the tides around new and full moons each month when the highs are highest and the lows are lowest. Spring tides come in summer, fall, and winter as well as spring. Confusing, isn't it? Around the new and full moon periods in most areas there is one major high and one major low daily, and the magnitude is much greater than at other times of the month. These are designated spring tides.

Neap Tides

Neap (pronounced *neep*) *tides* are the tides around the quarter-moon periods each month when tidal variation is minimal. During the "quarter" periods of the moon, in many areas there are two nearly equal highs and two lows each 24-hour period. Less water is moving on each tide, and both highs and lows vary less from mean low water.

Remember that the tides repeat themselves on two-week cycles, following the waxing and waning of the moon. And the tides also pretty much repeat themselves each year on a given moon cycle, so if there's a 4.90 high tide in your home port on this year's December full moon, it will be about the same next December. (Remember that the full moon won't come on exactly the same date, though, if you're planning a trip far in advance.)

Look Out!

Points along a shoreline can also cause increased tidal speeds as the water stacks up and hurries around the obstruction. Take care when passing close, particularly in a sailboat under sail or in a boat with minimal power.

Tide Sense

Watch natural tidal indicators to get a feel for the movement. The way a stick or a buoy carves the surface can tell you volumes about the flow, and will be much more accurate for your particular location than any forecast printed in a book. Take what the water gives you—many days, you'll find that the published tide tables and nature don't agree.

Learn to read the real-time clues. In general, current speeds are controlled by the difference between the highs and lows, and the time from the high to the low—lots of water moving over a short period of time means strong currents.

However, it also pays to understand how the geography of an estuary affects current speeds. Anywhere that lots of water has to fit through a narrow gap between islands or bars there will be a strong flow, even on moderate tidal periods. Some of these areas are obvious, as in the main pass coming out of a large bay. If the pass is narrow, the flow is going to boil through it. In fact, the currents in those areas have created the channels. A big, deep channel equals lots of current, so be wary on new and full moons.

Seasonal Variations

Summer tides are generous; winter tides are stingy in many areas. Remember that when you think about running your boat across a shallow flat on a December full-moon low. In summer, the only tides that go below mean low or zero are the spring tides on the few days around the new and full moon. But in winter, it's not uncommon for a week on either side of the moons to be at or below zero at extreme low.

For example, on the full moon in May, the lowest tide might be –0.27 at St. Petersburg Pier in Tampa Bay. On the December full moon at the same spot, the lowest tide might be –0.50, about 0.3 lower. That doesn't sound like a lot, but it's enough to make hundreds of acres go bare in the gentle topography of Florida's west coast. It's also enough to ruin your lower unit if you're not careful where you drive.

The highs are higher in spring and summer as well—the max on the June full moon might typically be +2.91 at St. Pete, while the high on the December full moon is likely to be around +2.20, more than .7 foot lower.

Wind Tides

The predicted tides are based on the pull of the moon, sun, and earth, but they can't take into account the effect of winds. In winter on the west coast of Florida, it's very common to get 20- to 30-knot winds out of the northeast after a front, and these can move another 6 inches to a foot of water out on the extreme lows. Conversely, these same winds pile water into the inlets on the east coast. And in summer, strong winds out of the southwest are not uncommon along the Gulf Coast. These tend to make the already tall summer tides even higher. On the Atlantic Coast of southern Florida, the trade winds that blow from the east make the high tides taller in summer.

Winds can even create tides in freshwater. In winter, strong north winds over several days pile 6 inches to a foot of water up on the south shore of Florida's 25-mile-wide Lake Okeechobee. The same effect occurs on many big lakes, but most of them don't happen to have the height-above-sea-level measuring devices they have at Okeechobee, so the result is less obvious.

To learn more about tides, currents, and intensive coastal navigation, you can find dozens of useful books on any web search engine, or take a look at *Chapman's Piloting*, mentioned earlier.

The Least You Need to Know

- ♦ In coastal areas, boaters must be familiar with tide cycles for safe navigation.
- ♦ The tide tables give the necessary data for cruising throughout U.S. waters.
- ♦ Tides control not only water depth, but also currents.
- ♦ Sustained winds can have major local effects on tide movements.

Part 5

Staying Safe Afloat

If you've read this far, you know most of the basics of spending a day afloat. But don't ignore these very important chapters on keeping yourself and your crew safe.

You'll want to make sure your boat's equipment meets the federal requirements for safety gear before you leave the docks that first time.

It's also wise to remember that the best defense is a good offense, particularly when it comes to avoiding problems afloat—see Chapter 18 for some important cautions.

Real emergencies afloat are rare, but the smart skipper is prepared in advance to deal with whatever comes along, and this part also offers some advice on situations that might someday happen on your boat.

Chapter 17

Gearing Up for Safety

In This Chapter

- ◆ Determining your boat's class
- ◆ Choosing a personal flotation device (PFD)
- ◆ Distinguishing between extinguishers
- ◆ Stocking your first-aid kit
- ◆ A look at other safety gear that's good to have

Before you leave the docks for the first time, you have to equip your boat with a set of federally required gear that experience has proven to be essential for basic safety afloat, whether you're boating in a 10-foot jon boat or a 60-foot yacht.

This might not be the most fascinating topic, but it's stuff you have to understand well enough to gear up, so persevere. And should the day ever come when you *need* a PFD or other safety gear, you'll be extremely glad you have the necessaries aboard.

In this chapter, you'll learn the types of life preservers, the most basic piece of gear aboard any boat, as well as a bit about all the other equipment that might someday come in handy in an emergency. (Okay, maybe you'll be lucky and never have an emergency, but you'll need all the stuff in this chapter anyway when the Marine Patrol comes calling—they'll send you back to the docks and maybe give you a citation if you fail to have the required gear aboard.)

A Touch of Class

Before tackling the gear, it's necessary to understand how boats are classified by size, because the different classes require different gear. There are four classes of boats based on length, each requiring slightly different levels of safety gear:

- **Class A.** This class covers the smallest boats, under 16 feet long. More than half the recreational boats in the United States are in this class.

- **Class 1.** (Why isn't this called class B? Just to separate the salts from the land-lubbers, I guess.) This class includes boats from 16 feet to less than 26 feet long. Over 90 percent of the boats in U.S. waters are this size or smaller.

- **Class 2.** This class includes boats from 26 to 40 feet, the size that starts to make your banker sit up and take notice.

- **Class 3.** This class includes boats from 40 to 65 feet, the realm of the privileged few.

Why the distinctions? Because the larger the boat, the more likely it is to be taken far offshore; therefore, the more likely it is to need more extensive safety equipment.

Nautical Notes

Note that whatever the class, if it's powered by machinery, it will require state registration numbers, usually available through county tax collectors' offices. This is like the license plate on your car, and it must be renewed every year for an added fee. The numbers are displayed on both sides of the bow for most boats. Boats smaller than a designated size and those without power are exempt in most states.

The ABCs of PFDs

The Coast Guard calls life jackets *personal flotation devices* because it's longer. Then they shorten it to *PFDs* because it's shorter. Those of you who have been in the military instinctively understand.

Whatever you call them, they are intended to keep you afloat. You *must* have one aboard for each crew member. If the Marine Patrol catches you without enough PFDs aboard for your crew, you're heading back to the dock—it's a mistake no officer will ignore.

If you have kids aboard, you must have life jackets sized to fit them. In many states, children under 6 must wear the jackets while onboard and even while on the docks; in some states, all children under 12 must wear life jackets at all times, except in larger cabin boats, where the gear can be taken off while below-decks.

 Salt Talk

PFDs are **personal flotation devices,** commonly known as life jackets, although they can be any type of Coast Guard-approved flotation device, including a buoyant cushion or a flotation ring.

The dock rule is important as well, because it is very easy for a kid to wander off a dock (adults too, for that matter) and it is very hard to get back onto a dock.

Types of PFDs

PFDs are classified into five types.

Type I is the top-quality offshore jacket with lots of buoyancy or lifting force (22 pounds or more, by law), and it's fitted in a jacket that will stay in place even in rough seas. This type will turn an unconscious wearer face up, a must for high-performance boats and big-water kayakers and canoeists. These jackets are bulky and most are made with blaze-orange shells. They're a bit more expensive than the weekend-type jacket (about $30 to $60), but worth it.

Type II is the "horse-collar" or near-shore life jacket, with 15.5 pounds of buoyancy. It's not designed to turn an unconscious wearer face up, and it won't necessarily stay on in rough water. But it's inexpensive (under $10). These are the bright-orange jackets you see sold in every discount store. Are they adequate? Maybe, if the only time you ever need one is on a quiet pond where shore is only a few yards away. For the most part, boaters using bigger waters should stay clear of type II jackets—a type I or type III jacket (discussed next) is a better choice.

Type III is the most popular type of life jacket because it's both comfortable and affordable. It's made of foam so it flexes with the body, and is finished in attractive colors and materials, often with plenty of pockets to store gear. Type III jackets carry 15.5 pounds of flotation and stay on well due to zippers and straps. They provide good thermal insulation in cold weather and are easy to store because they fold flat.

Prices start at $15. Some high-performance models, with more straps and fasteners to make sure you stay in the jacket, cost up to $80.

Look Out!

If you have small children aboard, you *must* have vests sized for them. Kids will slip right through an adult-size vest in the water. In fact, in many states, kids under 12 *must* wear their vests at all times when the boat is underway, unless they're below decks on a cabin boat.

The disadvantages of type III jackets: In rough water, they float low, and you might have a hard time breathing as waves splash in your face. They also do not turn unconscious users right side up.

Type IV is not a jacket at all, but either a throwable cushion with straps or a foam life ring. At least one is required aboard all boats over 16 feet long. The idea is to throw this to someone who falls overboard without a regular life jacket, giving him something to cling to until you get the boat to him. The throwables are not intended to do much more than that.

Boat Bytes

There are also life vests for dogs (the small ones also fit most cats), recommended if you take your pet offshore with you. Dogs have a way of going overboard when you least expect them to, and the jacket helps them stay on top of the water and makes them easier to see. Inshore, don't worry about it—just about any dog can swim to any land within visible range. (In the Florida Keys a few years back, a Lab swam 8 miles after falling off a boat beyond the barrier reefs.)

Who will throw you the type IV cushion if you are boating solo? Nobody, but you're still required to have it onboard. Most wind up as seats, although that's not a good idea over the long term because it crushes the flotation material.

Type V PFDs include survival suits, which are the best of all life preservers, but they're so heavy and hot that they're only worn in rain or in cold-climate boating. They're both rainproof and packed with thermal insulation—you can survive for hours in cold water or for days in moderate temperatures in one of these suits. They're also very expensive, costing several hundred dollars each.

Type V also includes the new breed of inflatable PFDs that might be the answer to people who don't like to wear other kinds of life jackets. These devices come in the form of suspenders or belt packs, and they're so small and unobtrusive that you'll forget you're wearing one until you need it, and then you simply pull a cord to inflate it. (Not all inflatable PFDs are approved by the Coast Guard. Look for the tag before you buy.) Like any contrivance, the CO_2 cartridge that inflates the device can fail, but there are manual tubes you can use to blow up the inflatable if that becomes necessary. The big negative is price; they typically cost $70 to $200 each, which adds up if you're equipping an entire crew.

Inflatable PFDs are now approved for use on recreational boats. They're small and comfortable, which means more people are willing to wear them all day long, greatly increasing safety.

(Stearns Mfg.)

Which types of PFDs do you need on your boat by law? This is an easy one:

- Class A boats—One of any type of PFD for each person
- Class 1, 2, and 3 boats—One wearable preserver per person (not a type IV cushion), plus a single type IV throwable

Wearing PFDs

Does anybody actually *wear* these life-saving devices?

Surprisingly, many don't.

There's no law requiring adults to wear PFDs aboard, so most don't. Look in any boating magazine and you'll be hard pressed to find a single boater wearing a PFD—unless there's a story about why you should wear PFDs! The fact is that almost nobody wears them, except Coast Guard and Marine Patrol officers on duty. This, despite the fact that nearly every boating advice book tells you that you should wear a PFD any time you're afloat, and despite the fact that boating-related drownings would be cut to a fraction if everyone wore them.

People give many reasons for not wearing their PFDs: because they're bulky, hot, and unstylish; because the crew is in a hurry to get started; and because they don't want to give the appearance of being boating dorks. People participating in boat races and in most bass-fishing tournaments, where high-performance boats are involved, almost always wear their life jackets, but that's often because the rules require that they be worn in these events.

When the chips are down, you had better have the jackets close at hand, however. Mine go on everybody when there's a tough inlet to run or when a squall line stands between us and the harbor. And any time we have nonswimmers aboard, they wear them dock-to-dock.

When PFDs are not being worn, keep them in a location that's quick to get to, that everyone aboard knows about, and that will allow them to float free if the boat capsizes. If they're buried in the cabin under the bunks, they won't do you much good in an emergency.

Storing PFDs

PFDs are mold magnets. Put them in a damp boat locker for two days and you'll see a major colony sprouting. The only way to avoid this is to dry the PFDs in the sun after each trip. It's not a bad idea to hit mold spots with Lysol or a similar antiseptic spray before you lay them out to dry. Then stow them inside your garage, or even better, inside your air-conditioned house.

The big problem with stowing PFDs outside the boat is that it's easy to forget them when you load up to head for the ramp. One good trick is to clip the boat ignition key to one of the jackets. You might forget the jackets, but you won't forget the boat key. (Usually, that is. I did it once, and had to make a 20-mile drive to retrieve both while the rather abusive crew waited at the ramp. I pointed out to them that we couldn't go out until we had the jackets, anyway, so leaving the key with the jackets is still a good idea.)

If you choose to store PFDs in your boat, place a mildew-preventer such as Star-Brite mildew control bags in the storage compartment. The downside is that this stuff smells so bad that it might ward off your passengers, too.

Fire Extinguishers

Federal law also requires a fire extinguisher aboard any boat over 26 feet, and aboard those 26 feet and less where flammable gases can be entrapped below decks. In general, you are required to carry an extinguisher if …

- ◆ You have inboard or inboard/outboard engines.

- ◆ You have closed compartments where fuel is stored. (This includes portable fuel tanks.)

- ◆ You have permanently installed fuel tanks.

- ◆ Your boat has a double bottom not sealed to the hull with foam.

- ◆ Your boat has enclosed living spaces.

- ◆ Your boat has closed compartments where flammables are stored.

In short, pretty much *any* powerboat beyond a jon boat is required to carry an extinguisher. Sailboats with gas or diesel power must also have them.

> **Boat Bytes** _____
>
> Fire extinguishers must be checked regularly to make sure they're maintaining a full charge. Some are recommended for recharge every 6 months, some every 12 months. Most have a gauge on top indicating the charge level—check it often, but be aware that it might not be accurate. Weighing the extinguisher is the best way to check it for a full charge.

Like everything else required by federal regulations, there are classes of fire extinguishers. Basically, the designations include a number, which comes first and indicates the size of the extinguisher (the higher the number, the larger the volume of the extinguisher), and a letter, or sometimes several letters, indicating the types of fire the extinguisher will put out. Type A fires occur in combustible solids, such as wood, rubber, and fiberglass. Type B fires are flammable liquids including boat fuels, and type C fires are electrical. The type of extinguisher that recreational boaters are required to carry handles B and C fires, but you might as well buy a combination extinguisher that will work well on A, B, and C fires. You might see this sort of designation on a combo unit: "1-A, 10-BC, which means the extinguisher has a volume equivalent of 1 for fires in solids, and of 10 for fuel or electrical fires—a good combo for any small recreational boat. You can buy these for around $22 to $25 from discount supply houses. For larger boats, you'll want larger extinguishers, and several of them.

The federal regulations require boats to 26 feet to carry one size 1-BC extinguisher. Those 26 to 40 feet need two 1-BC models, and those over 40 feet need three 1-BC units. In the larger two classes, you can substitute a single larger BC type, which contains the same fire-quenching substances but more of them.

> **Look Out!** _____
>
> Never store your extinguisher in an aft compartment, where fuel and batteries are often found. Any fire is likely to start there, and you won't be able to get to your extinguisher for the flames.

Fire extinguishers should be stored where you can get to them quickly, just like PFDs. Upright clamp brackets that mount on the lower part of the console just to one side of the steering wheel are probably best. An extinguisher mounted here is always within reach of the skipper.

A nice extra on powerboats with enclosed engine compartments is an automatic fire-suppression system. It includes a heat-sensitive spray nozzle (like those used in fire-protection systems in hotels) and a fire extinguisher. If temperature gets too high in the engine compartment, the seal on the nozzle lets go and the contents shoot out to put out the fire.

Vents and Electrical Fans

All boats with inboard and inboard/outboard engines are required to have vents and electrical fans to suck flammable gases out of the engine area. Any boat you buy is likely to have the required vent system in place, but check to make sure the fans still function and the hoses still reach to the lowest part of the bilge, the area where the fumes are most likely to gather.

Sound Signals

Boats to 39.4 feet in length must have some sort of sound signal aboard—an electric horn is fine, as is an air horn with a compressed-air can attached. Boats over 39.4 feet must have a signal that can be heard at a half-mile and must also have a ship's bell.

Arresting Flame Development

All inboard and inboard/outboards have a backfire flame arrester atop the air intake. You can't distinguish it from an air cleaner by looking at the outside, but there's a series of fine metal or other nonflammable grids inside. These block any ignited gases that "backfire" inside the firing chamber from escaping back up into the engine compartment. This will be in place when you buy the boat, but don't remove it in the hopes of improving performance; this makes your boat both illegal and dangerous.

Visual Distress Signals

Powerboats more than 16 feet long are required to carry visual distress signals to let other vessels nearby know when immediate help is needed. Of course, you hope your radio will do the job on this, but the visual signals are your backup.

The most basic signal is an orange flag with a black square and disc. Orange smoke signals are also acceptable, as are red flares. Handheld signals, such as flags, are the simplest and least expensive, but signals that can be fired into the air are more visible.

A problem with the smoke- and flare-type signals is that they might not function if they get wet. And all have an expiration date, typically 36 to 42 months after the manufacturing date, stamped on the device. After that time, they no longer legally fulfill the requirement.

Boat Bytes _____

If you ever need to use visual distress signals, make sure you don't waste them. If there are no boats or aircraft in sight, there might not be anyone near enough to help. People are often tempted to fire the flares immediately when they start taking on water, in the hope of immediate rescue. But you'll be more certain to survive if you save the distress signals for when you're sure a potential rescuer is within range. If you travel far offshore regularly, invest in powerful, long-burning flares and plenty of them—you might be glad you did someday.

It's a good idea to keep your expired flares; they'll usually function even after the expiration date and provide a backup to your updated flares. (Just be sure to boldly mark the expired ones so you'll know which is which.)

All incendiary-type flares should be stored in your most waterproof compartment and should be sealed inside locking plastic bags.

Flares such as these from Skyblazer include their own launching system, which sends them up to 450 feet into the air. They burn for up to 6 seconds and can be seen for more than 20 miles in clear conditions.

(Martin Flory Group)

First Aid Afloat

Every boat should carry a basic first-aid kit containing antiseptic ointments; rubbing alcohol; an assortment of bandages, pads, and tape; tweezers; sunburn lotion; aspirin; diarrhea treatment; eye-drops; plastic gloves; and antiseptic soap for minor injuries and sicknesses that occasionally occur. Those who take longer voyages many hours from medical help ashore need more complete first-aid gear and the training in how to use it.

It's also wise for you, as skipper, to take a first-aid course that includes basic CPR and the Heimlich Maneuver to aid choking victims.

Good to Have: Common-Sense Gear

The following items are not necessarily required by law, but common sense dictates you should have them aboard anyway:

- **An anchor and line** can be used to keep you from drifting out to sea or into shipping lanes if your motor dies or the wind stops blowing.

- **An electric bilge pump, manual pump, or even a bailing bucket** should be part of the gear on every boat. A bucket is a good idea even if you have an electric pump—they're notorious for jamming up at the worst possible moments (for more on bilge pumps, see Chapter 19).

- **A second means of propulsion** for smaller boats, up through class 1 (this is actually required by many states). This can be oars, a push pole, a little kicker motor, or an electric troller—something that will get you home, slowly but surely, should the day come when the motor won't run.

Safety to the Max: Other Gear

A peace-of-mind extra is a waterproof strobe light that pins to your PFD. The strobe can be seen for a couple of miles at night and can make all the difference if you ever go into the water. They can also help a towboat locate you if you break down after dark. At $25 to $45, strobe lights are worth the price.

Emergency Position Indicating Radio Beacons (EPIRBs) are the best insurance for rescue offshore. When activated, they send out an emergency signal that can reach 300 miles both across the water and into the air, which means it's very likely the signal will be picked up by passing airliners, if not by other boats or ships. These are for serious, life-threatening emergencies only—such as a sinking boat or a massive heart-attack on board—but they do the job when needed.

EPIRBs are self-contained and are designed to be mounted on an open area of the boat where they can float to the surface if the craft sinks. Seawater activates most models; you don't have to turn them on.

If you venture out of VHF range regularly, it's a good idea to invest in one of these life-savers. The current models, designated Category I or Category II, are priced from $800 to $1,400, and the higher-priced models include a GPS sending unit that will transmit your latitude/longitude position as well as act as a homing beacon.

Personal EPIRB's that can be attached to a life jacket go for about $600. They're slightly larger than a deck of cards and weigh only a few ounces. For those who deal with extreme rough weather, they're a good investment.

> **Boat Bytes**
>
> Batteries on EPIRBs last anywhere from two to five years. They have a test-light to confirm battery charge; check it regularly. New batteries cost $120 to $240. They should be installed by a dealer to confirm that the water-proofing and functionality of the unit are preserved.

If you only need an EPIRB for a short period, such as a vacation cruise, you can rent them for about $50 a week from suppliers like Boat U.S.

Man the Lifeboats

For the casual boater, a raft is overkill, but for those who regularly make long cruises beyond soundings, they're a wise investment. However, buying a raft is a major investment. Prices range from around $2,000 to $4,000 for self-inflating models with a canopy to protect against rain and sun. They're built with the same quality as the toughest of full-size inflatable boats, thus the high prices. Most come equipped with survival kits that include a supply of fresh water, a knife, lights, flares, fishing gear, and more.

It's a very good idea to stock your boat with enough water and nonperishable food to last your entire crew at least three days, if you go offshore at all. The extra supplies will probably never be needed, but they're wonderful to have should you ever have to wait all night for someone to locate you.

If you go offshore a lot, a "watermaker," which converts seawater to freshwater, is a nice extra—they're about $500.

The Least You Need to Know

- The most basic gear on any boat is a PFD for every passenger—don't leave the docks without them.

- Fire afloat is rare, but a good extinguisher, regularly recharged, is insurance you must have.

- Gear to create sound, vent your engine compartment, and signal distress is also required in every state.

- Other gear that's good to have (but that's not legally required) includes an electric bilge pump, oars or a spare motor, and a waterproof strobe light. Emergency rations and extra water should also be standard issue.

The Best Defense Is Common Sense

In This Chapter

- ◆ Filing a float plan
- ◆ Making your boat secure when a storm comes up
- ◆ Staying safe while swimming, diving, and water-skiing
- ◆ Watching your speed
- ◆ The importance of keeping a clear head while operating a boat

The best way to deal with problems afloat (or ashore, for that matter) is to avoid getting into them in the first place. Of course, that's easier said than done, and looking in that rearview mirror often makes things much clearer than they were through the windshield. But a bit of caution judiciously applied can prevent most difficult situations before they get started.

In this chapter, I'll give you some added tips for keeping your crew and your boat safe.

Tell Someone Where You're Going

A *float plan* is a simple written communication that tells those ashore where you're going and when you expect to return. If you don't come back on time, they know where to start looking.

The float plan should include the following items:

♦ The skipper's name and home phone—this lets potential rescuers call your house to make sure you didn't slip home without telling anyone.

♦ A description of your boat, including registration numbers, length, and color.

♦ The itinerary of your trip—where you are going (including latitude/longitude for offshore locations), where you are putting in, and the approximate time you expect to return.

♦ Emergency numbers to call in case you don't return on time. The Coast Guard, sheriff's office, and Marine Patrol should be included.

Boat Bytes

If you leave a float plan with a pal, be absolutely sure to check in when you return. If you forget, causing your protector to launch a series of desperate but un-needed calls to authorities, it's unlikely your designee will ever again pay any attention to your float plans. One way to remember is to tape a reminder to your boat's ignition key.

You simply give this information to a friend, relative, or cooperative marina operator, and then check in with the person when you're back ashore.

An easy way to handle float plans is to make a template on your computer with the basic information that remains the same each time—your boat description, phone numbers, and so on. Leave space to write in the variables such as exactly where you're going and when you expect to return. Just print out a sheet and fill it in for each trip.

Storm Warnings

Storms cause millions of dollars in damages to recreational boats each year. Most of it could be avoided if the skippers took precautions well in advance of the storms.

Get Your Boat Out of the Water or into a Hurricane Hole

If a major storm such as a hurricane is forecast well in advance, the best move is to get your boat out of the water and away from the waterfront. The force of many sea storms abates dramatically just a few miles inland, and if you move your boat out of the strike zone, it's unlikely to suffer problems.

For trailered boats stored outside, remove all gear and add extra tie-downs at the bow and stern but pull the drain-plug. High-sided boats can hold so much rainwater they might break the trailer springs. Block the trailer wheels as well—you don't want the rig taking a drive by itself.

Look Out!

Don't forget "storm surge" as a factor in selecting a hurricane hole. A harbor protected by a jetty that's 5 feet above the normal high tide might go underwater in storm tides, allowing open ocean waves to roll right into your "safe" spot!

Boats too large for trailering have to be left in the water, and the trick is to find a "hurricane hole" where they will be protected from winds and seas. Deep coastal rivers are favorites for this, providing narrow waterways, often with steep banks to keep out the winds.

Even in these areas, it's necessary to make the boat extra secure by putting out two or even three anchors and tying off on large trees ashore. (Don't trust trees too much, though—they might blow down and drift away in a really severe hurricane!)

In moderate storms, including minimal hurricanes, many boaters take their chances with leaving their boats at a marina. As long as the storm doesn't make a direct hit, most of these boats survive. But it does take special preparation to see that they do.

Dock lines have to be lengthened significantly to allow for tides that might be three to five times the normal height. Spring lines have to be positioned so that the boat is cradled in place over its slip even though rising water elevates it above the tops of the pilings. (One of the major damages to boats is being holed by these pilings as the hull rocks in the waves.)

Take all your electronics, bedding, and personal belongings off the boat. The driving force of the wind will push water into every crevice, soaking anything that remains. And it's not uncommon for looters to visit the marinas just after a storm, so beat them to the punch by storing your gear safely at home.

Leave Your Boat Behind

One thing you shouldn't do is to stay with your boat in the hopes of saving it in a major storm. No boat is worth your life, and that's what you put on the line when you decide to stay after the evacuation order comes.

When the roads are flooded and the power lines are down, there will be no one to help you and no way out; make your boat as secure as possible, give it a farewell kiss, and then head inland when the hurricane flags fly.

Swimming and Diving

Most boaters use their boats for swimming at one time or another. Diving, both snorkeling and scuba, is also among the major reasons for being a boat owner.

But hopping overboard does pose some potential problems. The first story I wrote for *Reader's Digest* some 25 years ago was on a young woman and her husband who left their boat to snorkel in the clear waters off Homosassa, Florida, one summer morning and wound up in a struggle for survival that didn't end, for her, until some 24 hours later.

Their mistake? They left no one aboard to pick them up. In the strong currents flowing that day, they soon found themselves so far from the boat that getting back was a struggle. The husband made a decision to leave his wife in hopes that he could get to the boat and rescue her, but when he finally made it to the boat the sun was down and he couldn't find her. She spent a long night treading water, breathing through her snorkel, and hoping no sharks found her. The story had a happy ending the next day when the two were reunited, but it could just as well have been a tragedy.

The moral of the story, obviously, is that divers and swimmers must never leave the boat uncaptained in waters where the current can make return difficult.

Snorkeling for scallops is fun, but who's left in the boat to pick up this swimmer if he gets tired? This boat also lacks the legally required "diver down" flag to warn other boaters there's a diver in the water.

(Frank Sargeant)

In fact, one of the best ways to explore a reef, search for scallops, or simply snorkel over a grass flat is to let the boat drift right along with the swimmers on the tide movements. When anyone gets tired, the boat is only a few strokes away. An alternative is to swim up-current when exploring from an anchored boat. That way, when you get tired, you simply stop swimming and ride the current back to the boat. (Watch out for that tide change, though!)

Any time you divers overboard, make sure to display an orange and white "diver down" flag, which will warn any passing boaters to stay well clear—it's a legal requirement, as well as a great safety factor.

Waterskiing

Waterskiing, slaloming, and wakeboarding can be great fun, but they can also involve some dangers. The best way to avoid problems is to assign one person as the designated "observer" who faces aft and keeps an eye on the skier at all times, while the skipper keeps his or her mind fully on operating the boat. (An "observer" is required by law in some states.)

The major danger in operating a boat near skiers is that the prop will be rotating at fairly close proximity to them after a fall or when they want to be picked up. The best policy is to steer a circular course approaching the skier and then shut off the motor, rather than putting it in idle, as you let the boat slip sideways near enough for them to board.

Let the skier swim the last few yards to the boat, rather than trying to motor close to him or her.

> **Look Out!**
>
> The motor should never be running when anyone is on or near the boarding ladder at the stern. Have your designated observer remind you of this fact any time you forget.

Skiers must wear PFDs, of course, and should also learn the basic hand signals for communication with the boat. They are as follows:

- **Thumbs up**—Increase speed
- **Thumbs down**—Slow down
- **Hand up**—Stop
- **Chopping motion at the neck**—Shut off the motor

Skiers should also be aware that they are hard to see when they're down in the water—raising a ski over the head will make them more visible to oncoming traffic.

Waterskiing, slaloming, and wakeboarding are great sports for the whole family, but a few simple safety precautions are in order. The skier must wear a PFD and should know basic hand signals to communicate with the driver.

(Tracker Marine)

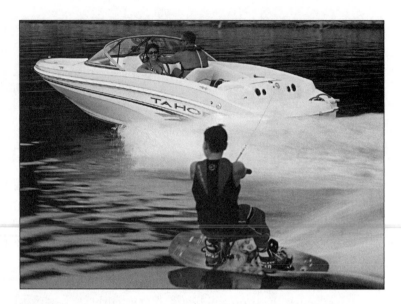

Loading—And Overloading

One of the most common causes of accidents in small boats is overloading. Although it might be fun to see how many teenagers will fit into a 10-foot jon boat, if that boat is moved anywhere away from the docks loaded with more than the capacity plate recommends, it's probably going to swamp. (The capacity plate, you'll recall, is mounted on the console or transom by the manufacturer. It lists safe load capacity in all boats, as well as maximum legal horsepower for outboard boats.)

Even fairly large boats can be overloaded easily. One of the more common mistakes is to seat too many adults in front of the walk-through windshield of bow-rider boats. There might be enough sitting room for four or five people, but the bow doesn't have the buoyancy to support 700 or 1,000 pounds up front. If the boat meets a wave of any height—a tugboat wake, for example—water will pour over the bow and it will swamp. That same load distributed aft might cause no problems, because the wider beam and decreased vee toward the rear of most boats can support more weight.

Excess weight doesn't have to come in the form of live bodies. A 40-gallon livewell filled with water at 8 pounds per gallon can considerably decrease the seaworthiness of a flats boat that already has minimal freeboard. If you're loaded to the max with passengers, the added weight of the water can make the boat sit dangerously low.

Rainwater can collect in the bilge of some boats and create a weight problem as well. Always pump out the bilges when preparing for a day on the water—the boat will float higher, run faster, and burn less fuel.

Look Out! _____

Large amounts of rainwater or water from leaks accumulating in a deep bilge can sink a boat that appears to be without problems at the dock. The boat might go on plane almost normally, but run in a bow-high position due to the water aft. When the hull drops off plane, the stern squats, sending all the water on the boat rushing toward the transom. The added weight concentrated aft can cause the stern to go under.

Speed Thrills, But Also Kills

One bit of advice given to me by an old skipper when I first became a coastal boater has served me well many times: "Go slow and you get in trouble slow," was the way he put it. This is particularly true with larger boats, where mistakes often have to be avoided early if they are to be avoided at all.

If you see a patch of lighter-colored water ahead and you wonder whether it might be a shoal, don't keep on motoring forward at flank speed to let your lower unit answer the question! Slow down to idle, send a crewman forward with a sounding pole (a pole long enough to probe for safe depth), and check it out. If the water is too shallow, back away while you still can.

The same sort of caution will take you far in dozens of other situations. In boating, remember that you are not out there to prove you are the fastest and toughest guy on the freeway, but rather to enjoy a few hours of leisure away from the rush.

Slow is good.

See another boat approaching from the left, which means you have the right-of-way, but he's not slowing down? You could speed up and cut him off, asserting your legal rights. But if he doesn't slow down, the legality of your actions and his might be left to your heirs and attorneys to sort out. Life is too short as it is—why take the risk? Besides, he's not really showing he's more macho than you, only more ignorant of the rules of the road.

Slow speeds are particularly appropriate for docking in most situations. You never know when the motor will die just when you need it to slow down before plowing into a piling, so be wise and approach your slip with caution, with fenders over the side and boat hooks at the ready.

All of this is not to say that there's no place for high-performance boats on the water. On the contrary, I enjoy mile-a-minute speeds as much as anybody—in the right place and at the right time. On open ocean or a broad lake or bay where traffic is minimal, there's no reason not to let your rig show its stuff on a calm, sunny day.

But in a winding residential canal, on the Intracoastal Waterway, in bad weather, or after dark a lot of unfortunate things can happen if the skipper can't keep his hand out of the fuel injectors.

High-performance boats offer a fast, exciting ride with very little risk on open water during calm weather. Larger models like this one are easy to drive and not so touchy as smaller, lighter, high-speed rigs.

(Donzi Marine)

Keep a Clear Head: Don't Drink and Boat

When the sun drops below the yardarm, many boaters like to enjoy an adult beverage or two aboard. There's nothing wrong with that, as long as the boat is securely anchored or tied to the docks for the night. But as I've already mentioned in Chapter 7, *operating* a boat under the influence of alcohol or drugs is asking for big trouble. The majority of boating fatalities nationwide each year involve *boating while intoxicated* (*BWI*).

The designated-driver rule that applies ashore goes double afloat; although you might not mind if your passengers party on, the person at the wheel must be a teetotaler until the engines are shut down for the day.

All states have BWI laws, and it doesn't take a lot of alcohol to put you over the legal limits that range from .05 to .08. For most men, three to four beers will do the job, and two or three might do it for small-bodied women.

You don't have to be legally drunk, though, to be incapacitated as a skipper. Researchers say the effects of alcohol can be more pronounced on the water than ashore.

Dehydration from exposure to sun and wind, plus the rocking of waves and the tiredness that comes toward the end of a day of boating, can all contribute toward making you more tipsy after a given number of drinks than you might be back on shore.

Don't take chances—steer clear of alcohol. The best policy is to keep your mind completely clear any time you might be called on to make decisions affecting the safety of your crew or your boat. (This caution also goes for mind-altering drugs, both the illegal kind and prescriptions—avoid anything that might slow your decision-making.)

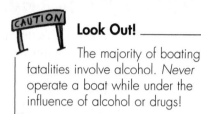

Look Out!

The majority of boating fatalities involve alcohol. *Never* operate a boat while under the influence of alcohol or drugs!

Running Out of Gas

Pretending to run out of gas might be a nice ploy to get cozy with a prospective mate, but the real thing isn't very amusing when you're miles from shore with no other boats in sight.

As I've mentioned earlier, fuel gauges are notoriously inaccurate, and the safest course is to top off the fuel tank before you head out.

If you know how far you intend to travel and about how many gallons per hour your boat burns, or what the miles-per-gallon figures are, you'll have a pretty good idea of whether or not your gas gauge is telling you tales. In general, fuel economy is likely to be best at near-idle speeds, as in slow-trolling at 1,000 rpms, with a second peak almost as good somewhere between 3,000 and 4,500 rpms for outboards, 3,000 and 4,000 for gas inboards and sterndrives.

But some beginning boaters don't realize that proceeding at off-plane speeds can make your fuel gauge drop like the stock market in October. Some boats, when operated in a stern-down, bow-high position between 2,000 and 3,000 rpms, actually burn *more* fuel than at wide-open throttle, even though their speed might be only one-third as fast. As a result, if you plow along at this speed assuming you're saving fuel for the ride home, you might make a sad discovery while you're still many miles from the dock.

Boat Bytes

A fuel-flow meter is a useful tool aboard—most offer both gallons-per-hour and miles-per-gallon readouts so that you can remain in the most efficient operating range.

Some boats come with an auxiliary fuel tank installed—when the main tank runs dry, you flip a lever and tap into the extra tank to get you home safe. If your boat doesn't have one of these tanks, consider carrying a spare portable fuel tank. The three-gallon size takes up little space and can save lots of headaches.

Getting Smart in a Hurry

Boating common sense is developed with years of experience, also known as trial-and-error. But one way for beginners to avoid a lot of mistakes is to take a boating course from the Coast Guard Auxiliary, U.S. Power Squadron, or a commercial provider like Sea School.

Many states license boat operators and check their knowledge with some sort of test, so these classes can be a great help in meeting legal requirements, too.

For boating classes near you, call 1-800-336-BOAT, or visit the Coast Guard Auxiliary website at www.cgaux.org, or the U.S. Power Squadron site at www.usps.org.

The Least You Need to Know

- Make sure someone somewhere knows where you are and when you expect to return any time you're on your boat.

- Make your boat as stormproof as possible, but never stay with it in a severe storm.

- High-speed driving has its place, but crowded waterways and harbors are not among them.

- For your safety and the safety of your crew and other boaters around you, never operate a boat while drinking alcohol or taking drugs.

Chapter 19

Common Emergencies (If There Are Such Things)

In This Chapter

- ◆ What to do if you run aground
- ◆ Coping with hypothermia
- ◆ Rescuing a person who falls overboard
- ◆ Survival tips if you fall overboard
- ◆ Dealing with leaks, fires, and other onboard emergencies
- ◆ When to call the Coast Guard for help

You might go through your entire boating life without ever facing a single emergency worthy of the name. Most casual skippers do—boating is not a dangerous sport compared to many. And sometimes an "emergency" is in the eye of the beholder. Is running aground an emergency? Sort of, if the tide is going out, the sun is going down, and the mosquitoes are coming in.

On the other hand, some boaters take an unplanned visit to a bar in stride and have an oyster roast on the shells while they wait for the water to come back up.

But it's also true that a short hop across a quiet suburban pond can very quickly and unexpectedly become what everyone would agree is an emergency, a disaster in the making.

Note that having an emergency does not necessarily mean a tragedy. It's often your rapid response to the situation that determines the outcome. This chapter touches on both the mild and the serious forms of emergencies and how to deal with them.

> **Boat Bytes**
>
> The first step when you go aground is to determine where the nearest water deep enough to float your boat lies. There's probably good water behind you, but there might be a drop-off just ahead or to one side, and sometimes it's easier to go forward than back if you've slid to the back side of a bar.

> **Nautical Notes**
>
> If you're aground but barely so, a likely solution in boats powered with outboards or sterndrives is to tilt up the lower unit to the point where the prop is just beneath the surface and try to back off. Many times, this is all it takes. For sailboats, sometimes all it takes is to tip the boat to one side, raising the keel a bit and hopefully putting the hull back afloat.

You're Grounded—Now What?

There are times in every boatman's life when the bottom is too close to the top. You're grounded, for the first time since you were a teenager. It happens to everybody, from boat designers to skippers with 20 years under their belts, and sooner or later it will happen to you.

One approach to the situation is to pretend it hasn't happened. Just tell your crew that this looks like a good place to drop anchor for a few hours and have lunch. Then assess the situation. How bad is it?

Determining Your Options

If the motors sporadically started laboring, the boat bumped a few times and then slid to a stop, you're probably going to be fine. You're stuck, but not bad, and the bottom is soft. However, if the boat suddenly came to a halt and flopped over on one side of the bottom, this is not a good sign. You are up where only the flounder and stingrays can swim.

If there were loud crunching or grinding noises when you hit and you stopped with a jolt, you might have struck rock rather than soft sand or mud. There could be damage to the prop, lower unit, skeg, rudder, shaft, or even the hull itself. This is the worst-case scenario.

The tides are also a factor to consider. If it's low tide and you had a soft grounding, you're probably in luck. Just relax, do lunch, tell a few grounding jokes, and the tide will come back within a short time and float you off. You might want to put out an anchor in the direction of deep water and keep tension on that line as the tide rises—often, this will pull you off. At least, it will keep the wind from pushing you farther up on the bar as you start to float.

Props pull better in forward than in reverse. So if the deep water lies behind you, you might want to try spinning the boat 180 degrees so that you can leave the bar with the gears in forward. On small boats, this can be done with muscle power, sometimes via a stout push pole or oar, but more often by going over the side and putting your shoulder to the bow.

If you have an outboard or sterndrive, be sure to tilt up your lower unit far enough so that it does not touch bottom before you attempt to push the bow to one side or to force the boat backward. The lower unit is the lowest part of the boat when tilted down, and it will block your efforts if it's not tilted up.

In fact, if the water is wading depth, it's best if everybody gets out—sometimes this reduction in weight raises the boat several inches and it floats free. Sometimes, just moving passengers from the bow, which is the deepest section of many boats, to the stern will bring you free. It's worth a try.

 Look Out!

If you hit hard bottom at speed, after you've freed yourself check things out before you head for deeper water. Better to be grounded than sunk! A hard strike on rocks can put a hole in the hull. Open the bilge hatch and make sure no water is coming in.

Tow, Tow, Tow Your Boat

Are seas rough, wind rising, or a storm coming? Is the tide falling? If so, you can't be casual about getting free. Use your cell phone or your VHF via channel 16 to contact a commercial towing service such as Sea Tow or TowBOAT/U.S. (for details, see Appendix B). These towing services will tow you clear for a price. Or flag down a passing boat—and do it quickly!

However, be aware that some unscrupulous types have claimed salvage rights, and won, after lending an apparently friendly helping hand to a boat in distress. It's by far best if you can get a tow from a friend—an unknown passerby is the last resort.

If you need a tow, use your anchor line for the towline—it's probably the strongest line on the

 Boat Bytes

Towing with the current usually works better than pulling against it. And sometimes whipsawing the boat—turning it 180 degrees—will do the job when a straight pull won't.

boat. Dock lines won't do the job. And secure the line to the bow eye (the ring at the bow to which a trailer's winch hook is attached), not to the cleats, which are sometimes held down by small screws—they'll be snatched out. (Ditto if you're ever called on to tow a boat—use the transom lifting eyes, which are through-bolted in the transom rather than screwed down like some cleats.)

Secure a heavy towline to the bow eye of the towed boat. Note the bridle or yoke attached to the aft lifting eyes of the towboat, rather than attaching the towline to one of the cleats.

(Frank Sargeant)

With I/Os and outboards, tilt your drive up out of the water before a tow to prevent damage to the prop or skeg. With inboards, consider the damage that might be done by towing—you can't be pulled backward without ruining the drive components, prop, shaft, and strut, and maybe allowing water to get in around the shaft log. And even a pull forward over a shallow bar might damage the running gear. You might have to wait for higher water.

There are times when even the most inventive efforts will not get a grounded boat free. It's then necessary to wait for the peak of an incoming tide.

Sometimes, with big, heavy boats grounded on high tide in protected waters, the least expensive thing to do is leave the boat there until the monthly tide cycles peak, as they do every two weeks, bringing added water to the shoal and gently floating the hull free. (Don't try this as an excuse to extend your vacation a couple of weeks.) Secure the boat, take the dinghy ashore, and forget about your little indiscretion until the full moon erases your mistake.

Person Overboard!

One of the most common potential emergencies is one of your crew going over the side. It happens sooner or later to just about everybody who spends a lot of time on the water, and whether or not it becomes an emergency depends on the conditions.

A fall from an anchored boat into calm water in the middle of a Georgia summer day by a good swimmer is an amusement, not an emergency. Give the swimmer a hand getting back aboard and no harm done. But falling off a sailboat during a fast downwind leg on a chilly fall evening in Maine when you're dressed heavily to keep out the cold can be deadly serious. Without fast action, it can become a tragedy.

Here are the steps in bringing someone safely back aboard:

1. **Don't lose sight of the victim.** If you can't find him, he's going to have to tread water a lot longer—maybe too long. Consequently, it's best if one crewperson does nothing but keep an eye on the swimmer, pointing at him steadily from the bow so the helmsperson knows where to steer for the recovery.

2. **Shut off the power immediately if there's any danger of the prop striking the swimmer.** If you're on a sailboat, turn the boat into the wind to stop the forward motion. (There has to be some hasty sail handling here, to be sure, if the spinnaker is set.)

3. **If the person is within throwing range, toss a life ring or flotation cushion to him.** (If there's wind or a current, be sure to toss it on the upwind or up-current side so it drifts down to the person.)

4. **Swing the boat back to the person to make the recovery.** He knows you've seen him and he's got flotation, so he hopefully won't panic.

   In a shallow-draft boat like a houseboat or pontoon boat that tends to "kite" or blow sideways in the wind, it's probably best to come to the person from downwind. Coming in upwind might result in the boat being blown right past him, or even over him. With deep-vees and keeled sailboats less likely to be pushed around by the wind, coming in from upwind allows you to shut off the motor and drift close enough to throw a line to the swimmer. The hull creates a lee from wind and waves as well.

5. **Draw the person in close, get a swim ladder over the side, and help him back aboard.** If the person is heavily dressed in waterlogged clothes, elderly, injured, or has been exposed to cold water, he might not have the strength to make it aboard himself. Haul him in with the help of two or three strong crew members, pulling on both arms and the back of the PFD he's hopefully wearing.

On sailboats with high freeboards, the boom's block and tackle (see Chapter 23) is sometimes used to hoist exhausted swimmers aboard, via a sling under their arms.

Hypothermia

Those who fall overboard in cold water and even those in warmer water for long periods might have their core body temperature reduced to the point where they lose strength and mental acuity—they are suffering from *hypothermia*. Longer exposure brings unconsciousness or death.

What are the symptoms of hypothermia? They can be varied depending on the temperature and the length of exposure, but suspect hypothermia if the victim ...

Salt Talk

Hypothermia is a lowering of body temperature that results from extended exposure to cold. It occurs much more rapidly in water than in air because water conducts heat away from the body faster than air.

- Shivers uncontrollably.
- Complains of being numb.
- Complains of being dizzy.
- Seems to be in a trance or not alert.
- Goes to sleep suddenly.
- Has an irregular or slow pulse.
- Breathes irregularly.

In water below 40 degrees, a person might become unconscious in as little as 15 minutes, according to the Coast Guard. Water from 40 to 50 degrees brings unconsciousness in 30 minutes to an hour, and from 50 to 60 degrees, in 1 to 2 hours.

Nautical Notes

It doesn't even take a fall overboard to become hypothermic; getting wet from a rainstorm accompanied by howling winds can do the job, even when air temperatures are moderate. If you stay dry, you're much less likely to become chilled. Get your rain suit out sooner rather than later, even during a summer squall.

In warmer weather, the prospects are much better. Water temperatures from 60 to 70 degrees can be endured for up to 7 hours for healthy adults, and from 70 to 80 degrees, survival time can exceed 12 hours.

In short, in extremely cold water, rescues have to be nearly immediate to have much chance of saving the victim.

To treat a victim of hypothermia, follow these steps:

1. Strip off the victim's wet clothes and dry him thoroughly.

2. Cover the victim with blankets or a sleeping bag (but no hot baths; the body should be warmed slowly).

3. Give hot liquids if the victim is thoroughly awake.

4. Monitor the victim's heartbeat and breathing and be ready to give CPR if needed.

5. In cases where mental acuity, heart rate, or breathing are affected, get the victim to a physician as soon as possible.

If You Fall Overboard

It's a horrible feeling to be left swimming in the open sea as your boat chugs off toward the horizon, according to those who have been there. Odds are huge that it won't ever happen to you, but there are several cases every year, and the larger the boat, the more likely it is that if you slip over the side, no one will notice. Having a boat sink out from under you can also force you to go for a swim when you'd rather not.

In either case, you're in immeasurably better shape if you've got on your PFD; you don't have to worry about staying afloat and can devote your attention to conserving body heat and to being found by rescuers.

Survival swimming experts suggest the following to improve your chances of survival:

- Don't take off your clothes so that you can swim better. Even wet clothes conserve heat. (If your clothes are so heavy you can't swim at all in them, however, shuck them.) Slip off your shoes, though—it will make it easier to kick.

- Use the Heat Escape Lessening Position (H.E.L.P) to conserve body heat. Basically, you pull your knees to your chest and hold them there with your arms. This only works if you're wearing a PFD—otherwise, you'll sink when you try it.

- If you're in cold water, try to keep your head out of the water. The head is the body's radiator, and immersing your face will cause you to lose heat rapidly.

- If you're in the water due to a capsize, stay with the boat and try to climb out of the water onto the boat, if possible. Air transfers heat slower than water, so you'll maintain body heat longer on the boat. It also provides flotation and makes it much easier for rescuers to find you.

- If you're in warm water, use the survival floating technique, in which you allow yourself to float face down between breaths, to help conserve energy.

- ◆ If you are tossed a lifeline by rescuers, make a loop around your chest and knot it securely. Your chilled hands might not be strong enough to hold on when the line is drawn in.

- ◆ Stay away from the propellers if the rescue boat approaches with its engines running.

That Sinking Feeling

Recreational powerboats 20 feet and under are all equipped with full foam flotation that's supposed to keep them afloat in an upright position should the hull get a hole in it. Larger boats are not required to contain this flotation, and many do not—they can sink like stones. Obviously, when you buy a boat, you should give special consideration to those of whatever size that contain flotation to keep you and your crew safe no matter what.

Sinking is rare in any well-maintained boat. Leaks, however, are not. And when the water comes in faster than you can get it out, the boat fills up.

Even a boat with full flotation might not stay upright when it gets loaded down with hundreds of pounds of water. When buoyancy is lost, waves can roll over the gunnels and complete the swamping process—in rough water, the boat is likely to turn over.

If Your Boat Springs a Leak

Bilge pumps are the devices that stand between you and any leaks. A 2,000 gallon-per-hour pump costs only $50 more than a 500 gallon-per-hour pump, so it makes sense to check your bilge pump, and if it's not a jumbo, replace it with a larger pump. It's very inexpensive insurance.

Look Out!

Bilge pumps have to operate in the dirtiest part of any boat, the bilge, where all the sand, shells, busted screws, and other debris accumulate. As a consequence they can jam, and often do so at the worst possible time. Keep your bilge clean, and clean out the pump strainer regularly.

Pumps should be hooked to an automatic float switch that turns the pump on anytime several inches of water gathers in the bilge. This way, you don't have to worry about a leak getting a big head start on you before you realize it; and just as important, you won't forget to turn off the pump, run it dry for hours, and burn it up.

Most leaks aboard fiberglass and aluminum boats result from malfunctioning through-hull fittings or hoses for bait wells and wash-down systems, and are not large enough to overcome the pumping ability of the bilge pump. However, for safety's sake, it's a good idea to carry some rubber stoppers that will plug your fittings in case something goes wrong with the valve or hose.

If you get a *big* leak, resulting from striking a submerged object, you might have to make some emergency hull repairs. Stuffing anything that will fit into the hull is the obvious and most practiced solution—extra PFDs and cushions do the job best, particularly when backed up with T-shirts and towels in the smaller cracks. You'll still have water coming in, but it might not flow so fast that the pump can't keep up with it. If the pumps can keep up with it, you can head for the boat ramp or marina. If they can't, head for the nearest beach or sandbar. And if the flow is too fast for that, break out the VHF and call for assistance, pronto.

Boat Bytes

Bilge pumps can burn out over time. If you're going on an extended cruise, particularly to a remote area, carry a spare or two for security.

Fire Aboard

Fires afloat are rare but scary, because the only solution for a serious fire is to go into the water and watch the burning boat drift away.

Although you're required to carry at least one fire extinguisher aboard almost any powerboat, the discharge time of that extinguisher will be less than 30 seconds. Clearly, if you have a fire, you have to attack it early and hit the base immediately or you won't be able to control it.

Fires in the engine room or anywhere near fuel lines or fuel tanks are particularly dangerous because a fuel explosion can take place at any time. A fire in proximity to fuel means everyone should put on PFDs immediately and prepare to jump overboard at a moment's notice.

Small fires in other parts of the boat, still dangerous, are usually less critical—although they can get big in a hurry, particularly if strong winds are fanning them. If possible, turn the boat so that the fire blows off the boat, rather than into it. This will slow the spread of the flames and give you a few added minutes to fight them.

Cabin boats sometimes have galley fires. A handy flame retardant for grease fires is baking soda, a staple on most boats to keep the refrigerator or cooler smelling fresh. Throw loose handfuls of baking soda at the base of the flame. Don't use water— it can spread the flames.

Other cabin fires involving clothing or upholstery can be put out with your most abundant extinguisher on a boat, water brought below via a bucket or the boat's wash-down system.

Calling for Help

You can call the Coast Guard for advice or aid when you have problems, to be sure, but never issue the famous MAYDAY … MAYDAY … MAYDAY call to the Coast Guard unless you have a life-threatening emergency. (Running out of gas 20 miles at sea doesn't qualify.) The Coast Guard will help you in contacting other boats nearby to render aid, hook you up with a commercial towing service, or send members of the all-volunteer Coast Guard Auxiliary to assist you. They will also call the commercial towing services for you if you can't raise them yourself.

Getting caught in a storm that scares the bejeepers out of you is not an adequate reason to use the distress signal. However, a boat that is sinking rapidly, or drifting powerless toward a rocky shore and an enraged surf, or aflame in a fire so severe that abandoning ship will probably be required, all qualify as emergencies. So does a passenger who is severely ill with a heart attack, stroke, and so on.

Issuing the call for lesser problems will result in a very grim-faced encounter with Coast Guard officers when they arrive to find you alive and reasonably well.

The U.S. Coast Guard responds only to serious, life-threatening emergencies. Small problems like running out of gas are handled by commercial tow services.

(Frank Sargeant)

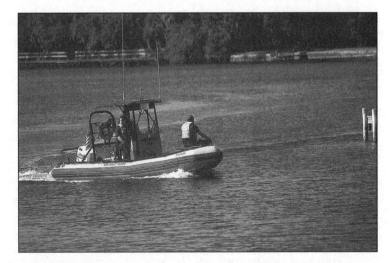

The call is issued on channel 16, which is constantly monitored by the Coast Guard. The proper format is to start with the MAYDAY call, repeated three times—this alerts any nearby boaters as well as the Coast Guard monitor that you have a very serious problem. Don't yell, even if you're under duress—it will only make your transmission harder to understand. Speak loudly and clearly.

Be sure to include the following information in your call:

- ◆ Your boat's name

- ◆ A full description of your position, including latitude/longitude

- ◆ The nature of your emergency

- ◆ A description of your boat, including length and color, so the Coast Guard can spot you when they arrive

> ### Nautical Notes
>
> If you hear a MAYDAY call from another boat and you're close by, you're legally obligated to render assistance and stand by until the Coast Guard or other authorities arrive, as long as doing so doesn't endanger your own boat or crew. It's not uncommon for a Coast Guard helicopter to zoom in and wave nearby recreational boats to the rescue if they don't have a boat of their own in the area.

Other drastic emergency procedures are to make use of visual distress signals: lighting up flares, firing a parachute flare skyward, or waving down another boat using objects of clothing as a flag. The point is to do whatever it takes to get someone's attention promptly.

The Least You Need to Know

- ◆ Not all emergencies result in disaster—be prepared and you can come through most situations safely.

- ◆ Carrying appropriate emergency gear, including extra bilge pumps and a fire extinguisher, can save your boat in the event of a leak or fire onboard.

- ◆ Knowing what to do in the event that you or one of your crew falls overboard can prevent a tragedy.

- ◆ Know the procedures for calling for help when your own remedies don't solve the problem.

Part 6

Boating Maintenance

Whether you own a house, a car, or a boat, you'll find that there's a bit of upkeep involved. Fortunately, boat maintenance is simple compared to some jobs, and most boaters find they can handle the majority of it on their own. (You can also save a bundle of money by doing many jobs yourself, and the skills you learn might be very helpful when something breaks and you're many miles from the nearest boatyard or marina.)

This section covers clean-ups essential to avoid corrosion and fouling, tips on keeping your boat's gel coat gleaming, and some advice on keeping the interior new-looking. (Remember the more shipshape you keep your boat, the more money you'll get back at trade-in time.)

And it's always smart to be aware of a few emergency repairs that can help your motor get you home when something goes wrong. You'll learn the basics in Chapter 22 and also get some advice on basic tools and spare parts you'll probably want to carry.

20

The Well-Equipped Nautical Toolbox

In This Chapter

- ◆ Gearing up for outboards
- ◆ Supplies and tools for inboards
- ◆ The universal tool kit
- ◆ Taking care of your tools
- ◆ Electrical tools and extras

Maybe you don't like grease on your hands and oil in your hair—for reasons not understandable to those who love the noise, heat, and smell of an engine running right, some folks don't. But there are times in every boater's life afloat when a few repairs are needed, and you're the only "mechanic" in sight.

With the right supplies, good tools, and a bit of know-how, you can solve many common problems on the spot, without so much as resorting to your cell phone to call your friendly marine mechanic ashore. (Although it's a very good idea to have a friendly marine mechanic ashore, and to keep his phone number in your cell phone, just in case!)

Part of keeping things humming is having the right tools aboard to do the various jobs necessary to maintain your boat.

In this chapter, you'll learn what goes into the basic marine tool kit as well as a bit about selecting boat batteries and the chargers that keep them well fed.

The Most Important Tool

The most important tool you can have for any boat is an engine repair manual dedicated to your particular year and model of motor. These shop manuals cost $25 to $35 each, and if it helps you make one repair you couldn't have made without it, it has paid for itself many times over. Manuals are available through local marine dealers as well as large bookstores.

Gearing Up for Outboard Boats

If your boat has a two-cycle outboard, you've got to be sure that it gets a steady supply of oil to burn with the gas. Small two-cycles and a few larger economy models don't have automatic oil injection, so you have to measure and mix the proper quantity of oil each time you add gasoline. The usual mix is 50 to 100 parts gasoline per 1 part oil, by liquid measure. There is usually a chart on the back of the oil container and a measuring device on the side of the container.

You need aboard …

- A supply of TCW-3 oil, used to refill the oil injection reservoir. Make sure to always buy extra oil when you refill the reservoir—you can't operate the motor without it, and if you run out miles from a marina you'll have a major problem.

Look Out!

Running a two-cycle outboard without oil will ruin the powerhead in minutes. Always make sure to mix oil with the gas, or to keep the oil tank full on motors with automatic oil injection. With four-strokes, you don't need to mix oil with the gas, but should change the oil and filter every 100 hours of operation.

Most outboard manufacturers distribute their own brand of oil, but any National Marine Manufacturer's Association (NMMA)–approved TCW-3 oil, including the much less expensive brands you can get at discount stores, will work fine and will not void your motor's warranty. Buy it by the gallon to save money.

- A funnel to get the oil into the tank without spilling it down into the bilge. The bigger the funnel reservoir, the better. Those with flexible plastic nozzles are easiest to use in the tight confines of a hatch.

You can make a serviceable funnel by simply cutting the bottom out of a plastic, one-quart oil bottle. Inverted, the small filler neck fits inside the oil-tank filler as you pour.

- Spare spark plugs. Make sure they're the same type used by the manufacturer.

- A spark plug wrench, including a soft insert to protect the ceramic insulator.

- On motors to 75 horses, a starter rope. Some larger motors can be pull-started, but only by rather burly mechanics. The starter rope is your insurance against a dead battery.

- On portable motors, a spare shear pin for the propeller.

- A spare propeller, prop nut, washer, and cotter pin.

- A wrench to fit the prop nut.

> **Boat Bytes** _____
>
> Funnels used for oil create a sticky mess if not stowed properly. Wipe out the funnel with paper towels and stow it inside a gallon-size plastic bag with an airtight locking seal to keep things clean.

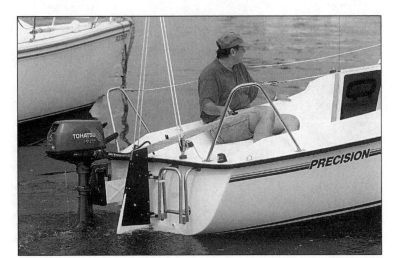

Four-stroke outboards like this one don't require oil to be mixed with the gasoline, but manufacturers recommend an oil change and new filter after every 100 hours of operation.

(Tohatsu Outboards)

Inboard Supplies

Four-stroke outboards as well as nearly all inboards and I/Os, both gasoline and diesel, get their oil from inside the oil pan attached to the bottom of the engine and burn very little of it with their fuel. Consequently, you don't have to add oil as often—although a marine diesel will very likely want a small sip every morning, gasoline inboards are likely not to need a refill for weeks at a time.

Still, extra oil and a means to get it into the engine are necessary, as is some other gear. Here's a recommended list:

- At least a quart of oil for a gasoline engine and four quarts for a diesel. (Note that oil for diesels is not the same as oil for gasoline engines.)

- A funnel to fit the filler on top of the engine.

- Fuel filter elements and gaskets. Particularly with diesels, the filters have to be cleaned regularly.

- Spark plugs and wrench.

- A spare propeller, prop nut, washer, and cotter pin.

- Spare drive belts and a knowledge of how to install them.

A spare propeller can be useful added gear, especially when boating in shallow areas. You also need a wrench to fit the prop nut and a new cotter pin.

(Frank Sargeant)

Universal Spares

Some spare parts are likely to be useful on almost any boat and in almost any situation. Make up a kit of the most common things to have aboard, and you'll be ready to fix many problems that crop up. Here's what I recommend every boater have:

- ◆ Nylon tie-wraps in various sizes, good for anything from securing a fishing reel to a rod to fixing a broken radio antenna.

- ◆ Stainless-steel screw clamps. Get them in several sizes to fit everything from fuel hoses to bilge-pump connections.

- ◆ An assortment of screws, washers, nuts, and bolts, preferably in stainless steel, carried in a plastic divider box that keeps them sorted by size. Marine stores sell kits that contain the most common sizes, all sorted in plastic bins.

- ◆ Wire coat hangers. The wire can be bent into all sorts of useful tools for retrieving dropped gear, securing loose stuff, hanging up tools, and so on. Keep several on board. (Remember, they will rust around saltwater—they're for temporary use only.)

Sticky Stuff

Something is always coming loose, flying around the cockpit, or springing a leak on a boat. You need an assortment of "sticky stuff" to take care of these little annoyances. Here's what I recommend: a large roll of duct tape, a tube of marine seal (particularly the tough, stick-to-anything type known as 5200 Sealer from 3M), several sticks of "hot-glue" (you can use a cigarette lighter to melt them), and epoxy-resin-based auto-body filler, which has endless uses.

Tool Time

Some guys believe you can never have enough tools, but it's probably more accurate to say that a few tools that you know how to use and that you keep where you can find them are more helpful than a 200-pound chest full of unsorted equipment.

One Size Fits All: Adjustable Tools

If you're not into owning large tool sets, adjustable tools can go a long way toward solving most mechanical problems.

Adjustable tools enable one tool to do the work of a half-dozen, so they take up less space and add less weight to your tool kit than conventional tools—plus they save you money.

The first tool you'll want in your basic one-size-fits-all box is probably the venerable locking pliers, which works both as pliers and a wrench when necessary. Get two of them, a 9-inch and a 5-inch, and you'll be ready to tackle most anything.

Crescent wrenches are equally useful. Get a 12-incher, an 8-incher, and a 6-incher, and you can cover most jobs, down to tightening the nut on your trailer hitch.

Third in your one-size-fits-all box is a slip-joint pliers, about 10 inches long, that enables you to lock on to pipes and large nuts.

Other Tools You'll Need

One of the first tools any boater should buy is a magnetic "wand" designed to retrieve bolts or other tools that fall down into the bilge under the engine. It's worth its weight in gold at times, and available at most automotive parts shops.

You'll also need large and small Phillips-head and flat screwdrivers. It's a good idea to get an extra flat driver with a 12- to 14-inch shaft if you own an inboard or stern-drive; the extra reach is often handy in the tight confines of the engine box.

It's also useful to carry a set of ratcheting socket drives (U.S. or metric, depending on the nuts and bolts on your engine) in $^3/_8$'' drive.

A set of hex keys, ideally all fitted together into a single tool like a locking knife, will often come in handy.

A claw hammer is occasionally useful, as well—fiberglass-handle models give fewer problems around the water because they won't warp or rot. A tool most anglers will want is a pair of stainless-steel side-cutter pliers. These are used for making wire leaders for toothy species, cutting monofilament lines, and removing fish hooks. Wear them in a holster on your belt so they don't get misplaced.

A pair of electrical pliers, including wire strippers and screw cutters, will pay for themselves dozens of times.

You can get most of these tools in a fitted plastic kit for $50 to $80, and the kit has slots so you can always keep everything in place.

Tool Care

Tools and water don't mix. Even if you never get your tools wet, water and salt mist will find a way to reach them, rust and corrode them, and eventually make them useless unless you take special care. The best way to keep tools bright is to wipe them down after every use with an oiled rag. My favorite corrosion-resisting oil is a thin blue liquid called Corrosion-X, but there are many good ones, including Bo-Shield and others. All are available at boating supply stores and many hardware stores.

It's also a good idea to store your tools inside a watertight box, and put that box inside a dry-storage box aboard.

A Slippery Subject: Grease Guns

If you tow your boat on a trailer, you *must* have a grease gun and plenty of waterproof grease. If you don't shoot a few shots of grease to the wheel bearings after every long trip, you will absolutely, positively, have fried bearings before long, possibly resulting in a locked-up wheel, resulting in a flat tire—you get the idea. It's a lot easier to grease the bearings.

The grease gun is also useful for lubing your outboard motor, steering cables, and all other moving, mechanical parts aboard. The best way to handle this messy job is with a cartridge-type grease gun—it keeps the worst of the mess off your hands. Even at that, though, you need plenty of paper towels, and the gun should be stowed inside a sealed plastic bag so that it doesn't ooze grease all over the compartment.

Electrical Extras

Electrical wiring causes frequent problems aboard. Carry several fuses that will fit each of the circuits you have on your boat (most newer boats have circuit breakers that do not require fuses), insulating electrical tape, and several spare pieces of insulated wire in various sizes.

Nautical Notes

Bolts and screws used around water have a habit of freezing in place, and when you try to remove them they break off. The solution to getting the broken section out of the hole is a tool called the "EZ Out," which enables you to get leverage on the offender. It's available at some marine dealers and all auto parts stores.

You might someday ruin the threads on engine parts by overtightening a bolt, particularly in aluminum heads. You can make temporary repairs with an epoxy material that is rubbed on the threads. When it sets, it has enough strength to let the bolt grab once again. (Long-term repairs are better made by inserting a metal coil that will remake the threads.)

Current Events: Marine Batteries

Batteries aren't exactly tools in the sense of being used to fix something that has gone wrong, but they are essential for keeping your powerboat running. There are two types of batteries used for boats:

- The basic starting battery, which is much like the battery in your car, is designed to provide a lot of power for short periods of time. Starting batteries don't do well if drawn below 50 percent of their amp capacity repeatedly. (The amp capacity is a way of measuring the available electrical energy of a battery.)

- The "deep-cycle" battery is designed to provide long-term power to low-amp draws like trolling motors and boat lights. These batteries can survive many complete discharges without damage.

Most batteries of both types are filled with a liquid acid that can spill out if the battery turns over. Sealed batteries avoid this problem; they cost a little more, but they can't spill and you never have to add water.

Boat Bytes

One of the most important "tools" you can carry on your boat is a spare battery. When your main 12-volt source dies, a back-up is a godsend, and having two or more batteries also splits the load for many operations, enabling both to live longer. You might want to swap them every month or so, keeping both fresh.

Gel cell batteries, which replace the liquid with a thick jelly-like acid, last about twice as long as conventional acid-filled batteries, but they cost three times as much. A typical 85-amp gel cell goes for around $175, compared to about $75 for the same thing in a standard battery. But if your batteries are in a tough-to-reach spot where installation and removal is difficult, the gels are worth considering. If you have a big inboard to crank, you need a really big battery—some of these develop over 200 amps—and weigh over 120 pounds! The gel cells' longer life will allow you to go longer between changing out these monsters.

Get a Jump on Things

A set of jumper cables should also be part of your basic boating gear. These allow you to tap power from one battery to another, getting the motor restarted when the main battery is otherwise too tired to do the job. It can also be used to borrow a start from another boat. Buy heavy-duty copper cables, not the cheap aluminum ones—the copper carries the power much better and will last much longer. A waterproof storage bag for the cables is a must—copper doesn't get along well with salt air.

Getting a Charge Out of Chargers

Alternating current (AC) battery chargers are an extra most boaters want sooner or later to give their boat's alternator an assist. You'll find the charger particularly useful if you make use of your boat for overnights, have a lot of electrical accessories, or use an electric trolling motor.

A basic 10-amp single or 20-amp two-battery charger is adequate to keep trolling motor batteries charged, and some of these units are so compact they mount inside the boat and stay there. To use them, you simply fit a special plug into the trolling motor panel. They're inexpensive, ranging from $40 to $100.

For jumbo boat accessory batteries, you need a marine charger. Many of these have a special "amp boost" feature that gives a short jolt of added power if your engine is balky at starting, and they put out lots of power, up to 50 amps, to keep all your accessories operational.

The best chargers are multistage—they charge the battery rapidly up to about 50 percent of full charge, and then reduce the flow to gradually finish off the job without danger of overcharging. They're also shockproof, which many chargers designed for automotive use are not. Prices range from $200 to $500.

Solar panel battery chargers are useful for keeping batteries topped off while you're on the water or at the dock. They lie flat on a cabin roof, are unobtrusive, and you never have to do anything to them. They do need a controller to prevent overcharging, though. They range in price from $100 to $300, plus an added $100 for the controller.

Got a Light?

Without being able to see what you're doing down in the engine box, all the rest of your tools are worthless. Thus, you should have several good flashlights onboard. These should be waterproof, plastic, rubber-coated, or stainless steel. The Krypton bulbs used in some models put out a lot more light than the standard, although they burn up the batteries faster. (Even waterproof flashlights should be protected from salt spray—keep them in the console, or in a plastic bag in dry storage until needed, and store fresh batteries with them.)

A spotlight can be worth a lot when you're looking for an unlighted marker on a dark night. They come in sizes from small up to what are called "owl-roasters," which can send a blaze of up to 1.5 million candlepower into the night. This is laserlike, and you don't want to shine it in your eyes, or in the eyes of another skipper, but it's tremendous for seeing at night. They're surprisingly inexpensive—from $20 to $75. For big boats, you can also buy remote-controlled spotlights to mount on the bow. These cost about $200 to $500.

The Least You Need to Know

- ◆ An engine repair manual is the most important tool you can have aboard.

- ◆ A basic kit of adjustable tools should be kept aboard every boat.

- ◆ Without a flashlight, all your other tools can sometimes be useless. Keep several good-quality flashlights aboard.

Chapter 21

Keeping Your Boat Shipshape

In This Chapter

♦ Keeping your boat clean

♦ Mildew-busting strategies for the cabin

♦ Protecting your bottom from algae, barnacles, and other marine growth

♦ Hull repairs in fiberglass and aluminum

Fiberglass boats don't take a lot of care. In fact, if you're so inclined, you can pretty much leave the cleanup chores to the rain and the wind and still have a serviceable boat, year after year.

Of course, it will look like heck and it won't be worth much when you want to sell it. But there's very little that you *have* to do to keep a fiberglass boat working.

Most of us, however, take a certain pride keeping our boats shipshape and new-looking, and a clean hull actually runs better and saves fuel. And the hours of elbow grease spent keeping a boat clean are often repaid when it's time to sell the boat—appearance is everything when it comes to moving a used boat.

In this chapter, you'll learn tricks for cleaning and polishing your boat, some tips on the use of anti-fouling paints, and a bit about patching small holes or leaks that might develop in your hull.

Washing Down

Although boats live in water, they get dirty. Those used for fishing get *very* dirty. To keep a boat looking new and functioning well, it has to be washed regularly—and those used in saltwater must be washed after every day on the water.

The standard wash-down is with soap and freshwater. Wash-and-wax–type car-wash soaps do a nice job and leave a protective coating on the *gel coat*, but plain old dish soap is okay, too.

A large sponge or wash mitt works best on flat surfaces, but use a scrub brush on skidproof decking and around the crevices and screws on metal work. (Washing all metal parts is particularly important on coastal boats, because just a bit of salt left in place will cause electrolytic corrosion—that green crud.) A scrub brush with a telescoping handle is handy for use on larger boats to reach areas below the waterline.

Salt Talk _____

The **gel coat** is the outer layer of a fiberglass boat, the "skin" that gives the hull its shine and color. It's a hard resin, thicker and more durable than paint.

Boat Bytes _____

Got a green scum line on your hull? Spray it with straight bleach. The stuff vaporizes algae, so that you scarcely have to scrub—just be sure to hose it off with freshwater. (This doesn't work if there's oil or other goop in the line, however.)

Fishing offal (or *awful*, as it's better termed) comes off best with a bleach solution—use about a cup of bleach per gallon of water. Remember, bleach will eat your clothes and your bare feet and hands; wear old clothes and use a long-handled scrub brush. Wash it off thoroughly with plenty of freshwater.

You can pour undiluted bleach into the live wells to get rid of the fishy smell—but be sure to rinse it out very thoroughly, or you'll come up with some very white but very dead baitfish next trip.

Kitchen cleansers with bleach, in a spray bottle, are very handy for spot-cleaning. (Clorox Clean-Up is the best I've found.) Spray it on any dark spots on the finish, let it set a few minutes, and wipe the spots away. (Remember, bleach can corrode metal, so keep it off the engine, cleats, and any other metal parts.)

It's a good idea to apply a fiberglass cleaner about twice a year to remove chalking caused by the sun. This brings back the shine, which can then be preserved by using a fiberglass wax.

Some new polishes include PTFE, the compound on which Teflon is based, and they're particularly good at keeping dirt from re-attaching itself to your hull. Also, you might try some of the new "micropolish" waxes, which not only clean off the crud but also fill the microscopic cracks and hills of the gel coat, creating a like-new shine. Most of these polishes also include a UV inhibitor, which prevents sun from fading the gel coat.

Boat Bytes

Many soaps and cleaners can be harmful to marine life. Use biodegradable cleaners and avoid letting phosphates run into the water by washing your boat on shore when possible.

Although it might be tempting to try an abrasive cleansing powder on a dulled fiberglass finish, don't do it. The stuff eats right through the gel coat, making it impossible to ever get a shine again. Microabrasives or cleaners like Soft Scrub do the job with gentle pressure but don't destroy the gel coat.

Sailboat Rigging

Sailboat rigging takes special care because there are lots of complicated metal parts that trap salt and might rust or corrode over time, weakening gear that must endure tremendous loads when the boat is under sail.

After use in saltwater, all the rigging should be hosed down thoroughly with freshwater, and at least weekly all metal parts of the rigging should get a soap-and-water bath. A soft-bristled scrub brush is the best tool for getting salt out of crevices.

Get Waxed

After a boat has been thoroughly washed and allowed to dry, it's wise to add a good paste wax designed for gel coats, at least twice yearly. The wax cuts down on ultraviolet oxidation and also causes some dirt to slide off, as well as making your gel coat look brighter.

Special formulas for glass, such as Rain-X and Rain View, are well worth buying for offshore boaters who regularly get water on

Look Out!

Fiberglass remains shiny longer if waxed regularly, but never put wax on walking surfaces. With a bit of water added, this becomes as slippery as an ice rink. Soap and water only on decks and walk-on gunnels, please.

their windshields. The products make the glass so slippery that most water simply slides off, giving much better visibility even without windshield washers. (Salt crusts on the shield when it dries, though, so you still have to wash it down later.)

Rain-X is so slippery that some boaters apply it to their boat bottoms to keep algae from forming a scum line. Just rub it on and wipe it off—a treatment once a month helps a lot.

Cabin Cleanups

If your boat has a cabin, it's probably got mildew. The best way to keep mildew out of a cabin is with a low-powered heater like the "Golden Rod," which dehumidifies the compartment. (These heaters only work when attached to 110-volt AC, however.)

Mildew preventives such as Damp-Rid and No-Damp are chemical dehumidifiers that help a lot in compartments that are closed tightly. And mildew-killing sprays such as Lysol will also help keep the black crud from getting started.

Boat Bytes

When possible, bring upholstery and life jackets topside to dry in the sun. Eliminating moisture and applying UV (ultraviolet) rays will help prevent mildew.

If you have vinyl sleeping pads below, treat them with a vinyl preservative once a year. This keeps them looking new and helps them retain their flexibility. Use the stuff monthly on any upholstery such as cushions in the cockpit, too, because vinyl exposed to the sun dries out and starts to crack quickly without it. It's a good idea to stow your cockpit upholstery in the shade of the cabin or your garage when the boat is not in use.

Clean Your Bottoms

The most significant cleaning job on any boat is the bottom. If the running surfaces are not kept clean and smooth, performance suffers.

So what's to make them dirty down there in the water, you ask?

In freshwater, there's algae, scum, and over the last 15 years, zebra mussels. Along the coast, a variety of sea life attaches itself to boat bottoms, but barnacles are the fastest-growing and most tenacious.

In warm weather, barnacles large enough for you to see and feel will grow on a boat left in the water just one week. The growth slows as the water cools, stopping completely in areas where water drops into the 40s in the winter. But in warmer climates like Florida, the little critters are down there digging in year-round—it takes them a couple weeks to show in winter, but they'll be there. Growth can be amazingly rapid, particularly on boats left at the docks for long periods of time. Small shellfish are no problem to remove—they can be scrubbed away with a light chlorine solution (about a cup in a gallon of water) and a medium-bristled brush. (Better wear rubber gloves if your hands are not barnacle-tough.)

If left until they become the size of a dime, barnacles become unbelievably difficult to get off. Some gel-acid cleaners do the job, but they're so powerful they will also clean the skin right off any part of you they happen to contact—risky stuff for the amateur to handle. Scraping and power-sanding is the more common solution, and the sanding knocks off the gel coat so you then have to paint the bottom. So clearly, it's wise not to let the growth go past the initial stages. In warm weather, 10 days is about the max.

For larger boats that must be left in the water, it's a good idea to don a mask and fins and go over the side to give the bottom a monthly scrubbing with a firm brush, particularly in the summer. It's possible to hire a diver to perform this task for you, with costs typically $25 to $40, varying with the size of the boat. If you wait too long between cleanups, the hull will have to be hauled out at considerable expense and scraped down.

The easy way to avoid problems is not to leave your boat in the water for more than a few days at a time. Although the larval forms might latch on to your hull if it sits still for only a few hours, they quickly die and fall off if the boat is pulled out and allowed to dry.

You can get some of the scum off yourself, either with a brush and long handle, or you can snorkel-clean the bottom, but we find the small fee to the diver well worth it.

Paint Your Bottoms

Another solution, most common for large boats that have to be left in the water, is to use anti-fouling paint. This is a paint that contains elements toxic to barnacles and other marine organisms. The most commonly used anti-fouling paints include copper as the toxicant.

There are leaching paints, in which the copper leaches through the paint but leaves the surface itself fairly intact, and ablative paints, which wear away in layers, revealing fresh copper as the top layers disappear.

With either type of paint, a layer of gel-coat primer, applied after a thorough fine-grit sanding, is usually needed to make the anti-fouling paint stick. Not all types are compatible with each other—check with your dealer or read the cans for advice.

Take your checkbook with you when you go shopping for anti-fouling paint—it's horrendously expensive compared to conventional paints. Prices of $75 to $125 per gallon are typical, and you need about a gallon to do the bottom of a typical 24-footer.

Anti-Fouling Aluminum and Wood

Boat Bytes _____

Applying anti-fouling paint is a lot of work. For boats kept in freshwater lakes, it's much easier to use a growth-repelling bottom wax like Easy On, which keeps zebra mussels and algae from taking hold. (Unfortunately, it's not effective against saltwater barnacles.)

Bottom-painting is definitely one of the nastier jobs in boat maintenance; you might consider paying the boatyard to do the job. But having the bottom of a large boat painted by a boatyard can be an expensive proposition—many hours of labor plus the cost of the materials add up. Shop around and get several estimates, in writing, before you make a choice. Be sure the estimate includes the cost of hauling your boat out of the water and setting it on blocks.

However, if you're a do-it-yourselfer, all you need to do is purchase anti-fouling paint and follow the directions on the can.

Anti-Fouling Aluminum

Aluminum gets a different paint, usually one with copper thiocyonate, which does not cause electrolysis as does the standard cuprous oxide used in most anti-fouling paints. (Tin-based paints are also used for metal boats, but must be applied by specialists because they are considered hazardous materials.)

Look Out! _____

Some types of antifouling paint lose their effectiveness if allowed to dry out. Keep the boat in the water if you use one of these types of paint or you'll have wasted your painting effort.

The surface is sandblasted (you can rent a sandblaster and try this yourself, but beware: too much pressure or too long in one spot and you'll need to know how to repair holes in aluminum boats!), then coated with metal primer, then epoxy primer, sanded, more epoxy primer, and then two finish coats of tin-based or other aluminum-type anti-fouling paint. Whew! This definitely sounds like one for the boatyard.

Teak Treatment

Teak is a lovely, durable wood that is a tradition in fine boat building. But teak is, to put it mildly, a pain in the stern to care for. For that reason, a lot of modern builders have eliminated it completely, replacing fittings such as rod holders and cup holders with composite plastics. They don't look nearly as good, but they never require care.

If you have teak aboard, however, you do have to take care of it to keep it from looking like driftwood.

Teak cleaners are strong acids or corrosives designed to bleach away oils and dirt. They have to be applied while wearing rubber gloves. You let them set on the wood for a few minutes, brush them down, and then rinse with freshwater.

When the teak dries after this treatment, it turns almost white. To restore the golden glow, you add teak oil, available at all marine dealers. Just rub it on, let it dry, and then rub on a second or third coat. The oil makes water bead up rather than penetrate, helping to keep the wood clean.

Keeping Stuff Dry

Most boats have dry boxes. They're sort of like those water-resistant watches that work fine until they get anywhere near water. Dry boxes or storage compartments that are truly dry are almost nonexistent. Most makers don't build hatch lids that are adequately guttered, and fewer still are gasketed. This means rain, spray, and washdown water gets in.

Condensation is also a problem, gathering on the inside of the lids during the cool of night, dripping into the compartment as the sun rises. (This is avoided on a few well-made boats with insulated lids.) And a bit of salt on anything stowed in a box will draw water out of the air, making everything else in the box damp.

The solution? Put a truly watertight box inside the dry box. Plastic boxes with snap-on lids are the ticket. And with sensitive stuff like toilet paper that you really want to keep dry, it's not a bad idea to put the item inside a Ziploc bag, then place the bag inside a plastic box, and then place the plastic box inside the dry box. It's sort of like those trick birthday presents that come in a very large box, inside of which is a smaller box, inside of which is an even smaller box, and so on, but it works.

Basic Hull Repairs

With fiberglass, when you get a hole, you fill it with more fiberglass. In fact, tiny holes can be repaired with filled polyester resin putty, which contains a thickener and small glass fibers.

It spreads like peanut butter (but smells worse) and hardens to about the same density as the glass. You then sand it smooth, finishing with 600-grit sandpaper, and spray on gel coat, feathering it in at the edges. Finish with rubbing compound.

Patching Bigger Holes

It's not easy to punch a big hole in a fiberglass boat, but it can be done. Boatyards sometimes manage the trick by dropping boats off forklifts. At sea, running into a submerged post or rock will do it—and give you a lot more problems than simply how to patch it so it looks nice. (See Chapter 19 on emergency procedures for suggestions. Quick!)

Bigger holes require a patch be inserted from inside the hull. You might have to cut a hole in the floor to insert the patch, and then patch that as well. (It's one of those deals where you start out to tighten a drip from a pipe under the sink, and then you find that to get at that drip you have to remove the sink, and then the sink molding breaks when you're taking it out … been there?)

Patching small fiberglass holes on your own is potentially a home-handyperson type of job because the stuff is relatively simple to work with. Expect to get fiberglass dust up your nose, little pieces of glass in your arms, resin under your fingernails. If you're not into this sort of thing, just do what the pros do—send your boat down to the nearest boat hospital and hope your credit card won't melt down over the bill. (Boat-repair guys don't get quite what heart surgeons do, but they're not far behind.)

Patching Aluminum Boats

In truth, most patches in aluminum fail sooner or later. It's very difficult to get anything to stick to aluminum permanently, and the different flex rates between the patch and the expanding and contracting metal eventually cause those tiny leaks to start again.

> **Look Out!**
>
> Acetone, the best cleaner for polyester resin-coated tools, is extremely flammable and hazardous if inhaled in high concentrations. Keep this product well clear of heat and flames and use it only in open, well-ventilated areas.

However, the same epoxy/fiberglass compounds used for fiberglass boats also offer good initial adhesion to aluminum, as long as the parts are thoroughly roughsanded and wiped down with acetone, the standard solvent for epoxy resins.

So-called "liquid aluminum" patching material that comes in tubes also works, but it's basically epoxy resin with an aluminum and/or fiberglass filler.

Aluminum hulls more than .025-inch thick can be repaired by heli-arc welding at an aluminum shop, but the thinner material on most jon boats and canoes simply burns into a larger hole if welding is attempted.

Hull Painting

It's usually not necessary to paint fiberglass boats because the gel coat lasts for decades, particularly if you apply UV-inhibiting polish once or twice a year.

There are a few paints designed for fiberglass, though, that can make an old hull look like new, and that will stay put on the smooth surface. It's not something most boaters can do for themselves and come out with a respectable finish, however, because the paint is best sprayed to lay properly, and on smooth, vertical surfaces spray-painting can be a challenge.

If you truly feel the need to restore the finish on a badly dulled boat, this is a chore that's best left to the pros. Your best course of action is to regularly perform the cleanup duties on your hull to make sure painting will never be necessary.

The Least You Need to Know

- Time spent cleaning your boat is repaid in less maintenance and a better resale value.

- Keeping your boat's bottom clean is a continuous chore for the owners of boats left afloat.

- Simple hull repairs of small holes are easy to do at home, but larger holes take more work and might be better left to the pros.

Chapter 22

Keeping Your Engine Happy

In This Chapter

♦ Basic engine maintenance

♦ Fight back against corrosion

♦ Trouble afloat—and how to fix it

Modern marine engines typically don't require a lot of care, but they do need a bit of attention from time to time to keep them purring. A few minutes of engine care before every boating day will be repaid with reliable starts, longer engine life, and much less chance of trouble when you're far from land, so it's time well spent. And it can save you a boatload of money—it's a lot cheaper to add a quart of oil today than to rebuild the engine tomorrow.

This chapter looks at general engine maintenance and also includes a few tips for minor troubleshooting when something goes wrong. (Thankfully, the tinkering that used to be a part of many outings has nearly disappeared with ever-more-reliable marine engines.)

Let's Get Oiled

The most obvious but probably most forgotten part of engine care is keeping oil in the tank of two-cycle engines with oil injection. Although there are warning horns and *speed-limiters* to prevent you from overlooking this duty for long, many boaters have learned that by the time the horns go off and the limiters kick in, it's too late—your next cruise is to the $40-an-hour repair shop.

Two-cycles engines, unlike four-cycles engines, rely on delivery of lubricating oil with the gasoline to control friction and heat in the cylinders and bearings, so if you don't make sure there's always oil available to mix with the gas, your engine will have a short, unhappy life. (Four-cycles have a pool of oil in a pan at the bottom of the engine and don't require it to be mixed with their fuel.)

Salt Talk

A **speed-limiter** (or "rev-limiter") is used on many marine engines, both to prevent winding past the redline or recommended top limit for revolutions-per-minute, and to slow the engine to near idle speed if anything goes wrong with the lubrication or cooling systems.

Most outboards of four cylinders or more have protective systems to prevent damage resulting from operation without oil. Most have warning horns (electronic beepers mounted in the dash or throttle box) that give an audible signal when you need to add oil or when the engine is running hot.

On four-stroke outboards, sterndrives, and inboards, both gas and diesel, check the oil dipstick religiously before every trip, and at each stop along the way on longer cruises. A four-cycle engine kept full of oil is a happy four-cycle.

Tighten Your Belt

When the belt on your trousers gets loose, it's good. When your engine's belts get loose, it's bad. Outboards use rubber and fabric belts to drive their alternators, and inboards and I/Os use them to drive water pumps, alternators, power steering, and more. The heat and vibration of operation on the water causes these belts to gradually go slack, and when they do they begin to slip. The more they slip, the faster they wear and the looser they get in a vicious circle that ultimately ends when the belts finally break.

Keep the belts tight (most have an idler arm—a moveable pulley—or other adjuster) and you'll eliminate this potential problem. Also, at least yearly, look at the underside of the belts for fraying or missing pieces. Any damage at all means it's time for a replacement. This also goes for water hoses; give them an occasional light squeeze, as if you were checking a peach for ripeness, to detect any softness that may mean they're about to fail.

Torque Time

At 5,000 revolutions per minute, there are a lot of vibrations in a marine engine. Vibration makes nuts, bolts, and screws work loose.

To keep something unfortunate from happening, it's wise to check your engine every four or five trips for anything that might be coming loose and retighten all suspects.

In engines with aluminum heads and blocks, including all outboards, it's easy to strip the threads by putting too much pressure on a stainless-steel bolt or screw. Use a torque wrench, along with the shop manual suggesting how many foot-pounds can safely be applied to each fastener.

It's also a good idea to regularly check the mounting toggles on small, portable outboards; vibrations and compression of the transom can cause them to work loose over a period of months or years, and if they get too loose, they can jump right off the transom.

Lube Job

Because the steering systems on outboards and sterndrives are constantly exposed to water and to salt in coastal areas, they require frequent lubrication. The fittings and brackets support a lot of weight, and unless you keep them lubricated, they will be difficult to steer.

The throttle cables can also benefit from a shot of lube regularly to allow for easy speed adjustment.

Hydraulic and power steering systems are filled with oil (not motor oil, but hydraulic steering fluid), but unless they leak, you'll rarely need to add any fluid. If you open the system to add fluid, you might have to bleed air from it—a job better left to a pro if you're not inclined to tinker.

While you're examining the steering system, check it for any binding or excessive play, grating noises, or loose fasteners. Any problems in this system can lead to disaster, obviously, so if you even suspect problems, take the boat to a shop.

Check the Oil, Please

The lower unit of outboards and sterndrives is filled with gear oil, and this should be checked regularly. Do so by opening the upper inspection hole, which is sealed with a flush-mounted screw. A slight amount of the oil will run out when you pull the screw if the unit is properly filled.

The oil should be dark and clear. If it's milky-looking, there's water in the lower unit and you need to visit the repair shop promptly to find out why. (Usually it's a prop-shaft seal, but sometimes it's a crack in the housing, the result of striking an obstruction.)

If the unit needs oil, it has to be added from the bottom. Oil added from the top traps air, creates bubbles, and makes a mess.

The oil filler screw is on the bottom side of the gear housing, just above the skeg. Don't remove it until you put the upper screw back into place unless you want to drain the unit and refill it completely. The air lock formed by the airtight housing will keep most oil from running out when you remove the lower screw.

Check the oil that comes out of the bottom hole for metal particles. If you see any, it's a sign that something is coming apart inside—have a mechanic take a look. If you don't see any debris, put the filler tube into the filler hole, and then slightly loosen the upper screw so that air can escape as you pump or squeeze oil into the lower tube.

When oil comes out the upper hole, tighten that screw to re-create the vacuum, and then quickly remove the filler tube and plug the hole with the lower screw. Now tighten both screws securely and wipe off any excess oil with paper towels.

Another hidden spot that might need a refill once a year is your tilt/trim reservoir. Check your owner's manual for location and access to the filler tube, and use only the recommended fluid.

Sparking Your Relationship

Without lots of fire, marine engines don't run well. On outboards, the spark plugs and the wires that lead to them stick out and can be bumped or loosened by contact with the cowl or by careless work on some other part of the engine.

Check the plug wires and connections regularly. Particularly on older motors, the connector insulation sometimes goes soft and sticky as a result of long exposure to gas fumes and loses its insulating capability. Replace any plug wires that are not firm and dry, and make sure the connectors snap securely on the spark plug contacts.

With diesels like this Yanmar, you can be sure that the spark plugs are not the problem. Diesels function without them.

(Yanmar Diesels)

It's not a bad idea to pull the spark plugs before the start of the boating season. Clean them with a wire brush, check the gaps and adjust them according to the manual, and then reinstall them.

Use a torque wrench to tighten the plugs. It's *very easy* to strip the threads in the aluminum heads by overtightening spark plugs—don't try to do this by "feel" unless you're an experienced mechanic.

When you fit the cowl back in place on an outboard, make sure that it doesn't hit any of the plugs or wires and cause problems.

The powerhead of an outboard runs in a mist of wet air, with lots of salt along the coast. This soon corrodes or causes electrolysis if the metals are not protected. Spray down your powerhead monthly with a water-replacing oil spray like Corrosion-X to keep corrosion away. The same products also help to keep rust and corrosion off inboards and sterndrives.

Look Out!

Any time you take the cowl off an outboard, make absolutely certain that the rubber seal at the bottom fits back into the casement around the powerhead. Any misfit here or any failure to properly clamp the cowl back into place will let water into areas where it shouldn't be, particularly if you use the boat in big seas.

Prop Problems?

Check the propeller several times a year, or immediately after you brush bottom. Any bent or damaged blades can cause vibration that might eventually ruin the seals in an outdrive or stuffing box in an outboard and lead to lots more problems. (A *stuffing box* is the sealing system that prevents water from entering around the hole where the drive shaft of an inboard passes through the bottom of the boat. A similar system is used around the post that supports the rudder on inboards and sailboats.)

It's not possible to correctly reshape the blades of a bent propeller without templates and other gear, so the best thing to do when you see damage is to send the prop to the shop.

Also, watch for fishing line on the prop shaft, next to the seals. If not removed, this can eventually work its way between the seal and the shaft and cause leaks.

Many boaters consistently flush their outboards with freshwater after every trip on saltwater. Most outboards these days have an attachment on the cowl allowing easy connection of a garden hose. If you use one of these, be sure to turn on the water *first*, and then start the motor to allow the water to flush it out. Starting the motor before you turn on the water can cause overheating. (I don't flush my motors after every trip but do attend to them at least once a month to prevent salt buildup in the cooling passages.)

Follow all these maintenance tips and your engine problems will be rare. However, there will be times when even the best cared-for motor will be balky.

Why Won't It Start? Basic Troubleshooting

Considering that V6 outboards and sterndrives now cost more than many cars, you'd think they'd start right up, first time, every time.

Some do, some don't. Carbureted motors are particularly cranky at times, which is one reason why they've just about disappeared from the new boat market, having been replaced by more dependable, cleaner-running, and more efficient fuel-injected two- and four-strokes. But with small motors as well as older motors in used rigs, there might be a bit of gasping and wheezing, and sometimes nothing at all. Even the latest and greatest motors might not start on occasion.

The loudest sound in the world is when, 20 miles from the nearest land, you turn the starter key and hear … nothing.

Before you face that situation, let's review some of the most common reasons why an engine might not start and how to fix the problem.

Nothing Happens When I Turn the Key

If you turn the key and nothing happens, check the position of the shift lever. Most marine engines have a lock-out that prevents them from starting in gear. And some shift levers don't have an obvious neutral detent. Try moving the shifter to reverse, forward, and then feeling for that center position.

Silence could also mean that wires to the ignition key or to the battery have come loose. Check the battery first—shifting of the batteries due to boat motion sometimes loosens wires, and corrosion building up on the terminals can also be a culprit.

Wiggle the large black and red wires attaching to the terminal posts to see if anything is loose. Look at the connectors and the posts to see if there's any sort of blue-green build-up that indicates corrosion. If so, remove them and scrape the inside of the connectors with a knife until they're bright, and then reattach them securely.

If the wires are tight and clean but the engine won't turn over, it's possible that the battery is dead. If you have auxiliary batteries aboard (those used for trolling motors, cabin lights, and so on) you can tap into these to get things going by using jumper cables.

Another possibility on many engines is that a main fuse has blown or a breaker has tripped. The fuses are usually found in a waterproof connector near the starter. Check and replace or reset as needed. (You'll want to carry a spare fuse of the proper amperage, obviously.)

Look Out! _____

Because direct current doesn't shock, people have a tendency to treat boat wiring with a lack of caution. But a 12-volt battery can generate instant, red-hot metal if you cross connections or drop a wrench that lands across both terminals. Always use caution when working on wiring.

Look Out! _____

Using jumper cables causes sparks, so always make sure there's no gas leak in the engine compartment before you use them. And remember, black goes to the negative post, red to the positive posts—otherwise you'll get some real fireworks!

It Turns Over but It Won't Start

The most obvious solution here is that there's no fuel reaching the firing chamber. To get it there, you hit the choke or "prime" button. About 98 percent of the time on cold-start with an engine that's not fuel-injected, the problem is too little fuel.

With small carbureted outboards, it might simply be that the motor was stored in a position that let the fuel run out of the carburetor bowl; storing a motor at the full-tilt position will cause this to happen in some motors. First try tilting the motor down, so that it's upright in the running position.

Squeeze the primer bulb, located near the motor in the fuel line, to pump fuel from the tank into the fuel system. The bulb becomes firm when the system is ready to go.

Next, choke the engine, most commonly done by pushing in on the ignition key as you crank the starter. On manual-start motors, you pull a choke lever. The choke puts an air restrictor across the carburetor, reducing the amount of air that gets in, making the fuel/air mix richer. Some motors have a "primer" that squirts a shot of fuel into the intake manifold.

In either case, you're enriching the mix, getting explosive fuel into the air inside the cylinder, so that when the spark plug fires, the motor starts.

On fuel-injected motors, which now make up the majority of larger direct-injection two-strokes and virtually all large four strokes, starting is nearly immediate and almost 100 percent dependable, just as in your automobile.

On carbureted motors, it can be a bit trickier. The normal routine is this: You crank until the motor stumbles, and then you stop choking, turn the starter one more time, and it starts. You might need to press in on the key, in short blips, to keep it running after the first start-up, but after 15 to 20 seconds, it should smooth out.

> **Boat Bytes**
>
> If a cold motor stumbles, pops, or belches smoke, even for a second, the fuel is there—so stop choking it! If you continue, it will flood—get too much fuel for the amount of air—and not start because the spark plug won't fire liquid fuel nearly as well as vaporized fuel.

If the motor coughs and runs for a few seconds and then quits with a lot of smoking, don't choke it again just yet. Open the throttle a little and crank the motor once more. Often, it will pop right off.

If you crank 10 seconds more and don't get another cough and don't smell gasoline, give the engine another blip of choke until it coughs again, and then repeat the procedure.

I Flooded the Engine—Now What?

You can tell when your engine is flooded because you'll smell gasoline and the motor will sound "wet" when you crank it. To fix this problem, you have to add more air and cut off the fuel.

Make sure the choke is "off." Don't squeeze the prime bulb, but do open the throttle. (On outboards and sterndrives, you do this by pushing a button on the bottom of the throttle lever, which disengages the shifting rod and enables you to open the throttle without putting the motor into gear.) Crank for 10-second bursts, with 30 seconds in between, until the motor coughs or sputters. (If you're hand-cranking, do it until *you* cough or sputter.)

Don't keep the starter cranking for long periods; it will simply overheat and burn up. Crank the motor for no more than three or four 10-second bursts, and then rest it for several minutes to let the starter cool before you crank it again.

In a worst-case scenario, you might have to unplug the fuel hose, take out the spark plugs, crank the engine a bit with them out to blow out the excess fuel, dry off the plug elements, and then reinstall the spark plugs.

Don't choke the engine after this procedure; it should pop right off. (If you have a chronically troublesome engine, a shot of Quick Start or other fuel vapor into the spark plug hole will help.)

Most of the time when your motor won't start, it's the fuel/air mix. Each motor has a particular starting procedure that works best. Learn the idiosyncrasies of your motor and these problems will go away.

Look Out! _____

Never choke or prime a hot engine, because the fuel is already where it needs to be, and the motor will flood immediately if you add excess fuel.

Look Out! _____

A kill switch, or emergency stop connector, is found on a red lanyard near the ignition switch on most outboard-powered boats and many performance inboards and stern-drives. If this switch is tripped by pulling the cord, no matter how long you crank, the motor won't start.

Could I Be Out of Gas?

Dumb as it sounds, your boat might simply be out of gas. Never trust fuel gauges on boats. Because the floats bounce around so drastically, fuel gauges often get out of whack. So whenever you have the slightest doubt that you might be low on gas, add more. (It's a good idea to keep the tanks topped off, anyway, to prevent water condensation inside, which eventually builds up enough to cause rust and maybe even running problems.) Also, at least once a year you should calibrate your gas gauge by running almost all the fuel out of the tank (carry some spare gasoline in case you overdo it), then slowly fill the tank and note the readings on the pump at every quarter mark on the gauge.

To avoid low fuel problems afloat, the general rule of thumb is to use no more than one third of a tank for the trip out, no more than one third for the trip back, and save one third for reserve. Why leave so much in reserve? Because currents, wind, and waves working against you can suddenly convert your 5-miles-per-gallon motor into one that gets only 2 miles per gallon. (Anglers who troll for hours must reserve plenty for that, as well.)

I've Tried Everything and the Motor Still Won't Start!

If you've done everything right and still can't get the motor to start, check for loose fittings in the fuel line. At times, the quick-release connector on hoses for portable outboards pops loose at the engine cowling. Check for secure attachment here, and at the entry to the portable tank, if you have one.

The fuel hose could also be pinched—maybe someone set a heavy tackle box on top of it. Check the length of the hose, particularly if it's exposed in the cockpit.

On portable tanks, the vent might be closed. It's designed to prevent fuel spillage during transport, but it forms an airlock if left screwed shut when you try to start the engine. (Suspect this one in particular if the engine starts briefly but then shuts down and won't start again.) The vent is a small screw located on the filler cap.

The culprit could also be dirt in a fuel filter. Modern fuel-injected outboards and diesel inboards have several filters built into their fuel systems. If any of them clog, the motor won't start (or it will stumble when it does). Check the filters if simpler remedies fail.

Needless to say, you should have spare filters onboard. For boats that go offshore, you might consider a dual fuel system, where two filters are used in parallel, with a switch in between. When your filter clogs just as you come into a harbor, this can be a lifesaver.

Water in the fuel is another problem. It sometimes results from condensation in older tanks, or it can come from contaminated fuel at a gas station or marina. It's not a common problem, but it can happen. Keep a can of dry gas handy to add to your tank, just in case. (You might have to shoot Quick-Start down the air intake of your motor or through the spark plug holes to get the contaminated fuel clear.)

When the Motor Overheats

When the overheat warning buzzer comes on, it's usually because of weeds in the water intake, found on the lower unit housing slightly above the bullet or gear housing on most outboards and sterndrives. Plastic bags can also cover these intakes. And if you run aground, soft mud can jam them. Tilt up the lower unit and remove any obstructions, and you should be good to go. (If there's mud in the intake, you can clean it out with stiff leader wire.)

It's also possible, on outboards and stern-drives, that the lower unit—the part that sticks down into the water—is tilted up too high. If the water intake comes above the surface, the motor will get hot.

The third possible cause of overheating is a bad water pump—not a fun repair on most engines. See your owner's manual and break out the wrenches, or have the water pump repaired by a professional. (It's a good idea to carry a spare water pump impeller, just in case.)

> **Boat Bytes**
>
> All outboards have a "tell-tale" spout on the cowl that squirts a thin stream of water out to the side when the cooling system has proper pressure. Check this spray regularly, particularly when you pass through weeds, to head off overheating problems.

It Runs but It Doesn't Move

If the motor runs fine until you shift it into gear, and then it dies, you could be looking at some major surgery, as in broken shafts, gears, or other parts. But more often, it's a rope, wire crab trap, or other obstruction wrapped around the propeller.

The solution is to turn off the key, tilt up the lower unit on outboards and sterndrives, and work on the offending tangle with a knife, pliers, or wire cutters. On inboards, you have to put on your dive mask to get at the source—no fun at all in winter!

It's also possible that the shaft is turning but the propeller is not—indicating a broken cotter pin in small motors, a spun rubber impact hub in the prop on larger outboards and sterndrives. To replace a cotter pin, remove the propeller, tap out the old pin, and then insert the new one. You can also use a stout nail cut to size if you don't carry a spare pin.

If the prop has a spun hub (when the hub turns but the prop does not, indicating a failure of the breakaway connection between the two), you can't fix it yourself. However, most propellers will operate at idle speed, allowing you to get back to the dock. (If you speed up, the load is too much for the minimal friction in the hub and the prop won't turn.) Carrying a spare prop is the best way to deal with a spun hub.

The Least You Need to Know

◆ Many engine problems can be avoided with proper maintenance.

◆ Some apparent problems can be solved without ever touching a tool—think things through before you act.

◆ Fuel, air, and spark problems are the most common reasons why engines fail to start.

Part 7

Sailing, Sailing ...

Sailing offers a curious combination of peace and quiet and laid-back lifestyle with intellectual and physical challenge, depending on how you go about it.

This part details the language of sailors as well as the remarkable variety of types of sailing vessels, ranging from fly-weight sailboards to giant schooners big enough to take on transoceanic voyages.

And although getting started in sailing usually requires a bit of hands-on instruction, you can learn the basics through reading this part—from attaching and hoisting the sails to steering through all the points of sail from close-hauled to a downwind run.

You'll also find tips on selecting a sailing school, judging the wind, use of blocks and cleats, handling a sailboard, and lots more in this section.

23

How to Tell the Main from the Jib: A Sailor's Vocabulary

In This Chapter

- ◆ Sailing schools give you the basics, but hands-on instruction is best
- ◆ The names of all that stuff
- ◆ Learning the points of sail

Sailing is an art almost as old as boats themselves, and those who take the time to learn (it doesn't take much) are rewarded with voyages that offer peace and grace and blessed silence that many feel is more at one with the watery environment than the noise and the fumes generated by power-boats.

Sailing is a thinking person's mode of transportation, employing physics, geometry, and ergonomics. It's not for those who simply want to step aboard, turn the key, and take off. But with a bit of study, anyone can learn the basics of sailing in a long weekend. After that, it's a path you can follow as far as you like toward becoming a master.

And although sailing can be among the most tranquil of sports, it can also be among the most exciting and challenging. It holds a lifelong attraction, both for those who race avidly in competition and for those who only race avidly for the best sundown anchorage.

In this chapter, you'll become familiar with the names of all the parts of a sailboat and its rigging; the masts, sails, and lines that make it sail; as well as the points of sail and an assortment of other terms that will make sailing easier. It's a simple language, and one you'll pick up quickly as you spend a bit of time aboard.

Getting Started

It does take a bit of application to get started in sailing, but in retrospect, those who have learned feel it's almost intuitive. I once wrote in my newspaper column that sailing was a technical sport that took a fair amount of instruction. An avid sailor wrote back in a huff that sailing is *not* a technical sport. "Give me three full days and I can teach anybody to sail," he wrote.

I guess he meant it isn't technical in the sense that nuclear physics is technical. But compared to powerboating, it's pretty complex.

Note that there are hundreds of sailing schools throughout the world, but almost no "powerboat schools." This should tell you something.

> **Nautical Notes**
>
> The American Sailing Association (www.american-sailing.com, 310-822-7171) and the U.S. Sailing Association (www.ussailing.org, 401-683-0800) both offer listings of sailing schools nationwide. See Appendix B for more information.

The first difficulty you will encounter is the vocabulary. If you know what to call all the parts of a sailboat, instructions suddenly become much clearer.

You can't truly learn in a classroom, however, and all the good schools feature on-the-water instruction after a brief period of book learning.

Learning sailing is like learning German, not so tough if you're in-country with people who speak it, and, when they hand you a cup of coffee, tell you it's *eine Tasse Kaffee*. Sailing is like that. It's easier to learn by doing than by reading about it.

Go do it first, with a patient instructor, and then learn the terms. You can learn to get around the buoy and back in an hour. Doing it in style or with any hint of speed can take months and years of study and practice.

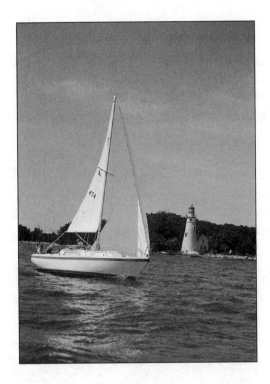

Sailing requires some know-how and practice, but the rewards are well worth it. This family uses a single-masted sailboat known as a sloop to visit an island in Lake Erie.

(Frank Sargeant)

Sailing with Class

Sailing classes are, by far, the easiest way to learn sailing. And you'll learn to do it right, from people dedicated to making sure you have a good experience.

Just as in learning to fly a small plane, the instructor typically starts you out with a form of "ground school" in the classroom or on the dock. You learn the terms, the principles, how to tie a knot or three, a bit about navigation on the water, and only then are you likely to step aboard for the first time.

Classes are available for all levels of sailing, from basic boot camp to fine-tuning for long-experienced racers or offshore cruisers.

Getting Started

Many schools offer an "Introduction to Sailing" class, which is basically a two- or three-hour boatride with other prospective students while an instructor goes over the essentials of what makes a boat sail—they give you a taste of what it's like to be on a boat pushed by the wind, so that you can decide if you want to pursue the sport further. Prices are modest, usually around $50, sometimes even free as a sales promotion.

Covering the Basics

The "Basic Sailing" classes typically last two full days, which is why most are scheduled for weekends. Or you might find classes meeting for several hours on weekday evenings, typically for five or six days straight. You can expect to pay around $800 to $1,000 for a quality course, including an instruction book and use of the school's boats. You will sail with two to five other students aboard, depending on the size of the instruction boats, with each of you taking turns at the tiller and managing the sails.

When you graduate, you will be more or less capable of taking a 20-foot sailboat out on your own and returning safely to the dock, so long as nothing unusual happens during the trip. And just as important, you will no longer have to turn down those invitations to crew on someone's sailboat because you don't know a jib from a jibe.

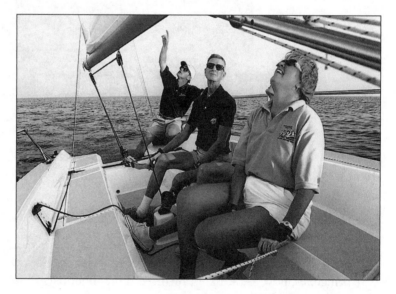

Learning the basics of sailing is easy if you attend a school. You'll be studying with others of your own skill level, some of whom are likely to become your sailing partners, too.

(Offshore Sailing School)

Cruising Along

If you want to do anything more than run a Hobie off the beach for an hour or two, you might eventually want to add a "Basic Cruising" class to your resumé. These typically include classroom and on-the-water work in navigation, rules of the road, weather, tides, sea conditions, and other essentials you need to sail on big water within sight of land. Again, they typically last two full days, and pricing—including boat use—is similar to the basic sailing classes.

It's All About Performance

Those who get serious about sailing soon become interested in getting the most out of their boat, and so "Performance Sailing" is likely to be next on the agenda. You'll learn handling of spinnakers, sail shaping, how to round a mark efficiently, heavy weather handling, and lots more in these classes, which usually are given over a weekend and are priced at around $500.

Big boat sailing, multi-hull sailing, long-distance cruising, and other classes might round out your education. Many move on to a little private instruction as a sort of "graduate school" to fine-tune their skills, and this typically costs $50 to $75 per hour plus the cost of renting the boat if you don't own your own.

Boat Bytes

Many sailors turn to racing as their skills develop. It's a great way to find out just how good a sailor you are by competing with others.

Choosing a Sailing School

Which school is best for you? Any of the reputable schools will do a good job of teaching you the basics. But you'll be more likely to have a good experience if you can visit several schools before making a choice. Here are some suggestions to help you make the best choice:

- Meet the individual who would be your instructor and try to get a feel for the type of person he or she is; type A personalities often make wonderful racing skippers but miserable instructors. Is he or she certified? It's not essential, and many good instructors are not, but you can be sure those who are certified know what they're doing.

- Check out the boats; are they reasonably new, well-maintained, and kept in a harbor where getting in and out does not take a traffic cop? Are they a design that interests you as a boat you might someday want to own?

- What is the ratio of students to instructors—a higher ratio means you get less one-on-one time, but might help keep course costs lower.

- Does the school offer U.S. Sailing certification?

From A to Z: Parts of a Sailboat

However you learn to sail, though, there are a considerable number of terms that you will eventually want to know, and the sooner you know them, the easier learning will be. Check the figure that appears after this list for an idea of what is located where.

Let's define these parts of a sailboat one by one (the numbers correspond to the accompanying illustration):

1. **Mainsail.** The large sail on the back side of the main mast.

2. **Jib.** The sail set on the front side of the main mast and supported by the head stay or forestay.

3. **Mast.** The vertically mounted pole used to support the sails and rigging.

4. **Boom.** The horizontal pole along the foot of a sail.

5. **Main sheet.** The line used to control the angle of the mainsail via the boom.

6. **Jib sheet.** The line used to control the angle of the jib. Most boats have two jib sheets, used one at a time depending on which side of the boat the wind is coming from.

7. **Halyards.** Lines used to hoist sails up the mast or stay.

8. **Luff.** The front edge of a sail. (When a sail is "luffing," it is flapping and loose, not creating lift.)

9. **Leech.** The back edge of a sail.

10. **Head.** The top corner of a sail. (Not to be confused with the marine toilet, which goes by the same name.)

11. **Foot.** The bottom edge of a sail.

12. **Clew.** The bottom rear corner of a sail. On a jib this is where the sheet attaches.

13. **Tack.** The bottom front corner of a sail. (To "tack," however, is also a term meaning to work back and forth into the wind. And "tack" can also refer to one leg of the zig-zag course steered when "tacking" upwind.)

14. **Backstay.** A tensioned support cable that runs from the top of the mast to the stern of the boat.

15. **Forestay.** A tensioned support cable that runs from a point near the top of the mast to the bow of the boat. If this stay goes all the way to the top of the mast, or masthead, it can also be called a head stay.

16. **Battens.** Stiffeners that insert into pockets in a sail's leech to improve the shape and the lifting ability, and to allow the mainsail to be larger than the triangle defined by the mast and boom.

17. **Keel or centerboard.** The fin on the bottom of the sailboat that keeps the boat from slipping sideways. Keels are usually ballasted or weighted to help prevent a

capsize. The centerboard is a moveable keel, unballasted, that's used on smaller boats. The swing-up keel makes it easier to beach or trailer the boat.

18. **Boom vang.** The line used to control how much the boom can pivot upward. It sits closer to the mast than the main sheet, which is also attached to the boom.

Run through this list a few times while studying the figure on the following page. When you know the names of all the parts without sneaking a peek at the key, you're ready for some on-the-water instruction.

1. Mainsail
2. Jib
3. Mast
4. Boom
5. Main sheet
6. Jib sheet
7. Halyards
8. Luff
9. Leech
10. Head
11. Foot
12. Clew
13. Tack
14. Backstay
15. Forestay
16. Battens
17. Keel or Centerboard
18. Boom vang

The parts of a sailboat's rigging or sailing gear have specialized names with which you'll want to become familiar.

The Points of Sail

A sailboat's heading in relation to the wind is everything in sailing. No boat can sail directly into the wind, and going directly downwind is, surprisingly to initiates, not the most efficient course unless you break out a special sail called a "spinnaker" (which we'll talk about in Chapter 26).

The headings in relation to the wind have a set of names (doesn't everything in sailing?) that you will want to be familiar with. They're shown in the following figure.

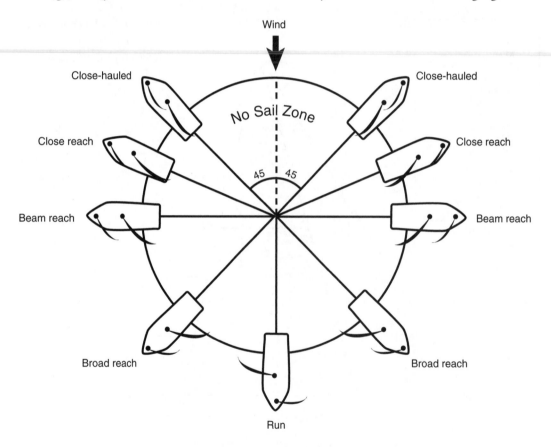

The terms for the points of sail—the boat's heading relative to the wind—are shown in this diagram. Note that all points of sail crossing the wind are known as "reaches," while the point of sail heading into the wind at about 45 degrees or less to the wind direction is known as a "beat." Note, too, the position of the boat's sails in each heading.

Here's the rundown on each of these terms:

- **Run.** This is a downwind leg, usually sailed with the main and the jib on opposite sides of the mast (also called sailing wing-on-wing).

- **Reach.** To sail across the wind at an angle that allows the main and the jib to work efficiently on the same side.

- **Broad reach.** To sail downwind at an angle greater than 90 degrees from the wind direction.

- **Beam reach.** To sail across the wind at 90 degrees.

- **Close reach.** To sail upwind at an angle less than 90 degrees but not into the wind as much as when sailing on a beat.

- **Close-hauled or beating.** To sail as nearly into the wind as the boat will allow for the purpose of making progress upwind. Most boats sail at about 45 degrees from the wind direction when they are sailing close-hauled.

Each point of sail requires a different adjustment of the sails for efficient travel (you'll learn more about these adjustments in Chapter 25). But in general, the reaches are the most efficient points of sail—that is to say, you go fastest with a given amount of wind.

Sailing Magic: Going Upwind

Sailboats obviously can't sail directly into the wind, but they can easily reach upwind locations by *tacking*, or beating into the wind. This is sailing a series of legs or tacks back and forth across the wind, as shown in the following figure.

Note that there's an area of about 90 degrees going into the wind (45 degrees on either side of straight upwind) where most sailboats can't function. Most modern performance-oriented boats can sail 5 or 10 degrees nearer the wind when properly handled, but for most basic trainers, you can't sail closer than 45 degrees to the wind.

Also note that in common usage, a boat on a *port tack* (bearing to the right of the wind direction) has the wind coming in over the port side. On a *starboard tack*, the boat is steered to the left of the wind direction so that the wind comes from the starboard or right side. Racing

Salt Talk

Tacking is sailing back and forth on a series of legs to work toward an upwind objective. The process of working the boat upwind in this manner can also be called "beating to windward" or "beating into the wind."

sailors will point out that technically, the boom determines which tack a boat is on; if the boom is on the left side of the boat, the boat is on a starboard tack, and vice versa.

Beating into the wind in a series of direction changes is slow going, but it's the only way for a sailboat to reach an upwind location. The art and intellect come into play when you try to predict repetitive wind shifts, and then time your tacks so that you are always sailing on the "lifted" tack. This will get your boat to a windward destination by sailing less distance through the water.

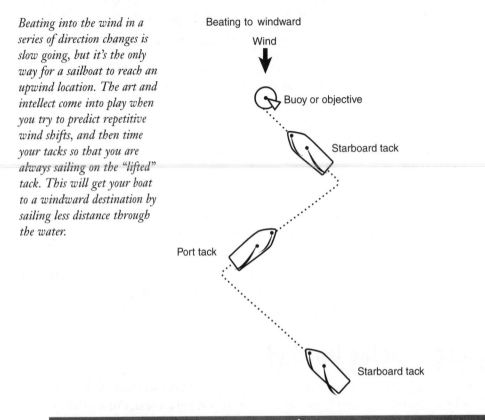

Nautical Notes

For thousands of years, ships were steered by a steering oar, usually on the starboard side. As a new sailor you will discover very quickly that to get a good view of a boat approaching on the opposite tack, you must look under the sails from the "low" side of the boat, or the side of the boat opposite the source of the wind. And that is why starboard tack has right-of-way over port—the Viking steering the longboat on port tack can see what's coming on the other tack, but the one on starboard tack has a blind spot.

Terms for Downwind

When sailing on a beam reach, a broad reach, or a run, it's also necessary to turn downwind across the wind at times, which is called *jibing*. In this maneuver, the bow swings through the direct downwind position, the exact opposite of changing tacks on an upwind beat. Note the position of the sails in the following figure.

Jibing

Wind

Boom and mainsail swing

To jibe is to turn away from the wind, swinging the bow through the downwind position and back out the other side. Because the boom can swing rapidly (and sometimes unexpectedly) on this maneuver, caution is required.

Blocks, Shackles, Cleats, and Winches: The Hardware of Sailing

The mechanical hardware of sailing enables you to control the sails and the boom with minimal effort. Familiarize yourself with the following hardware vocabulary:

◆ **Blocks.** The pulleys of various sizes mounted on the boom, the deck, and the mast. The more blocks, the less effort to haul on a line, but the more line you have to haul to get a given amount of movement.

◆ **Cam cleats.** These are cleats that depend on eccentric or off-center wheels to lock lines in place—they are faster to use than conventional cleats, so they are favored for sheets that might need frequent adjustment and that sometimes need to be released quickly for safety.

◆ **Shackles.** These are the metal attaching devices that connect the sails to the halyards, the anchor to the anchor chain, and anything else aboard that requires a strong but removable connection.

◆ **Winches.** The revolving drums that make it easier to handle the heavy work aboard, such as hoisting the mainsail on a large boat. Internal gears give them a mechanical advantage. You insert a long handle and crank to snug the line.

Look Out!

Lines under pressure on a winch can slip suddenly, and if you have your hands in the wrong place, your fingers can be pinched between line and drum. Remove any rings when working on a winch, and if you wear gloves, make sure they fit closely.

Winches provide a mechanical advantage when handling heavy loads on larger boats with big sails. Mechanical advantages of as much as 56 to 1 are common for large winches. Self-tailing winches like this one do not require a second person to hold tension on the line.

(Harken, Inc.)

Other Handy Terms to Know

There are a number of other components on most sailboats, as well as sailing terms, that might someday be useful to know as you become more practiced. Here are some of them:

- ◆ **Apparent wind.** The wind as it affects a sailboat in motion. Apparent wind on a downwind run is minimal because you're moving along at close to the speed of the wind, while on a close reach the felt wind is near maximum, combining wind speed with the forward motion of the boat.

- ◆ **Bosun's chair.** A sling used to hoist a crewperson up the mast to inspect and repair rigging.

The bosun's chair is used to hoist a crewperson aloft (carefully!) to clean the standing rigging or to untangle or retrieve fouled halyards.

(Frank Sargeant)

- ◆ **Coming about.** To change direction or change tacks so that the wind comes from the other side of the boat and the sails fill from the other side.

- ◆ **Genoa.** A large jib sail that overlaps the mast.

- ◆ **Heeling.** Leaning to one side from the force of the wind on the sails.

- ◆ **In irons.** A boat is said to be in irons when it is stuck pointing directly upwind and the sails cannot be filled to begin sailing again.

- ◆ **Leeward.** Away from the wind.

- ◆ **Lifelines.** A safety rail usually made of steel cable that circles the deck of larger boats to keep the crew from falling overboard. (Note that international ocean racing safety rules now prohibit plastic coating on lifelines installed after January 1999. The plastic coating makes it difficult to detect badly corroded wire, and a number of accidents have been attributed to failed lifelines that appeared to be in good condition.)

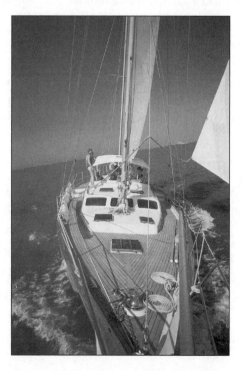

The lifelines or safety rails on this yacht protect the crew from falling overboard.

(Frank Sargeant)

- ◆ **Outhaul.** A line used to tension the foot of a sail along a boom.

- ◆ **Reefing.** To reduce the sail area by partially lowering the sail and rolling or tying it to the boom.

- **Roller furling.** A system of storing sails by rolling them up around the forestay or headstay.

- **Running rigging.** Refers to all the adjustable lines and gear used to raise and tension the sails. It is adjusted frequently as winds and course change.

- **Shrouds.** Support wires that run from the mast to the sides of the boat, part of the standing rigging.

- **Slot.** The space between the headsail and the mainsail, where much of the lift or propelling force is generated.

- **Spinnaker.** A lightweight, three-cornered sail with a parachute-like shape used for adding speed on downwind runs.

- **Standing rigging.** The stays and shrouds that hold the mast upright. It is more or less fixed rigging.

- **Telltales.** Small bits of yarn or other lightweight materials that are attached to the sail or other readily visible spot to indicate wind direction and flow.

- **Windward.** Toward the wind.

All the terms listed here might seem a jumble as you read them, but take this book with you aboard and think about the name of each piece of gear as you rig it, and about the names of the maneuvers as you perform them, and you'll have it locked within a trip or two.

The Least You Need to Know

- The easiest way to get started in sailing is with hands-on learning from a good instructor.

- The *best* way to get started is as a small child with a sailing dinghy. Even if you are no longer a small child, you will still learn the most from the smallest boat.

- Learning the sailor's vocabulary helps communication between teacher and student.

- The best way to learn the vocabulary is aboard a boat.

Chapter 24

Types of Sailboats

In This Chapter

- ◆ How to tell the difference between a sloop and a schooner
- ◆ Sailboats with single, double, and triple hulls
- ◆ Types of sails
- ◆ Taking care of your sails and hardware

It doesn't matter, in terms of your success and enjoyment of sailing, whether you ever learn the names of all the types of rigging, hulls, and the categories of sails. Plenty of very happy and very good sailors never do.

But as your experience grows, it's likely that you'll want to be able to converse with others who do know these terms, so this chapter presents a brief review.

What Do You Call It?

Sailboats are generally classified according to the number and position of the masts. The size doesn't matter in this case, simply the way the mast or masts are put on the boat.

Single-Mast Sailing

Most modern sailboats are sloops. Sloops have a single mast that's stepped, or set, into the deck and/or hull a bit forward of amidships. The mast supports two sails—a main on the back side of the mast and a jib in front. Sloops range in size from under 10 feet to more than 80 feet long. If the mast is at the very front of the boat and only has a main, it is called a catboat, and if the mast is set farther back and has a main and two jibs, it is called a cutter.

Single-mast boats are generally smaller, less expensive, and easier to sail than two-mast boats—your first sailboat should be a single-master, even if you are Bill Gates's only heir.

Single-mast sailboats include sloops, cutters, and catboats. The number and location of the sails is the determining factor in how the boat is cat-egorized.

Two-Mast Sailing

Larger boats can handle more sail power and need it for reasonable performance. Two masts can support more sail area than one without any single sail becoming too large to handle, so two-mast rigs are common among offshore voyagers. Two-masters begin at around 40 feet and stretch out to over a majestic 150 feet long.

A *ketch*-rigged two-master has the taller or main mast in front, and a smaller "mizzen" mast aft, but in front of the wheel or tiller.

A *schooner*, once the most common rig for island traders and other large sailboats, has a foremast that's shorter than the mainmast, which sits well aft. Large schooners can have more than two masts, but as long as the foremast is shorter than the main, it's still a schooner.

A *yawl* is like a ketch except that the mizzen or aft mast is stepped behind the wheel or tiller. It's a rare rig these days.

Two-masted sailboats include ketches, schooners, and yawls. Both ketches and yawls feature a taller main mast forward and a shorter mizzen mast aft, while schooners have the tallest mast aft. Some sailors like two-masted boats because of their traditional look, or because it gives them more flexibility in choosing sails.

One Hull or Two?

If one hull is good, can two be better? How about three? It depends on what you want to do with the boat, and what you can afford.

Monohulls

The vast majority of sailboats are *monohulls*, which means they have a single hull—they look like a boat is "supposed" to look.

Monohulls have the grace of line that appeals to many, and they're sometimes more affordable than a catamaran of equivalent size, particularly in cruising sailboats, because it takes far less fiberglass to build one hull than two. The narrower beam of a monohull also makes it easier to trailer and easier to fit into your garage (with the mast folded down).

The interior of a yacht-class sailboat is a match for the finest homes ashore. The cabin of this Beneteau 57 offers a combination of spacious luxury with the durability required for years at sea.

(Beneteau Yachts)

Catamarans and Trimarans

However, *catamarans* or two-hull sailboats ("cats," not to be confused with catboats) and even *trimarans*, with three hulls, are becoming increasingly popular. One reason is that they're tremendously stable, even without a ballasted keel. The broad spread between the hulls creates powerful leverage to help keep the boat upright.

Cats are also noted for a soft ride in rough head seas, and in cruising boats, the great span of the beam allows space below decks that makes any monohull seem like a tunnel.

When operated on auxiliary power, catamarans are also highly fuel-efficient, another advantage for long-range cruising.

Catamarans like this Endeavour 34 offer remarkable stability plus an enormous amount of space belowdecks. This particular boat has a 15-foot beam, far wider than the typical monohull.

(Endeavour Yachts)

Are there any negatives about catamarans? Maybe a few: Some say that the cabin space divided by the bridge, or connecting structure, between the hulls is inconvenient on some models. Cats are also somewhat less graceful to the eye than a sleek monohull, and some models cost more at a given length. But there's enough to like about cats that you should give them a try to see if they suit you and your family.

Sink or Capsize?

If you took a conventional monohull cruising sailboat, even a very small one, and placed it in the water completely upside down, it would turn itself upright. The deck and cabin are strong and watertight (that's why sailboats have such small windows compared to powerboats) and there is usually enough lead ballast in the keel to right the boat in short order without any assistance from the crew. If you did the same thing with a catamaran or trimaran, it would stay upside down. Even with rescue boats on the scene, righting a large multihull is difficult.

But if you punch a hole in the hull of a typical monohull cruising boat, it will fill with water and sink to the bottom. Punch the same hole in the cat or tri, and it will fill with water but still float. There is no ballast to pull it down, and the hull material is usually made of a very buoyant fiberglass and foam sandwich construction.

Although some designs (monohulls with extra flotation) are both self-righting and unsinkable, you usually have to choose one or the other when you decide on the number of hulls. In practice, however, very few yachts are lost to either capsize or sinking. Most cruising boats are lost during collisions, fires, and explosions, or from being stranding on reefs.

Daysailers, Cruisers, and Racers

Daysailers are the most popular and affordable of all sailboats, and include everything from the tiniest dinghy to 30-footers that can handle a crew of a half-dozen. They have no overnight accommodations, however—just a cockpit where the crew can sit. (That's why they call them *day*sailers.)

Sailing *cruisers* are the largest and most comfortable of sailboats, distinguished by overnight accommodations belowdecks. These can range from nothing more than a vee-berth—a pair of sleeping pads that form a vee inside the bow—to very plush multistateroom digs. Traditional cruisers usually have full-length keels that make the boats very stable, while the more modern performance cruisers mimic race boats with their fin keels and lightweight hull forms.

Beautiful motorsailing cruisers like this one are more than a match for the world's finest powerboats and are, in competent hands, seaworthy enough to take on all the world's oceans. Motorsailers have larger engines than other cruising sailboats, and generally smaller sail rigging.

(Beneteau Yachts)

Some unique racing hulls like those used in the America's Cup are much like oversized (and unbelievably expensive) dinghies. They have no accommodations, not a pound of extra weight devoted to creature comforts, but they're loaded to the gills with high-tech sails, winches, and navigational gear. They sport a fairly flat bottom, with a short but deep keel that is heavily ballasted.

Nautical Notes

Combine a surfboard with a sail and you have a *sailboard* (also known as a *Windsurfer*). This is an extremely lightweight and inexpensive boat that can be transported on the tops of the smallest cars. It's also very, very fast. In fact, sailboards are among the fastest sailboats in the world, with speeds exceeding 50 mph on special boards in the hands of experts. These boats can literally fly, traveling many yards through the air, when sailed off the tops of big waves.

Sport Cats

Sport catamarans are twin-hulled boats that can actually go as fast as some power-boats. The narrow hulls produce very little wave resistance, so they can achieve white-wake speeds, without the need to plane, in winds of as little as 15 mph. The Hobie Cat is the most famous of the breed, but there are many other well-known builders, including G-Cat, Prindle, and Nacra.

Sport catamarans have no cockpit, only a "trampoline" of mesh fabric or rope over the water where one or two people can sit. The wide spread between the hulls gives the boat great stability and resistance to heeling, and makes it possible for the crew to use their weight to leverage the boat flat against powerful winds.

Boat Bytes

If you think you might want to race your boat, consider buying one of the more popular types, so that you can easily find other people with similar boats to race against.

Because of their stability, larger sails can be used on catamarans, adding to their potential speed without dramatically increasing their chances of being knocked down. And, because the hulls are very narrow, there's very little drag.

Sport cats are light, easily trailered, shallow in draft so that they can be sailed off any beach, and reasonably economical—used 16-footers start as low as $600.

Some have no centerboard, instead depending on sharp keels to hold them stable against the sideways push of the sails. Others use a "daggerboard"-type centerboard, which is pushed straight down through the center of the boat.

The smallest Hobies and some others are "cat-rigged," meaning that they have a single sail. Others use a jib in front of the mast and are therefore "sloop-rigged."

Sport catamarans are light enough to be launched off the beach. They're moderately priced and offer great performance, although there are minimal creature comforts aboard the trampoline between the hulls.

(Hobie Sailing)

Flying on Water

Sport catamaran sailors are privy to one of the most spectacular forms of sailing, called "flying the hull." When a boat is flying the hull, its upwind hull is actually raised off the water by the heeling force on the sails. If allowed to go too far, flying can result in a capsizing, and you've got a long way to fall from the upwind side of a cat. But kept under control by steering slightly into the wind to luff the sails (or away from the wind to reduce the apparent wind speed) and hiking out on the windward side, it's an effective tactic for balancing a catamaran. (*Hiking out* is hanging off the high side of a sailboat when it heels to help keep the hull upright by moving the center of gravity to windward. Hiking straps across the trampoline secure your feet so you don't fall overboard.)

Cats with big sails sometimes call for "trapezing" in strong winds to keep them upright. This is done by attaching a cable from the mast to a harness around the helmsman, allowing him to stand on the rail with his body extended almost horizontally over the water—one of sailing's biggest rushes!

Sail Shapes

In addition to the names for different configurations of boats, there are also names for various types of sails—not something you have to drop into conversation when you're stepping aboard for the first time, but something you will want to know somewhere down the road.

The most common type of sail is the triangular "Marconi" rig, which is the sail you see on virtually all modern sailboats. Allegedly, it was originally named because the stays and shrouds holding up the mast reminded Depression-era sailors of the first radio towers set up by the Italian inventor. Short battens, of wood or plastic, are inserted into pockets sewn into the sails to help shape the back edge.

Sport catamarans have Marconi sails, but rather than the short battens on conventional sloops, they sport full-length battens that run from leech to luff, better shaping the sail and giving stronger performance. Lateen sails are spread by two spars: a lower boom that extends past the mast and a second that runs at an angle from the forward end of the boom to the top of the mast. It's the rig for some popular "board boats" such as the Sunfish.

> ### Nautical Notes
>
> One of the most thorough and interesting books on sail design, function, use, and care is *Sails* by Jeremy Howard-Williams (J. de Graff, 1983). It was first published in 1967, but it's been through umpteen editions since then and is still the definitive work for those who really want to get the best from sail-power.

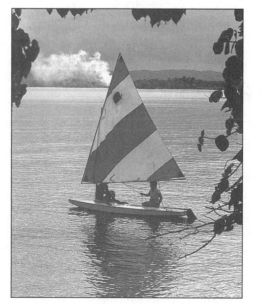

The very popular Sunfish class boats sport a lateen sail.

(Frank Sargeant)

Gaff rigs are still seen on classic catboats here and there along the east coast—they include a spar or "gaff" extending out along the sail's upper edge from about two thirds of the way up the mast.

Sail Care

Whatever the type of sail, it should be folded neatly at day's end. The accordion fold is most common, starting at the foot and working toward the head. Storing a sail via the accordion fold is called *flaking* and is designed to keep the sail neat without bending the fibers excessively.

It's not necessary to take the mainsail off the boom for overnight storage. It can be rolled up or flaked, with alternating folds on each side of the boom, and then secured in place with bungee cords so it's ready to go in the morning.

Boat Bytes

It's not necessary to wash down and dry sails for overnight storage, but you should brush away any sand or debris that might cause abrasion.

If you're putting the sail away, fold it over on itself several times or roll it up and store it in the bag it came in. Sails should be stowed out of the weather and kept away from excessive heat. Store them in an air-conditioned building when possible to ensure long life. Most sails are made of Dacron, a tough, low-stretch synthetic. Dacron sailcloth doesn't rot and has tremendous resistance to tearing. However, Dacron and all other sails should be washed with freshwater, and then dried thoroughly before winter storage to prevent mildew.

Caring for Your Hardware

Blocks, cam cleats, shackles, and winches, have moving parts, which salt and sand can cause to fail prematurely. At the end of each day on the water, give all your hardware a quick rinse down with the freshwater hose. And on a regular basis, wash each device with a soft-bristled brush and soapy water. Winches will need disassembly and interior cleaning and lubrication a couple times a year if you're in a year-round sailing area, or at the beginning and end of the season otherwise. A drop of oil to the bearings of other gear is usually enough to keep things rolling smoothly; keep an eye out for jamming sheaves or pulley wheels, however, which might warn of pending bearing or wheel failure.

The Least You Need to Know

- ◆ Sailboats are categorized by height, placement, and number of masts.

- ◆ Sailboats can have one, two, or even three hulls. Each type has its own advantages.

- ◆ Sailboards and sport cats offer some of the most exciting and demanding types of sailing.

- ◆ Modern sails are tough but take a bit of basic care to stay in top shape.

25

The Mechanics of Sailing

In This Chapter

- ◆ What makes a sailboat sail?
- ◆ Rigging the sails
- ◆ Getting underway on your first sailing trip
- ◆ Downwind turns and all that jibe
- ◆ Zig-zagging away: Sailing upwind and the art of tacking

By now you have some idea of the sailor's vocabulary and the different types of sailboats that are out there. But before you jump on board and sail off into the wild blue yonder, there are a few basics you need to know.

In this chapter, we'll tackle the nitty-gritty of sailing, including the basics of rigging the sails, and then leaving the dock and going for a sail across the bay under the power of the wind. You'll also learn the basics of turning under sail, going both upwind and down.

Why Sailboats Sail

A sailboat sails on the same principle that allows an aircraft to fly. Air passing over a rounded or convex section, be it a wing or a curved sail, goes faster than across a flat or concave section because it has to travel a greater distance to the aft edge. This creates a lower pressure on the convex side than on the concave side, according to Bernoulli's principle. (There's that pesky ninth grade science again.) So, there's less pressure on the convex or leeward side of the sail than on the concave or windward side, and a lifting force is exerted toward the convex side.

Actually, a sail is so thin that by this logic, the difference in speed between one side of a sail and the other would be negligible, and there would be no lift. Also, even if there *was* a big difference in distance traveled on the two sides of the sail, there is no law of physics that says that the air has to take the same amount of time to travel to the back of the sail on either side, and indeed wind tunnel demonstrations show that this condition is usually not met. So this explanation of lift is all wrong on several counts, but what the heck, it's still the one they use at the very best sailing schools ....

Lift is created in sails when air flows faster over the convex, leeward side than over the concave, windward side.

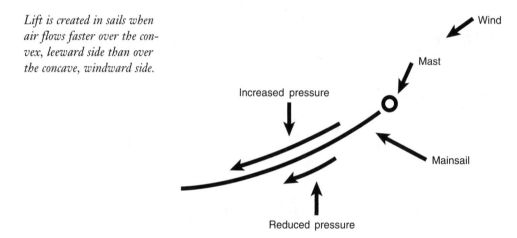

This gives lift in an aircraft wing and thrust in a sailboat. But in a sailboat, no mechanical power is required—you travel on the power of the flowing air alone—more like a glider than a powered aircraft.

A keel in the sailboat "stiffens" the boat, holding it from blowing sideways or even over on its beam ends with the pressure of the sail. (A boat rolled on its *beam ends* is flipped up on its side, on the verge of capsizing.) The keel acts on somewhat the same principle as the sail—it's a rounded "hydrofoil," and when directed slightly to windward by the rudder, it generates lift in that direction.

The force acting on the sail is balanced by appropriate steering with the force acting on the keel, and the boat goes straight ahead.

Many larger sailboats have weighted keels that function as "ballast," a righting force when winds threaten to capsize the boat. Smaller boats depend on movement of the crew from gunnel to gunnel to act as ballast.

These are the most basic principles of sailing—there are endless volumes on the finer points, but you don't need to know those now and you probably won't ever want to know them unless you become a serious racer or sail maker.

Note how the crew members on this big sloop make use of their weight to help keep the boat leveled despite the force of the wind against the sails. Crew shifts are even more important in smaller, unballasted sailboats.

(Beneteau Yachts)

Your First Sailing Trip

Step aboard a fully rigged sloop and you'll see it looks like a marine rats' nest of ropes, cables, winches, pulleys, and other unidentifiable stuff that could have come from the insides of a computer, and is just as expensive. Do you have to learn what all this does to go sailing?

Sort of.

All this equipment is used to keep the sails at an efficient angle to the wind and extract the most thrust or lift to push the boat forward.

But it's not as hard as it looks (of course, that's what your calculus teacher told you), at least not until you get to the competitive level. A couple of hours on a boat is adequate to get you started.

It's much easier if you have an instructor, either a pro who teaches for money, a friendly sailing club member, or a neighbor from the next slip. It's generally not a great idea to try learning sailing solo—too many things can go wrong, causing frustration, disappointment, and maybe even a bit of danger. It's much easier, faster, and more fun if you have experienced sailors around you.

Boat Bytes

Volunteering to crew on someone's boat is a great way to learn the basics! It's generally free instruction— at the price of a lot of winch turning.

The basic steps to getting started are not quite as simple as indicated in Chapter 23, but they're not a whole lot more difficult, either. Here they are, without any of the subtleties you'll learn as you gain experience:

1. With the boat in the water and tied to the dock, lower the centerboard and secure the rudder in place, then lay out the mainsail on deck next to the boom.

2. Locate the clew of the main (the rear corner that will go out to the tip of the boom) and feed it into the fittings in the track on top of the boom or into the groove designed to hold it. This is easier if one person fits the foot of the sail to the track while the other works it toward the outer end of the boom. If the mainsail is "loose footed" as many modern mainsails are, skip this step.

3. If the sail has batten pockets along the leech or trailing edge, insert the battens or sail stiffeners. They're often tapered—put the thinner end in first. They're not all the same size, so be sure to fit them to their proper pockets. Make sure the battens are properly locked in place. They should fit tight enough to stretch the pocket slightly around them, and secure enough so that they will not shake out if the sail flogs.

4. Straighten the leading edge (the luff) of the sail and get out any twists, and then secure the tack of the sail (the bottom front corner) to the fitting on the front or inside of the boom, near where it attaches to the mast. Pin the tack through the grommet in the corner.

5. Attach the clew to the outhaul at the other end of the boom. You've now got the foot of the sail secured. Cleat off the outhaul, keeping it lightly slack.

6. Now you're almost ready to hoist the sail. Check the main halyard to make sure it's not twisted around the mast or one of the stays (a common problem). Attach the halyard to the head of the sail through the grommet in the headboard via the shackle provided.

7. Attach the luff or the leading edge of the main sail to the mast via the slide attachments spaced along its edge, or feed the bolt rope into the mast groove.

8. If your boat has only a mainsail, or if you're only using one sail for your first trip—a very good idea—you can now lower the centerboard and make sure the rudder is secure and functioning.

9. Before you raise the sails, point and hold the boat into the wind so that the sails can't fill when first raised. You want the boat to sail, but not until you're ready. By pointing directly upwind, you put the boat "in irons"—unable to move in a controllable direction due to a lack of lift on the sails—and it can't go anywhere.

Go for it—go ahead and raise the main at this point, feeding the slides or bolt rope into the groove in the back of the mast as you pull on the main halyard. (Make sure the mainsheet and boom vang—the adjustment ropes that control the mainsail—are slack so the sail can't fill until you want it to.)

Cleat off the halyard on the mast, coil the leftover line neatly, and hang it below the cleat.

10. If your boat has a jib, the tack is first attached to a fitting near the bow, adjacent to the forestay, which supports the jib in the way the mast supports the mainsail.

    You can identify the jib tack because the angle there is wider than at the clew. On your own sails, it's not a bad idea to mark the tack in indelible ink. Most sailmakers put their company logo near the tack of the sail.

    When you're sorting through a pile of sail looking for the tack and the clew, it can be hard to tell which is which. The best way to find the tack of a mainsail is to look for the corner where the bolt ropes that attach to the boom and the mast meet. If there's only one rope, it's the clew (unless the sail is of modern loose-footed design, in which case if there's a headboard, it's the head, if there's no bolt rope, it's the clew, and if there's a bolt rope or sail slides but no head-board, it's the tack).

11. The jib is now attached to the forestay via the hanks or snaps along its luff. Start from the bottom of the sail up, not vice versa—that way the bottom section will be easier to attach.

12. Attach the jib sheets, using a bowline or shackles, and run the sheets through the pulleys (known as "blocks" to sailors) provided back to the cockpit—one goes to each side. Put a stopper knot, a figure eight, in the end of each so they don't slip back through the pulleys.

13. Attach the jib halyard to the head of the jib. On a windy day, it's very easy for the jib to be blown off the front deck. Have a crewperson sit on the jib until you're ready to hoist it. Some boats have bungee cords that will keep the jib in place.

That's it—you're ready to go, at last. Before you move the boat away from the dock, though, make one final check to make sure both jib sheets and the mainsheet are slack, so that the sails won't fill immediately when you push off.

Getting Underway

To get started sailing, raise the main first, if you haven't already done so as in step 9. Then raise the jib. Pull both taut to the top of the mast and cleat them off, coiling the halyards neatly. Never tie the halyards in a knot that could be difficult to release quickly, and always make sure the end coils are orderly. This is so that you can quickly lower the sails—your only way of stopping short of turning up into the wind—in an emergency.

Because the boat is still pointed directly into the wind, the only thing that happens at this point is that the sails start to flap fast and loud if there's a lot of wind.

Boat Bytes

Most small sailboats are tiller-steered, which means a straight handle at the stern rather than a steering wheel at a console controls the rudder. Tiller steering is different than wheel steering because you push the handle left to go right, and vice versa.

If you're in a crowded harbor, it's not a bad idea for the crew to man the paddles (or to start the auxiliary motor) and make your way out before the sails are trimmed. After the boat starts sailing, things can get pretty busy, and it's best to have open water ahead.

To make the sails fill, push the bow off the dock or paddle so that it turns a bit away from the wind, which will bring the bow beyond the "no-sail" area (where the boat is pointed almost dead into the wind and the sails have no lift). This will allow the wind to strike the sails at an angle greater than 45 degrees.

In close quarters, such as passing under a drawbridge, even the most experienced sailors often use their engines to assist the sails and maintain steerage.

(Frank Sargeant)

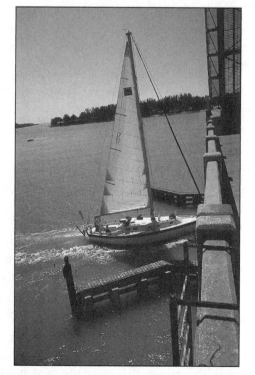

Backing the jib is using the jib sail to turn the boat enough to catch the wind, and is the usual course of experienced sailors for getting underway. It's done by a crewperson holding the clew of the jib out to one side of the bow, while the tiller is put over to the opposite side. The breeze catches the jib and swings the bow in the desired direction.

Trimming the Sails

Now you can tighten up the sheets, the main first. The sail will start to take shape but will flutter at first. Draw in or *trim* the mainsheet until the fluttering stops and the sail stiffens—you're sailing!

Trim the jib similarly to the main with the lee-side sheet and your speed will begin to increase.

The sails will remain properly trimmed as long as you hold this heading or as long as the wind remains steady from the same direction. If you turn, the sails will begin to flutter again and must be adjusted. Your first courses should be beam reaches, basically sailing across the wind (see Chapter 23).

Nautical Notes

How do you know where the wind is coming from? Keep an eye on the *telltales*, those bits of yarn or other lightweight material that are attached to the shrouds. They fly like flags, streaming away from the wind. Telltales are also sometimes stitched through the luff of the jib to check for the best sail trim. When the sail is trimmed at its most efficient angle for a given heading, the yarn on both sides of the sail streams directly aft.

To try a close reach (at an angle between 45 and 90 degrees from the wind direction), turn up into the wind slightly. The sails will begin to flutter but will tighten again as you draw in the sheets slightly.

As you point up even farther, you sail "close-hauled" to the wind, as near as you dare without going into the no-sail zone and losing power. As you do, the boat heels over. If the boat leans enough to make you nervous, let out the sails quickly and turn a few degrees back away from the wind and the hull will straighten up. Alternatively, you can turn into the wind and leave the sails trimmed—you may go into irons (stop moving), but that is much easier to recover from than a capsize.

For a broad reach (at an angle of more than 90 degrees but less than 180 degrees from the wind direction), turn away from the wind slightly, and let out the sheets a bit.

Safe Downwind Turns

Turning across the wind on a run is known as a *jibe*, and it requires coordination between skipper and crew.

As long as the wind comes from the side of the boat opposite the side that the boom is on, even at a modest angle, the boom is under control. When you turn directly downwind and then back to the other side, putting wind and boom on the same side of the boat, the boom is going to swing.

A controlled jibe requires you to warn the crew that you're about to turn across the wind, by saying "Ready to jibe." This tells them that the boom is going to come across the cockpit, although hopefully it will come slowly and under control of the mainsheet, which you or an assigned crew member will control.

When everybody is paying attention, you issue the command "Jibe ho" and make the turn, while a crewperson first draws in the mainsheet to start the boom swinging, and then gradually lets it back out as it crosses to the other side of the boat and begins to fill.

To anyone in the cockpit, the "Jibe ho" command should be a signal to duck his or her head, because many booms swing across at just about head level.

For more on jibing, see Chapter 23.

> **CAUTION**
>
> ## Look Out!
>
> Don't turn directly downwind or anywhere close to it at first, because a downwind run can cause an unintentional jibe, or crossing of the wind, which makes the boom swing across the cockpit at great speed if winds are strong and the sheet is loose. The boom can seriously injure crewpersons as well as knock them overboard.

Tackling Tacking

Tacking, as you'll recall from Chapter 23, is the procedure for sailing or beating toward an upwind objective. It's done in a series of close reaches, just greater than 45 degrees from being directly into the wind.

By running a zig-zag course, the boat eventually gets to the upwind target that it could never reach by sailing straight into the wind.

Tacking upwind is much like jibing downwind in terms of sail-handling. Again, you make sure the crew has their heads up (down, that is) by issuing the command "Ready to tack" or "Ready about." The crew uncleats the jib sheet and gets ready to slack it, and responds "Ready" to signify they know what's coming.

The helmsperson then commands "Tacking" or "Helm's alee" and turns the rudder to make the bow swing across the wind.

> **Boat Bytes** _____
>
> If your hands are not used to manual labor, you'll regret a day spent handling the sheets aboard a sailboat in strong winds unless you wear gloves. Sailing gloves are thin so you can work with the lines, and sometimes they are fingerless. A leather palm patch prevents sliding sheets from burning your skin. They sell for around $20. (A $1 pair of cotton gloves will also work fine for a while; if you forget your sailing gloves at home—just whack off the fingers and go for it.)

The sails begin to flap or luff as you come into the 90 degrees where there is no lift available, and the boom swings across the cockpit. It doesn't make the big, fast swing that it might on a jibe because it's controlled by the shortened mainsheet, so this is usually not a problem for the crew.

Come about smartly when tacking—if you let the boat lose forward motion, it might not complete the turn and you'll wind up in irons, with no sail power.

At this point, the crew lets go the jib sheet and switches sides to put their weight on the new windward side as the boat comes out the opposite side of the no-sail area and the sails begin to fill again. They then take in the new windward jib sheet and adjust it to stop the sails from luffing. The main is also readjusted, and the tack is complete.

Judging the Wind

Wind is a sailor's best friend—and potentially his or her worst enemy. The first things you'll want to know before you head out for a day of sailing is how much wind to expect, and what direction it will blow from.

Although weather forecasts give a good general idea, you'll want to check wind direction and speed yourself before hoisting any sail. Weather vanes, flags, and waves can tell you the direction, and the way a flag moves can also tell you a lot about wind speed. Or you might invest in one of the little handheld wind-speed devices, which are about the size of a cell phone.

If you're a beginning sailor in a small boat, you'll want to plan your first trips when winds are 5 to 10 knots, or just enough to extend a light flag off the pole. (Much less than 5 and most boats will barely sail, so these are days best spent mowing the lawn.)

Look Out!

Always remember that local winds are subject to dramatic and sudden changes, particularly if a thunderstorm approaches. Be alert for changes in wind direction, sudden changes in temperature or approaching squall lines, and be ready to adjust sails accordingly.

In larger boats and/or with more experience, you might take on winds of 10 to 15 knots, enough to stiffen a flag and create frequent whitecaps on the sea.

Only experienced sailors leave the docks at winds over 18 knots; the flags will be snapping, and you'll see whitecaps everywhere. In a boat that can handle it, winds to 25 knots can make for exhilarating sailing, but it will be rough and wet.

Over 25 knots, 99 percent of all sailors will be happier sitting on the dock and wishing they were offshore, rather than offshore wishing they were sitting on the dock.

The Least You Need to Know

♦ Understanding sail rigging from a book is harder than understanding it from a friendly teacher, so get some hands-on experience.

♦ When sails flap or luff, they have no lift and the boat will sit still.

♦ When sails fill and tighten, the boat starts to move—be ready to let go of the sheets if you're not quite ready to leave the docks.

♦ Always be wary of the boom on downwind runs, because an uncontrolled jibe can send it violently across the cockpit and endanger your crew.

♦ Be aware of wind direction and speed before you leave the dock, and keep an eye on wind changes so long as you're on the water.

Chapter 26

Handling Your Sailboat

In This Chapter

- Handling your sailboat around the docks
- Anchoring and mooring
- Planning a sailing route
- Learning the rules of the road for sailors
- Handling rough weather conditions

Sailboats present some unusual challenges in handling under sail; if you're not careful about how you maneuver, you can suddenly lose power just at the moment you need it most.

Of course, you can duck the issue by paddling, hanging an auxiliary outboard off a bracket on the stern of most small sailboats, or starting the inboard on larger rigs—and that's the way most people do it. If you choose this route, you'll have no more problems with handling than do powerboat people.

But serious sailors sometimes like to do it the "right" way, which is sometimes the hard way. And being able to handle your boat in tight situations under sail gives you a backup for the day when your auxiliary won't start. In this chapter, I'll direct you around some of the potential problems.

Sailing to the Dock

The major difference between sailboats and powerboats in docking is that in sailing, you have no real brakes except the wind. With a powerboat, reversing the propeller can bring most boats to a halt in less than a boatlength, but sailboats keep going for some distance after the sails are doused or lowered or the boat is headed up into the wind.

The trick in coming to a dock is to plan your landing so that you turn up into the wind at the last moment. This allows the momentum of your turn to push you sideways close enough to toss a line ashore or hook on to something with a boat hook, or to have a crew member step onto the dock and secure the bow line. The person should be at the bow ready to step on the dock with the bow line the instant the boat is within safe distance. With any amount of wind or current, the boat won't stay in position long, so the crew will need to look lively.

Look Out!

A large sailboat coming to the docks has a lot of momentum, and it can't be stopped by the casual push of a foot. Keep feet and hands out of the space between the rail and the pilings to avoid potential injuries.

An alternative is to sail very slowly to a point on the dock. Slow sailing is tricky, because the wind can be shifty, and boats tend to drift sideways more when going slowly. You need to learn how much above the desired docking point you need to point to reach it successfully. Learning how to "range," which means using several landmarks to make sure you are on a straight course, helps a lot.

Depending on the wind, you might come to a dock in a number of different ways and you might have to dock on a particular end of the structure, whether you want to or not, because of conditions or available space. You can then walk the boat to where you'll tie it up while you have lunch or stay overnight.

Three typical situations are shown in the following figures.

Docking with the wind blowing toward the dock is best avoided, but if there's no alternative, it's best accomplished by approaching with only a small jib flying. Turn the boat parallel to the dock and loose the jib sheet so the sail begins to luff as the hull swings sideways. Momentum from the turn carries the boat forward while the wind pushes it sideways to reach the dock. Fenders should be put over the side in advance to protect the hull. If the wind is strong, even a luffing jib can easily impart too much speed, so the safer strategy is to approach the dock under "bare poles," with no sails up at all. Unless there's a strong current, you'll have no trouble directing the boat downwind (or on a very broad reach) to the exact spot on the dock you want.

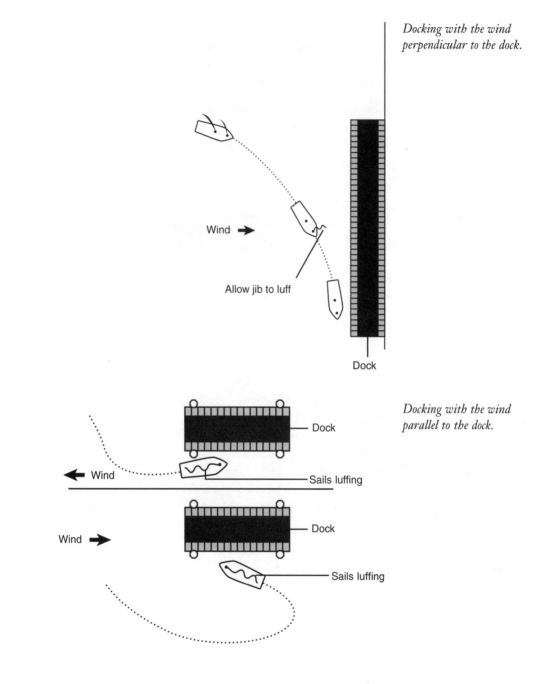

Docking with the wind perpendicular to the dock.

Wind ➡

Allow jib to luff

Dock

Docking with the wind parallel to the dock.

⬅ Wind

Dock

Sails luffing

Wind ➡

Dock

Sails luffing

Docking with the wind parallel to the dock is not difficult if you remember to head up into the wind as you near the landing point. Be sure to maintain your motion to maintain steerage—approaching too slowly might leave you dead in the water before you can heave a line to the dock.

The important skill to develop for this and other docking or mooring maneuvers is the ability to estimate with some accuracy just how far the boat will drift into the wind before it stops. A large boat in medium wind conditions and smooth water might go 10 boatlengths or more. A small boat in a good blow might barely make it 1 length into the wind.

Docking into the wind.

Docking into the wind is risky if there's no area where you can shoot past the dock, because your speed has to be calculated just right to stop the boat before it hits the dock, but not so soon that the dock is still out of reach. A sharp turn while still a boatlength or two off the dock might bring you in just right, but have a hand ready to heave a line in case you're too far out, and have the fenders over the side in case you're closer than you think. Remember that the rudder can also be a brake. Turning the tiller rapidly all the way to one side can cause the rudder blade to stall, which burns off a lot of boat speed. And, once again, you might prefer simply to sail as slowly as you can maintain headway, right up to the dock, by reducing sail and slacking sheets as needed.

Anchoring Under Sail

It's by far easiest to anchor under power, and if you have an auxiliary engine that's what you should do. However, if not, here's the procedure for doing it the way that Captain Cook and Magellan did it:

1. Drop the jib before you approach your selected anchorage. If you don't, it's going to be in the way of the person handling the anchor on the bow.

2. Select the spot where your anchor needs to go to allow lots of scope and hold you in place. If you're picking an overnight spot in a cruising sailboat, choose an

area where the boat can swing 360 degrees with any changes in wind and tide without going aground or bumping another boat.

Boat Bytes _____

To anchor in a harbor crowded with both powerboats and sailboats, choose a spot near the other sailboats. They are more influenced by current than wind due to their deep keels and will all swing at about the same rate, while the powerboats will swing mostly based on the wind direction. Besides, if you're a sailor you don't want to be in among all those generators and poodles.

3. Sail toward your drop spot and turn directly into the wind as you get within two or three boatlengths, or whatever your estimate of stopping distance is under the prevailing conditions. The sails will luff and the hull will coast to a stop.

4. Lower the anchor and pay out the rode as the wind pushes the boat backwards. (If there's not much wind, you might want to "back" the mainsail by pushing the boom out to one side so the sail fills and makes the boat sail backward.) Few sailboats will drift straight backward. You will probably be blown off to one side, and it might be important to take just enough strain on the rode as it pays out to keep the bow pointed more or less into the wind. If the boat turns away from the wind, you risk drifting or sailing over the rode and tangling it in the keel, propeller, or rudder.

   Depending on the boat and the conditions, you might need to lower the mainsail in addition to the jib in order to keep the boat stable at anchor. Otherwise, simply slack the sheet.

5. When you've released adequate scope (three to five times the water depth or more, as you'll recall from Chapter 8), pull on the rode and see if you can help the flukes (the hooks of the anchor) to work their way into the bottom. This step isn't necessary in a powerboat where the reversed engine puts pressure on the rode, but it's a good idea in a sailboat under light winds.

6. Cleat off the rode.

When you're ready to leave the spot, raise the mainsail if it has been taken down, tighten the sheet a little, and then pull in the rode until the bow is nearly over the anchor. Keep track of the angle of the rode at all times. The boat will try to sail around the anchor, and it's very easy to get the rode wrapped around the keel, propeller, or rudder if you are not careful. Agree on a set of hand signals between the bow and the helm. After the bow is over the anchor or slightly beyond, a few pulls usually breaks out the hook. Sometimes the pitching of the boat can be used to advantage here, taking up slack with each pitch down and using the buoyancy of the bow for power with each pitch up.

Getting to a Moored Boat

With large fixed-keel sailboats, it's common to leave the boat at a mooring well away from the dock, avoiding the handling problems of docking in a tight spot. The dinghy, or "dink," is a small boat used to travel back and forth from shore to the boat.

Boat Bytes

An inflatable dinghy also acts as a serviceable lifeboat in an emergency. It has the stability to survive in rough water and plenty of space to haul your entire crew to safety—something that most "hard" dinghies can't manage.

The dinghy is also a mobile fishing and diving platform that allows you to poke into shallows where the mother ship can't go. It's also useful for setting out a second anchor where necessary for overnights. (The anchor is lowered into the dinghy, and the rode paid out as the smaller boat moves away from the mother ship.) And there are times when it can serve as your tow boat, as well; even with a 4-horse outboard, a dinghy can tow a 40-footer out of the harbor, slowly but surely, so long as wind or current is not excessive.

Inflatables like this Zodiac make excellent dinghies because of their great load capacity and stability, and the soft sides don't mar the surface of the mother ship. They're also light enough to hoist aboard easily.

(Zodiac of North America)

A Route You Can Root For

Wind, tides, and seas control where you can go and how fast you can go there in a sailboat much more than in a powerboat, so a daylong voyage to an offshore island, for example, takes a bit of advance planning. Before embarking on the trip, you should do the following:

♦ Check the tidal currents for the area you'll be cruising. If the tide will be coming in when you're going out or vice versa, it would be better to leave earlier or later to have the tides in your favor. See Chapter 16 for more on tides.

♦ Study the weather forecast (see Chapter 15). If the winds are going to force a long beat in one direction, it might be better to select another destination where you can go and come on a reach.

♦ If you'll be sailing to windward on one leg, remember that this will take far longer than the run in the opposite direction. Allow plenty of time so that you can get home before sunset unless you feel experienced enough to try sailing after dark.

♦ Check the charts for tricky water with lots of shoals (see Chapter 11). It's often best to plan a much longer route that will avoid the shoals rather than try to pick your way through. The longer route will take less time if you figure in a couple of hours for working off a sandbar on the short route.

The Sailing Right-of-Way

The rules of the road for sailboats under sail are a little different than for powerboats. In general, a sailboat under sail has the right-of-way over a powerboat, no matter what the angle of approach between the two craft (unless the sailboat is overtaking). This is because the sailboat can't maneuver as rapidly as the powerboat. (When a sailboat is operating under motor power, it's considered a powerboat and must obey the same rules as all powerboats.)

In fact, powerboats are supposed to stay well clear of boats under sail. A large powerboat wake hitting a small daysailer can literally "knock the wind out of the sails" and cause

> **Look Out!**
>
> The passage of a large ship to windward of your boat can block your wind and make your sails luff. The wake of a fast-moving ship can also shake the wind from your sails as the boat hobby-horses back and forth. Give these sea monsters plenty of space!

the boat to lose steerage, and maybe even broach or make a rapid turn sideways to the sea, with some danger of swamping.

Powerboaters who see a boat flying a spinnaker can be sure it's sailing on a run or a broad reach and will have a hard time safely maneuvering if they pass too close on the bow.

(Endeavour Yachts)

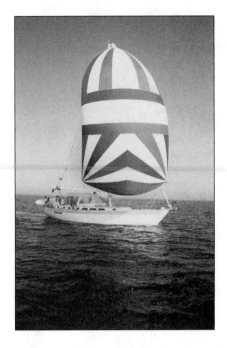

Sailboats on a run dead downwind can be forced into an unexpected jibe, complete with wildly sweeping boom, if forced to bear off by the close pass of a powerboat off the bow.

For these reasons, powerboats must give way to sailing boats unless the powered vessel is dead in the water, or is a deep-draft vessel with limited maneuverability because of water depth in a narrow channel, or if a fast sailboat is overtaking a relatively slow powerboat, not as unusual as one might think in windy sailing areas.

For sailboat meeting sailboat, there are three basic rules:

1. With two boats on the same tack, the leeward boat has the right-of-way.

2. With two boats on opposite tacks, the boat on a starboard tack has the right-of-way.

3. When one boat overtakes another, the one ahead has the right-of-way.

Dealing With the Draft—And the Drift

Keeled sailboats draw a lot of water compared to powerboats of similar size. Typically, they have twice the draft at a given length; that is, it takes twice the depth to keep them from going aground. The deeper the keel sits in the water, the better it works, because the greater the leverage to hold the boat upright when it begins to heel.

However, deep draft means that you will go aground in areas that even some fairly substantial powerboats cross with impunity. Don't assume that just because the sport-fisher in front of you got over the bar, you can do likewise. And when you sink a fixed keel deep into a mud flat under the power of full sail, it will be very difficult to get it back out under the power of the typical auxiliary engine on most sailboats. The good news is that the keel hits long before the propeller and usually protects the rudder as well. So a grounding will seldom cause any damage to the underwater gear.

A sharp lookout, polarized glasses to cut the glare, and good local knowledge can help you avoid most groundings. However, nobody, not even the most seasoned skipper, stays off the bottom all the time.

If you go on slowly in soft mud, you might be able to sail free, or to crank up the kicker and back off. Or if you have a moveable keel (a centerboard), just raise it up far enough to clear the bottom and go on your way.

If you're stuck hard, however, you'll have to apply other methods.

One is to raise the keel through heeling the boat—move everybody to the leeward side and you may gain a few precious inches of clearance so that you can sail clear. You might consider sending an athletic crewperson crawling out along the winged-out boom, with the mainsail down, to provide more heeling leverage. (Make sure he or she has on a PFD—this maneuver can send the person on an unexpected swim.)

If that doesn't work, you might have to get some weight off the boat. In calm, shallow water during the summer, the crew can simply hop overboard for a swim while the skipper stays aboard to steer for deeper water. All swimmers should wear PFDs, just in case the boat gets off quicker than expected. The crew can then swim to the edge of deeper water to be picked up on the next pass.

Boat Bytes

The best way to prevent your sailboat from grounding is to study the chart for the area. If you know the waters ahead, the tides, and your exact draft, and keep track of where you are at all times, you can avoid any risky areas. Keep an eye on your depth finder to alert you to shoaling water.

In high-current areas such as passes and narrow channels (where groundings are frequent), getting crew off the boat is not an option unless you have a dinghy. Make sure the dinghy is secured to the boat if the flow is strong, or your crew might take a fast ride down tide toward a nasty inlet.

It's also possible to use the anchor to "kedge" or pull your boat off a bar. The trick is to get the anchor well away from the boat, the full length of the anchor rode, so that holding power will be maximized. (Remember, the more scope, the better the anchor holds.) You can then use one of the winches aboard to inch the boat off by cranking in the anchor line.

A more elaborate strategy is to use two anchors: one to pull the boat forward, and one to heel the boat way over on its side to reduce draft. This heeling anchor is attached to a halyard and set off to one side of the boat. It pulls from the top of the mast via a halyard winch.

An even more time-consuming but often essential possibility is simply to sit and wait for the next high tide, unless, of course, you went aground on high tide. If you did, you're going to have to flag down a tow quickly or endure a very long wait through an entire tidal cycle. It's a good idea to put out an anchor toward deep water to prevent the boat from being pushed farther aground by wind or currents.

Heavy-Weather Sailing

Although sailors love wind, there's such a thing as too much of a good thing. But getting caught in a squall is a part of sailing; the moderate speeds available in most sailing craft mean there's no chance you can run for the docks in time to avoid a storm once the black clouds blot out the sun, as you sometimes can in a powerboat.

The best way to deal with bad weather is to watch it over a cup of hot tea from the clubhouse, and that requires you to carefully check all sources of weather information before you leave the docks. But even the most careful sailors sometimes find themselves in more weather than they want.

The basic response to a serious blow is to reduce sail. But when the first blast hits, it might be too late to inform your crew of your plans in time to avoid a capsize.

Any time the weather seems iffy, it's a good idea to review the basic heavy-weather plan, which should be followed in progressive order as the winds become more severe:

1. Before the storm arrives, make sure the sheets and halyards are clear and ready to run free as needed.

2. If members of the crew are not already wearing PFDs, they should put them on. Foul-weather gear is also a good idea, even in warm weather—the wind chill can be fierce with a 50-knot wind after you're soaked by rain or spray.

3. If you have an engine, get it started. You'll have more options than facing the storm under sail alone.

4. If the wind lays the boat over on its side, ease the sheets immediately and turn up into the wind.

5. If it's a major storm, drop the mainsail. If the boat is still heeling excessively, drop the jib as well. The idea is to get all that wind-catching sail area down on the deck so that the boat isn't pushed over on its side. (Lash the sails down to the boom or deck hardware—the wind might catch and tear them otherwise.)

6. You might find that you can't beat up into the wind, even under engine power, because the wind and seas stop all forward motion. If this is the case, turn downwind enough to take the seas on your stern quarter and head for the nearest protected area.

7. In a worst-case scenario, all sails down and the boat blowing down on a shoal, put the anchor over the bow, let the entire length of the rode run out, cleat it, and hope it catches!

Riding the Waves

Sailboat handling is a bit different than powerboat handling in large waves because of the minimal power available from the sail and/or auxiliary engine.

It's best to sail close-hauled into oncoming seas, letting the bow take the seas at an angle. This prevents the boat from rolling in the troughs and stabilizes the ride. On the other hand, sailing upwind in a blow will increase the apparent wind, while running downwind will reduce it. Your best strategy will depend on the kind of boat, the amount of sea room to leeward, the intensity of the wind and waves, and a dozen other factors.

Going downwind in a strong storm can make the boat go out of control because the waves from aft might throw the stern sideways. Sailboats that venture offshore should carry a "drogue" or sea anchor that can be trailed from the stern to keep the boat straight while underway, or from the bow to keep the head of the boat into the seas if you decide to heave-to.

A drogue or sea anchor behaves like a parachute to create drag and keep the stern from rolling into the trough in following seas.

Following seas (waves coming from astern or behind a boat)

Drogue

Righting a Capsize

Whoa! This isn't supposed to happen, but it's not uncommon for sailboats under 20 feet without weighted keels to be knocked down by a blast of wind that comes so fast no corrective action can be taken. Sailing a bit beyond the edge of your skill is also frequently to blame—if you wait a moment too long to ease the sheets as you enjoy the foam and noise of a boat practically on its beam ends, you might find yourself in the water.

This is a fairly predictable "emergency" in dinghy-class boats (small one-designs such as the Sunfish) designed to be righted by their crew, and it's one you should practice dealing with in calm winds and seas.

The drill is basically this:

1. The skipper should confirm that the crew is okay, free to move about, and floating or swimming safely. It's very important that all crew members keep one hand on the boat. In bad weather, the boat can blow away fairly quickly.

2. Grab any loose gear, such as PFDs and cushions, that might be in danger of floating off. Secure it to the boat.

3. The skipper should work his or her way around to the bottom of the boat and make sure the centerboard is down. The crew needs to support the mast at the gooseneck (where the boom fits on the mast) to keep the boat from "turning turtle" or completely turning upside down.

4. The skipper should get on the centerboard as quickly as possible to keep the boat floating sideways. This frees up the crew to search for the jib sheet from the "low side," or the side in the water. If the centerboard is high enough to stand or sit on, climb on up! If the centerboard floats well above the water, hanging on and working your upper body up should be enough.

5. Make sure the mainsheet is off. Chances are this is why you capsized to begin with, so make sure the mainsail is free.

6. When the crew has located the jib sheet, they should throw it over the hull to the skipper standing on, sitting on, or hanging from the centerboard. This provides the extra leverage to get the boat all the way upright. It takes a major pull to make the sail come clear of the water—don't be delicate. (On the other hand, don't stand on the very end of the centerboard—the leverage might be enough to break it off!)

7. The crew can now move into the middle of the boat hanging on lightly to the centerboard case, being careful not to put their full weight on it. This is called the "scoop position" because as the skipper rights the boat, the crew is "scooped" up into the interior. As the boat is mostly upright, the crew can help by kicking their legs and shifting their weight.

It's important that the skipper not right the boat until the crew is in the scoop position. If your crew is in the boat when it comes up, they can get the boat under control and keep it from capsizing again. Skippers should keep communicating with their crew.

If the boat comes up with no one in the scoop position, or if the crew doesn't make it in, don't panic. Just hoist one person into the boat as soon as possible to get it under control.

Boat Bytes

Small sailboats often get very wet, even if they don't capsize. If you carry equipment aboard that can be damaged by water or that could sink if the boat turns over—cameras, portable GPS or VHF, and so on—protect it in sealed, watertight bags tied to the boat or secured in latched compartments.

8. The crew in the boat can now assist the skipper in getting back in the boat. The best way to bring them in is over the stern (if possible). If you have difficulty getting them in, reverse the mainsheet through its cleat, tie a bowline as a foot strap, and hang it over the back of the boat. But keep in mind that some boats will turn downwind if someone in the water is holding on to the stern, and that will cause the mainsail to fill even if the sheet is uncleated. Therefore, in some conditions it might be better to pull crew back aboard up by the windward shrouds.

9. If it is very windy and the boat blows right over again as soon as you right it, do not keep trying until you are exhausted. With the boat on its side, uncleat the halyards and pull down the sails. Then try again—you'll be amazed how much easier it is.

10. Help any other crew back aboard. Make sure nothing important (like the rudder!) came loose and floated away during the spill.

11. Bail out excess water and go back to sailing—but this time ease the sheet! (If the boat is full of water to the gunnels, you might have to bail it out before you or anyone else gets back aboard. Tie a gallon bucket somewhere in the cockpit to be sure it's there when you need it.)

Obviously, capsizing is anything but routine in larger sailboats, and there's no way you're going to manually right a 25-footer that goes bottom-side up, but for the smallest sailing craft, it's a fairly common procedure.

The Least You Need to Know

- Sailboats can't be maneuvered quickly or stopped like powerboats, so more care is required when docking and anchoring them.

- Boats under sail have a different set of rules of the road than powerboats.

- The deep draft of many sailboat keels makes grounding frequent. Know the tricks for getting free.

- Sailboats can handle most rough weather easily if the crew prepares in advance.

Glossary

adrift   Loose from moorings or anchor, without power.

aft   Toward the rear section of a boat.

aground   When a boat is stuck on bottom.

amidships   Near the middle of the boat.

anchor   A device for securing a boat in place in open water, attached to the boat by an anchor rode or line.

anchor light   A white light displayed on the highest point of a boat at anchor, visible 360 degrees.

anchor rode   The rope or line leading from the boat to the anchor.

anchorage   A harbor or protected area where waves can't normally reach.

astern   Toward the back of a boat, or sometimes behind the stern of a boat.

autopilot   An automatic steering device designed to hold a compass course despite wind and current.

backstay   A supporting guywire running from a sailboat mast to the stern area.

barometer   A meter for measuring atmospheric pressure, indicative of weather changes.

battens   Thin strips of plastic used to stiffen or flatten the leech of a sail.

beam   The width of a boat.

bearing   The course in degrees toward a distant object.

beating   Sailing to windward via tacking.

bilge   The lowest area inside the bottom of a boat.

bitter end   The cut end of any line.

block-and-tackle   An assembly of pulleys and ropes to multiply force.

boat hook   A hook with rounded ends set on a long handle, designed to pull in or fend off other boats; distinguished from a gaff hook, a sharp-pointed hook designed to boat large fish.

boom   The horizontal pole that secures the bottom of the mainsail.

boom vang   Lines and fittings that secure the boom.

bosun's chair   A seat used to hoist sailors aloft to work on rigging on the mast.

bow   The forward part of a boat.

bow line   A line attached to the bow of a boat, used to secure it to a dock or mooring.

bowline   One of the most useful of boating knots, used to make a secure loop.

breakers   Waves rolling over on themselves to create white, disturbed, and often dangerous water.

bulkhead   A frame member or wall across the beam of a boat.

buoy   A floating navigational aid.

capsize   When a hull turns upside down.

cast off   Set free or loose, as in "cast off the dock lines."

catamaran   A twin-hulled boat.

cavitate   When a propeller loses its bite on the water and spins rapidly while losing forward thrust.

centerboard   A pivoting keel board that can be lowered to keep a sailboat from being pushed sideways by the wind.

chafing gear   Protective material secured around a dock line to prevent abrasion.

channel   The deeper portion of a waterway, often marked for navigation.

charts   Nautical road maps describing depths, aids to navigation, wrecks, and other navigational dangers.

chock   A U-shaped fitting designed to keep a line in place.

cleat   A two-horned fitting that makes it possible to rapidly secure lines without tying knots.

clove hitch   A tie-up created by using two loops crossed over each other on a piling.

coaming   A raised edge or lip on the gunnels, designed to prevent spray from dripping into the cockpit.

cockpit   The working area of a boat, aft of the wheel.

come about   To change directions, turn around.

compass   A magnetic navigational tool.

cotter pin   A wire or fastener used to secure nuts on bolts or to keep turnbuckles in place.

cunningham   A line used to control tension along a sail's luff.

davits   Stout lifting arms designed to hoist a boat onto a seawall or to bring a dinghy aboard a larger boat.

dead reckoning   Determining position based on distance, time, and speed.

deadrise   The angle between one side of the bottom and the horizontal, usually measured near the transom. Boats with a high degree of deadrise—deep-vee hulls—perform well in rough water.

deck   The floor or walking surface inside a boat.

dinghy   A small boat, also known as a "dink," that is used to travel back and forth from shore to a larger boat.

displacement   The weight of water displaced by a boat.

displacement hull   A boat that maintains a consistent draft while moving; a boat that does not plane. The speed of displacement hulls is limited mostly by their length, with longer boats traveling faster.

douse   To drop a sail quickly.

downwind   With the wind.

draft   Vertical distance from the waterline to the lowest point on a vessel.

ease   To let tension off a line gradually, as in adjusting a sail.

ebb   An outgoing flow of water; falling tide.

fathom   A unit of measurement that equals six feet.

fathometer   An electronic instrument used to measure depth.

fender   A cushion placed between two boats, or a boat and a dock, to prevent damage.

fetch   The distance over water the wind blows, which affects wave height.

flare   The outward curve of a boat's sides near the bow. Also, an emergency distress signal.

flood   An incoming flow of water; rising tide.

following seas   Waves that come from astern or behind.

forward   Toward the front section of a boat.

freeboard   The distance from the surface of the water to the gunwales.

gaff   A spar to support a sail. Also, a hooked tool to land fish.

gel coat   The outer layer of resin, usually colored, on a fiberglass boat.

gunwale   The upper edge of a boat's side, also spelled "gunnel."

hatch   Deck openings, usually fitted with watertight doors.

head   The upper corner of a sail. Also, a marine toilet.

heading   The direction in which the bow points.

heel   To tip to one side.

helm   The wheel, tiller, or steering control.

hull   The body or shell of a boat, not including interior liner, decks, cabin, and rigging.

in irons   A sailboat headed into the wind with sails luffing and unable to make headway is said to be in irons.

inboard   A powerboat with the engine inside the hull and the prop shaft running through the bottom of the boat.

inboard/outboard   Also known as an I/O or sterndrive, this propulsion system combines an inboard engine with a drive unit on the outside of the transom. The drive can be trimmed up or down to improve running attitude.

Intracoastal Waterway   The protected, marked, and often dredged inland waterway that runs along the U.S. coast from Maine to Florida and around the Gulf of Mexico.

jib   The triangular foresail.

jibe   To change directions on a sailboat on a downwind run so that the boom swings across the cockpit.

keel   The bottom center of the hull, bow to transom. Sailboat keels often project below the bottom of the boat.

ketch   A two-masted sailboat with the foremast taller than the aft mast, and the aft mast stepped ahead of the rudder post.

knot   One nautical mile per hour, equal to 1.15 statute or land miles per hour.

latitude   A measure of geographic distance north or south of the equator. Latitude lines on a chart run east and west.

lee shore   A shore lying downwind.

leeward   Away from the wind.

line   Rope or cord used aboard a boat.

longitude   A measure of geographic distance east or west of the prime meridian which runs through Greenwich, England. Longitude lines on a chart run north and south.

lubber's line   The line on a compass in line with the boat's keel, indicating the boat's direction.

luff   The leading edge of a sail. Also, when a sail flaps because it's improperly trimmed, it's said to be luffing.

mainsail   The sail on the back side of the main mast.

mast   An upright spar or pole to support rigging and sails.

mizzen   A smaller mast set aft of the main mast.

mooring   A permanent anchor attached to a buoy, allowing tie-ups without dropping the boat's anchor.

nautical mile   One minute of latitude, or 6,076 feet.

neap tides   The quarter-moon periods when tide movement is minimal.

outboard   An engine and drive system that attaches to a boat's transom.

painter   A line attached to the bow, usually of a dinghy.

piling   A support post for a pier.

piloting   Navigation by use of visible references.

planing hull   A hull designed to lift to near the surface, decreasing drag and increasing speed.

port   The left side, facing forward on a boat. Also, a harbor.

port tack   When a sailing vessel has the wind coming over the port side.

prop   Short for "propeller," used to push a boat through the water via mechanical power.

quartering seas   Waves that come from aft of amidships.

radar   An electronic navigation system used to "see" via reflected radio waves.

Radio Direction Finder   Also known as RDF, this is a radio with an antenna that can be tuned to locate the geographic position of distant stations and thus to locate a vessel's position.

reach   Sailing across the wind.

right-of-way   The boat with the legal right to continue course and speed in meeting situations. The other boat is said to be the "burdened" vessel.

rode   The anchor line and chain.

rudder   A vertical plate near the stern for steering a boat.

running lights   Vessel lights that are required by law to be shown between sundown and sunup.

running rigging   The adjustable lines on a sailboat, used to control spars and sails.

schooner   A vessel with two or more masts, with the forward masts shorter than the last aft mast.

scope   The ratio between the depth of water and the length of the anchor rope. A scope of 3:1 is the minimum for anchoring in protected water, and scopes up to 7:1 are recommended in exposed conditions.

sea anchor   Also known as a drogue or drift anchor, this is any device that is streamed to act as a drag from bow or stern and slow the drift of a boat.

sea cock   A through-hull fitting that controls water flow; a valve.

shackle   A U-shaped metal fitting used to bind together anchor and rode or sail and line.

shear pin   A soft metal pin designed to break when the prop hits an obstruction, thus preventing damage to prop or gears.

sheet   A line used to adjust sail trim.

shipshape   In clean, orderly condition.

shrouds   Fixed rigging that supports the mast from the sides of the boat.

slip   A berth for a boat with pilings and finger piers on both sides.

sloop   A sailboat with a single mast set slightly forward of amidships, usually equipped with a mainsail and a jib.

spars   The masts and booms of a sailboat.

spinnaker   A three-cornered, parachute-like sail, usually brightly colored, for sailing downwind.

splice   To permanently join two ropes by tucking strands of each over the other, creating a smoother joint than any knot.

spring line   Lines used to control fore and aft motion of a boat tied up in a slip.

spring tides   Periods around the new and full moons when high tides are higher than usual and low tides are lower than usual.

squall   A sudden storm accompanied by strong winds.

standing line   The main part of a line, the part not used in a knot.

starboard   The right side, facing forward on a boat.

starboard tack   When a sailboat has the wind coming over the starboard side.

stays   Wire rigging used to support the mast fore and aft.

stepped   Secured to the deck or keel, used in referring to sailboat masts.

stern   The rear part of a boat.

stern line   A line from the stern cleat to the dock.

sterndrive   Same as inboard/outboard or I/O.

stow   To put an item in a secure spot.

swamp When a boat fills with water over the gunnels, often prior to sinking.

tack The legs of an upwind beat in sailing. Also, the forward lower corner of a sail.

tacking Changing the heading of a sailing vessel so that the wind comes over the opposite rail.

tackle Pulleys and lines used to gain mechanical advantage. Also used to describe anchor gear and fishing gear.

telltale A wind indicator mounted on sail or stay.

thwart A brace running laterally across a boat.

tides The vertical rise and fall of sea water caused by the pull of the sun and moon.

tiller An arm or lever for steering.

transom The squared-off section of the stern.

trim To adjust the running attitude of a powerboat by moving the drives up or down or adjusting trim tabs. Also, to adjust sails for most effective sailing.

trimaran A boat with three hulls.

trip line A line attached to the lower part of an anchor so that it can be easily pulled free of bottom.

true wind The actual direction and force of the wind, as compared to "apparent wind" felt aboard a moving boat.

underway When a vessel is in motion, not at anchor.

upwind Toward the direction from which the wind is blowing.

v-bottom A hull with a sharp or v-shaped bottom, designed to split the waves and soften the ride. Also spelled "vee-bottom."

variation Compass error caused by the difference between geographic north and the magnetic north pole.

ventilate To pump fumes out of the bilge via an electric blower. Also, when a prop draws in air and loses its grip in the water.

VHF radio Very High Frequency radio, the most common boat-to-boat and boat-to-shore communication system on recreational boats.

wake The waves created by boat movement.

walk-through A passageway through the windshield via a folding section, most often found on bow-rider powerboats.

waterline The line where the surface of the water meets the sides of the boat, sometimes marked with a trim strip.

weather shore A shore lying upwind.

whipping Securing the loose ends of a cut strand of line with cord. Sometimes applied to securing the ends with heat, tape, or glue.

winch A circular drum used to provide a mechanical advantage when hauling in line or cable.

windward Toward the direction from which the wind is blowing.

yawl A two-masted sailboat with a forward main mast and a smaller aft mast stepped behind the rudder post.

Resources

Boating School Sources

U.S. Coast Guard Boating Safety Hotline
www.uscgboating.org; 1-800-368-5647

U.S. Coast Guard Auxiliary
www.cgaux.org; 1-800-336-2628

U.S. Power Squadron
www.usps.org; 1-800-FOR-USPS

BOAT U.S.
www.boatus.com; 703-823-9550

Sailing School Sources

American Sailing Association
13922 Marquesas Way
Marina del Rey, CA 90292
www.american-sailing.com; 310-822-7171

National Sailing Industry Association
200 E. Randolph Drive, Suite 5100
Chicago, IL 60601-6528
www.nmma.org; 1-800-535-SAIL

Marina Sailing (six California sailing schools)
www.marinasailing.com; 310-822-6617

Offshore Sailing School (eastern U.S. and British Virgin Islands)
www.offshore-sailing.com; 1-888-454-8002

U.S. Sailing Association
P.O. Box 1260
Portsmouth, RI 02871
www.ussailing.org; 401-683-0800

Sources of Charts and Publications

U.S. Coastal Waters and Great Lakes, NOAA
www.chartmaker.ncd.noaa.gov; 1-800-584-4683

Mississippi River, U.S. Army Corps of Engineers maps
www.mvr.usace.army.mil/NavCharts; 309-794-5501

Tennessee Valley Authority lakes and rivers
https://maps.tva.com; 1-800-MAPS-TVA

E-Charts and Guide Books

C-Map originated the e-chart phenomenon when it developed some of the first recreational electronic charts in the 1980s; the company was also instrumental in producing GPS chart plotters for many companies. Today they produce some 15,000 e-charts in a wide variety of formats covering most waters worldwide. Prices range from $100 to $300 depending on coverage (www.c-map.com; 508-477-8010). Other companies who make excellent e-chart products include Navionics, www.navionics.com; Nobeltec, www.nobeltec.com; Lowrance, www.lowrance.com; Garmin, www.garmin.com; and Maptech, www.maptech.com. Maptech also makes wonderful electronic topographic maps, which are super assets for planning backcountry hiking.

The *Waterway Guides* are a series of books that have long been the bibles for Intracoastal Waterway cruisers from Maine to Texas and throughout the Bahamas. The books feature complete maps of the routes plus descriptions of the approach to every harbor, attractions along the way, and more. They are priced at about $37 each (www.waterwayguide.com; 1-800-233-3359).

The *Embassy Boating Guides* are remarkably detailed, spiral-bound, full-color books on coastal boating, fishing, and diving. They include color charts of coastal areas, suggested GPS fishing hotspots, aerial photos of many harbor entrances, and even a list of fishing guides and their phone numbers. They sell for about $40 each (www.nboat.com; 1-800-248-3512).

Towing Services

Sea Tow offers members unlimited free towing in many coastal areas nationwide. The membership fee is around $120 per year (www.sseatow.com; 1-800-4SEATOW).

TowBOAT/U.S. is a service associated with BOAT U.S. It includes nationwide towing 24 hours a day (www.boatus.com/towing, 1-800-391-4869).

Other Resources

BOAT U.S. is the nation's largest recreational boating club. It lobbies for boating interests in state and federal legislatures and publishes a monthly newsletter. Club members get discounts on fuel and dockage at many marinas. The company also distributes a mail-order catalog that's an excellent source of all sorts of economically priced marine gear. The club loans life jackets to kids via yacht clubs and marinas nationwide. For information, contact 880 S. Pickett Street, Alexandria, VA 22304-4606; 703-823-9550; www.boatus.com.

One of the best websites for boat shopping is Boat Trader, www.boattraderonline.com. The site is a great tool for finding a particular make and model of boat, and for comparing prices throughout your region, state, or even nationwide.

BUC Information Services publishes the *BUC Used Boat Price Guide*, which is the "bluebook" for buying or selling a used boat. The company also has a website that lists thousands of used boats at www.bucnet.com. For information, contact BUC Information Services, 1314 NE 17th Ct., Fort Lauderdale, FL 33305; 1-800-327-6929.

Tidemaster produces a computerized yearly tide listing that's very handy for trip planning—it's about $50; www.zephyrs.com; 412-422-6600.

A good source for online tides is e-chart maker Nobeltec (www.tides.com), which gives free daily predictions for any area of the nation.

Index

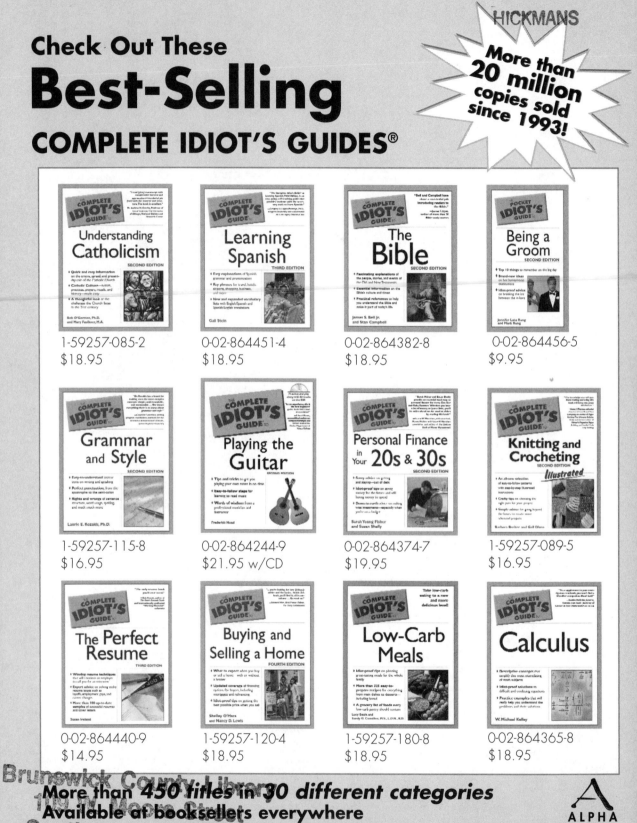
Brunswick County Library
109 W. Moore Street
Southport NC 28461